The Gulf Gourmet

presents

selected recipes

from

The Mississippi Gulf Coast

Westminster Academy PTA
Gulfport, Mississippi

The Gulf of Mexico and U.S Highway 90 are seen through live oaks along the Mississippi Gulf Coast. The oaks, now noted for their majestic beauty, were once a source for building ribs for wooden ships. Hundreds of these oaks stand as a background for the white sand beach extending for many scenic miles along the Mississippi Sound.

Photograph by Chauncey T. Hinman

Westminster Academy is a small school, kindergarten through sixth grade, dedicated to excellence in education and the individual development of each and every child. While small classrooms, enrichment programs, individual attention and expanded learning situations have almost become a thing of the past, Westminster Academy quietly pursues these ends. This approach to learning is an expensive process and the maintaining of our level of excellence is nearly prohibitive. Our cookbook, *the Gulf Gourmet,* evolved from a definite financial need within the school to sustain continued growth, to expand programs, to enlarge the physical plant yet maintain high academic integrity. Concurrently, the pride which we feel for our school and the quality of education it offers is directly reflected in the quality of our book as well. This being the case, may we express here our appreciation to those of you who support us in this endeavor and take great pleasure in knowing it will be well received.

Westminster Academy will always appreciate the work and continued support of all those who have contributed to *the Gulf Gourmet's* success and its subsequent financial contribution to the Academy. Their dedication will always be remembered and appreciated. Though space precludes a complete listing of the many who made a contribution it is only fitting that those ladies who served in major capacities compiling this book should herein be recognized: Mrs. Nita Bazzone, Mrs. Richard Graves, Mrs. Alben Hopkins, Mrs. Sam Morse, Mrs. Bill Smallwood, Mrs. Nancy Mize Sneed, Mrs. Dotie Clampffer. Past general chairmen include Mrs. Kent Lovelace, Mrs. William Rainey, Mrs. Jimmy D. Alexander, Mrs. Chevis Swetman, Mrs. Ronald Russell, and Mrs. James LaRose.

Mrs. Kent Lovelace, Jr., Editor; Mrs. William H. Murdock, Jr.; Mrs. William M. Rainey; and Mrs. Jack Thompson

COOKBOOK COMMITTEE–SIXTH PRINTING–REVISED EDITION

Mrs. Ronald Russell, chairman, Mrs. William Boyd, III, Mrs. James LaRose, Mrs. Danny Miller, Mrs. Chevis Swetman, Mrs. James Wetzel, and Mrs. William M. Rainey, Consultant.

Testing Committee: Mrs. Gerald Emil, Mrs. Lamar Gray, Mrs. Tom McCormick, Mrs. John McFarland, Mrs. Anna Mellen, Mrs. Samuel Robinson, Mrs. Craig Shier, Mrs. Gordon Stanfield, and Mrs. Richard Williams.

SEVENTH PRINTING WESTMINSTER ACADEMY PARENT-TEACHER ASSOCIATION COOKBOOK COMMITTEE: Debbie Harris LaRose, Chariman; Vicky Carol Carr, Gulf Gourmet Treasurer; Gina Dean Sessum, Mail-Order; Sonja Davis Gaddy, Anna Bieller Mellen, Kathy Slay Russell, Janet Owens Selig, Carol Palmer Threadgill, Caroline Eustice Wicks, Sales Representatives. PTA BOARD: Jan Tootle Salloum, President; Debbie Hirsch Golden, 1st Vice-President; Debbie Harris LaRose, 2nd Vice-President; Alice Lenora Bryant, Treasurer; Vicky Carol Carr, Asst. Treasurer; Barri Brent Wessler, Secretary.

Library of Congress Catalog Card Number 83-50196
ISBN 0-9611062-0-4

First Printing - September, 1978 - 4,000
Second Printing - September, 1979 - 10,000
Third Printing - September, 1981 - 5,000
Fourth Printing - August, 1983 - 10,000
Fifth Printing - December, 1985 - 10,000
Sixth Printing - July, 1991 - 10,000
Seventh Printing - February, 1996 - 5,000

Printed in the USA by

WIMMER
The Wimmer Companies, Inc.
Memphis

Table of Contents

. . . notes from times past

Since 1540 the Coast has been a melting pot of nationalities which is, of course, reflected in our cooking. All the eight flags, representing the different countries which have made claim to the Mississippi Gulf Coast, have brought with them their own particular foods. These foods were necessarily adapted to a new environment in a new land becoming new creations in the process. Today's descendants of Slavonians, Austrians, English, Italian, Irish, Swiss, German, Greek, Spanish, Indian and French have made a powerful impact on Coastal cooking. The most widely accepted influence still seems to be that of the French, whose dishes continue to delight the most discerning palate. Because of the availability of fresh seafood, coastal communities around the world seem to boast more than their share of cooking possibilities. The variety and abundance of fresh seafood quite naturally expands our own cooking repertoire, and the delicacies offered here make dining on the Mississippi Gulf Coast a memorable experience. This is not to say that our cooking expertise depends solely on seafood. The South itself has quite an established reputation for food preparation, and we on the Coast simply enjoy the best of both worlds.

Historically, the first of the eight flags to fly here on the Coast belonged to Spain. Hernando De Soto and his greedy soldiers, fresh from their spoils in South America entered Mississippi. They claimed the area for Spain, discovered the mouth of the Mississippi River and promptly left, for the acquisition yielded no vast riches in silver and gold.

Later, in 1682, the famous Rene Robert Cavalier Sieur de la Salle sailed down the Mississippi River from the Great Lakes region and subsequently entered our quiet coastal waters. He is reported to have remarked upon the beauty and determined that this was a country of ". . . gentle breezes and great, grey-bearded oak trees." This growth of live oaks so near the salt water's edge is peculiar to our area and was a distinguishing landmark to early explorers.

In 1699, the French-Canadian Le Moyne brothers, Pierre Le Moyne, Sieur D'Iberville and Jean Baptiste Le Moyne, Sieur de Bienville, approached our shores. They had been commissioned by Louis XIV to colonize the area called Louisiana which La Salle had earlier claimed for France. The French-Canadians with their two small frigates, *La Marin* and *La Badine*, and the guard ship, *Francois*, were first denied landing on Santa Rosa Island by the Spanish, who were already entrenched in that area. Then the small entourage moved westward, passing up the Mobile Bay area as being too shallow. Finding a natural harbor here and safety within the confines of our string of islands directly south, they dropped anchor at Ship Island. Only D'Iberville, a priest and an Indian scout in a small launch cautiously came ashore to greet the Biloxi Indians. The French explorers, interested in colonization, expressed respect for Indian ways and taboos and subsequently received much assistance from the gentle tribe. Fort Maurepas, a modest post, was erected according to D'Iberville, ". . . with four bastions; two of hewn timber, placed together, one foot and one half thick, nine feet high; the other two of double palisades. It is mounted with fifty four pieces of cannon and has a good outfit of ammunition." This fort, located at Ocean Springs, became the first capital of France in the Lower Mississippi Valley. Their poor establishment struggled, but a few gallant settlers were able to survive and to establish the Biloxi Bay Colony and New Biloxi, one of the very oldest cities in the United States.

The Le Moyne brothers left behind remarkable records, in the form of well-kept logs and journals, of their activities and efforts. D'Iberville departed from the coast shortly after erecting Fort Maurepas, leaving a friend in command as the King's Lieutenant, and his younger brother, Bienville, to explore the coastline more thoroughly. Though D'Iberville, called the Father of Louisiana, receives credit for the actual founding and discovery of the area, it was Bienville who made the more lasting contribution. It was Bienville who made detailed charts and maps of his explorations of the Lower Mississippi Valley, maps and charts which were indispensable to later explorers. He also cemented good relations with the Indians, learned their languages, established permanent settlements in Mobile and New Orleans, served as governor of the Territory and dominated affairs in Louisiana for forty years.

As the small Biloxi colony struggled, the shortage of marriageable women prompted a clever idea by the French government to properly colonize their new territory. Shiploads of young women, each in possession of a trunk of clothes from the French government, were sent to the new colony. The first shipload arrived on Dauphin Island, Alabama, and in 1719 and 1721 subsequent shiploads were sent to Ship Island. These ladies, of good reputation, were known as the "filles a la cassette" or the "Casquette Girls", deriving their name from the trunk given to them by the French government.

When the French were forced to relinquish their holdings in the Louisiana territory to the British in 1763, the coastal inhabitants of the era hardly noticed the change; and life continued under the massive oaks, much as it always had been. A slight attempt at private commerce emerged (a decided improvement over pirating) and charcoal and brick were traded between Mobile and New Orleans. The Indians continued their treks from the north to trade and to partake of the healing coastal waters and gentle breezes. By word of mouth they passed on tales and relayed messages keeping communication alive in this somewhat sleepy and very independent area.

The area did not remain sleepy long for the American struggle for independence from 1776 to 1781 demanded that the Coast recognize Spanish dominion and drive out the British or join the pro-American forces. Although the people had remained indomitably French, they were decidedly pro-American in feeling. Finally, on December 10, 1817, after much haggling, many border fights, and concessions by both sides, Mississippi became the twentieth state to enter the Union. The Coast then heaved a sigh as another flag unfurled its banner over these shores.

No concise statement can be made here to adequately describe the fantastic growth and bustle of the South prior to the War Between the States. Timber was sold, cotton was king, and trade with foreign countries flourished. The horrifying realities of the Civil War literally destroyed the South, and during this tragic time the Coast felt the pangs of war and death. Only one man in ten survived the war and returned to the Coast, finding life as it once was - gone. But, being a sturdy people, the South ignored adversity and ultimately triumphed; recovery came. With new railroads, ice plants, the development of canning processes for seafood, lumber mills and charcoal manufacturing, the Coast and the South rallied and grew once more.

The Coastal area has suffered much in the architecturally historical sense, losing many early landmarks (and 45,000 shoreline trees) to Hurricane Camille in 1969, but our cities and towns have rebuilt with resounding spirit. We still boast the beautiful sights of historic Fort Massachusetts on Ship Island, the gracious, lovely Beauvoir, last home of Jefferson Davis, President of the Confederate States of America, and many other beautiful homes of 1830 vintage. The quaint cities and towns of Bay St. Louis, Pass Christian, Long Beach, Gulfport, Handsboro, Mississippi City, Biloxi, Ocean Springs, Gautier, Moss Point and Pascagoula once again offer fine restaurants, shops and local art. Culturally, we boast a symphony, ballet companies, amateur and professional theater groups, and nationally known artists and writers. Our beautiful sunsets and sparkling waters, unusual cloud formations and the world's longest stretch of man-made beach provide a constant source of pleasure. The deep sea fishing and the many water sports available here provide an endless array of activities. In the colder months our string of protective islands, Cat, Ship, Deer, Horn, and Petit Bois, provide a haven for the many migratory birds who winter on our Gulf Islands National Seashore. The islands are all open to the visitor by private or charter boats, while Fort Massachusetts on Ship Island can be reached by excursion boats departing twice daily from both Gulfport and Biloxi.

Economically the Coast has always been a leader in the seafood industry, but in 1907, the fast-growing port of Gulfport also became the world's leading exporter of yellow pine. Before 1919 Gulfport welcomed its first banana boat into its harbor, and by 1973 this same port became the nation's leading importer of bananas. Freight trains and fleets of trucks, continuously loading, attest to the traffic in and out of the port of Gulfport.

More significantly, perhaps the Mississippi Gulf Coast is whatever anyone wants it to be. During a walk along the sandy shores one almost wistfully dreams of the quiet which first greeted the early explorers to our coastline. One can only imagine the bewilderment these gallant men might feel today if their wooden hulled vessels slipped quietly past these shores once more. No one will ever know, but one wonders if perhaps they too might feel again the beauty and serenity of the great, grey-bearded oak trees - majestic, silent sentinels beside a gentle shoreline.

Dee Rainey

Appetizers

Artichoke Dip

2 large cans artichokes, quartered
1 cup mayonnaise
1 tablespoon garlic powder

Paprika
1 cup grated Parmesan cheese
3 dashes hot sauce (optional)

Mix together all ingredients in 1 quart casserole. Bake 20 to 25 minutes in a 350° oven. Serve with plain or Ritz crackers. Serves 10 to 12.

Carole Joyner

Artichoke Balls

1 large can plain artichoke hearts,
    drained and mashed
1 cup bread crumbs
2 eggs, beaten

4 tablespoons Italian cheese,
    grated
4 garlic cloves, finely minced
6 tablespoons olive oil

Drain and mash artichoke hearts. Mix bread crumbs, eggs, and grated Italian cheese. Add to mashed artichoke hearts. Chop garlic cloves very fine and saute in olive oil until tender and just starting to brown. Add to artichoke mixture. Refrigerate at least 2 hours (better overnight) and form into small balls. Roll in mixture of dry bread crumbs and grated cheese.

Mrs. William Barrett

Artichoke Nibbler

2 (6 ounce) jars marinated artichoke
    hearts
1 small onion, finely chopped
4 eggs
1/4 cup fine, dry bread crumbs

1/4 teaspoon each: salt, pepper,
    oregano, and Tabasco
1/2 pound sharp cheddar cheese,
    shredded
2 tablespoons parsley, minced

Drain marinade from one jar of artichokes into skillet. Drain the other jar and chop all the artichokes. Add onion to the marinade in skillet and saute for 5 minutes. Beat eggs; add bread crumbs and seasonings. Stir in cheese, parsley, artichokes, and onion mixture. Turn into greased 7 x 11 baking pan and bake at 325° for 30-35 minutes. Cool 5 minutes and cut into squares. Serve immediately.

Mrs. John T. Marquez

THROWING A NET

A familiar sight along the Mississippi Gulf Coast stretch of man-made sand beach is the cast fisherman. Beginning in early depression days as a means of survival, cast fishing remains a viable method for "bringing home the bacon"...Biloxi Bacon, better known as mullet. Throwing a castnet in search of mullet seen jumping in schools across sparkling gulf waters is a time-honored craft still practiced today.

Photograph by Herb Welch,
Gulf Publishing Co. Inc.

Antipasto

1/2 pound feta cheese
6 ounces olive oil
1/8 teaspoon black pepper
1/4 teaspoon salt
1 teaspoon oregano
1 tablespoon parsley flakes

1 1/2 tablespoons sweet basil
3/4 tablespoon garlic powder
1 can black pitted medium olives,
    drained
2 diced tomatoes
1/2 diced green pepper

Mix cheese and olive oil well. Mix black pepper, salt, oregano, parsley, basil, and garlic powder. Mash until all cheese is broken up. Add olives. Mix and add tomatoes and green peppers and stir. Stir before serving. This is much better made the night before. Yield: Serves 6.

Dorrie Roney

Hot Broccoli Dip

1/2 cup chopped onion
1/2 cup chopped celery
1/2 cup chopped mushrooms
3 tablespoons butter or
    margarine

1 (10 ounce) package frozen
    chopped broccoli, cooked
    and drained well
1 (10 ounce) can cream of
    mushroom soup, undiluted
1 (6 ounce) package garlic cheese,
    diced

Saute onion, celery and mushrooms in butter until tender. Combine broccoli, soup, and cheese; cook over low heat until cheese melts, stirring occasionally. Add sauteed vegetables to broccoli mixture, stirring well. Serve hot. Yields 1 quart.

Mrs. Wallace G. Long

Caraway Celery Sticks

1 bunch celery, strings removed
1 cup thinly sliced white onion
1/2 cup chopped parsley
1/3 cup salad oil
1/4 cup white vinegar

1 tablespoon caraway seed
1 1/2 tablespoons salt
1 tablespoon sugar
1/2 tablespoon white pepper

Trim leaves from celery. Separate celery into ribs; cut ribs into 3-inch lengths; cut each length in four 1/4 inch wide sticks. Place celery in a large bowl. Add onions and parsley. Combine oil, vinegar, caraway seeds, salt, sugar, and white pepper. Mix well. Pour over celery mixture; toss well to coat. Cover and refrigerate overnight. This keeps well refrigerated for about 1 month. Men seem to like them.

Nancy Mize Sneed

Onion Pie

Crust:
   1 cup saltine cracker crumbs
   ¼ cup butter, melted

Mix together and press into a 9-inch pie pan. You may use a regular pie crust if you prefer.

Filling:

3 cups diced onion
¼ cup butter
½ pound Swiss cheese
˙ finely grated
1 tablespoon flour

1 teaspoon salt
¼ teaspoon cayenne pepper
3 eggs, beaten well
1 cup scalded milk

Saute onions in butter slowly, stirring constantly until golden. Remove from fire, drain and put into pie shell. Combine cheese, flour, salt, and cayenne; stir in eggs and milk. Pour over onions and bake in a 350⁰ oven for 40 minutes. Cut into small wedges and serve. Yields 8 or more servings. May be used as a main dish if hungry men are not to be fed.

Mrs. George P. Hopkins, Jr.

Hot Mushroom Turnovers

8 ounces cream cheese, softened
½ cup butter or margarine,
   softened
1½ cups all purpose flour
½ pound fresh mushrooms, minced
1 large onion, minced

1 teaspoon salt
¼ teaspoon thyme leaves
2 additional tablespoons flour
¼ cup sour cream
1 egg, beaten
3 tablespoons butter

Early in day: In large bowl with electric mixer at medium speed, beat cream cheese, ½ cup butter, and flour until soft dough forms. Wrap dough and chill at least 1 hour. In medium skillet, saute mushrooms and onion in 3 tablespoons butter until tender. Blend in salt, thyme, and 2 tablespoons flour. Stir in sour cream. Chill. On floured surface: Roll ½ of dough into 15" circle; cut 20 ¾" circles. Roll scraps into ball and chill. On ½ of each circle, place 1 teaspoon mushroom mixture. Brush edges with egg; fold over, press edges with fork; prick tops and place on an ungreased cookie sheet. Bake 12 minutes at 450⁰. Repeat with other half of chilled dough. Makes about 50 turnovers.

Mrs. William E. Smallwood

Spinach Dip for Crudites

1 package frozen chopped spinach,
   thawed and drained
¼ to ½ cup green onion tops,
   chopped

½ cup parsley, chopped
Salt and pepper to taste
2 cups mayonnaise

Combine all ingredients and chill. May be served with raw vegetables or crackers.

Mrs. Janette Jacobs

Spinach Cream Cheese Dip

1 package frozen chopped spinach
8 ounces cream cheese
Pod of garlic
Worcestershire sauce

Mayonnaise
Lemon juice
Parmesan cheese

Drop package of frozen spinach in boiling water for two minutes. Drain and press water out of it. Mix with cream cheese and add garlic which has been put through a press. Add Worcestershire sauce, mayonnaise, lemon juice, and Parmesan cheese to taste. Serve with crackers or crudites.

Mrs. George P. Hopkins, Jr.

Dip for Fresh Vegetables

3 ounces cream cheese, softened
½ cup mayonnaise
¼ cup sour cream
1 tablespoon lemon juice

1 teaspoon curry powder
  (or more, to taste)
½ teaspoon salt
1 (4½ ounce) can chopped
  ripe olives

Combine softened cream cheese, mayonnaise and sour cream until smooth. Add seasonings. Fold in chopped ripe olives.

Mrs. William H. Murdock, Jr.

Dill Dip for Vegetables

1 pint sour cream
⅔ cup mayonnaise
½ teaspoon dill weed
½ teaspoon sesame seeds

½ teaspoon celery salt
½ teaspoon garlic salt
½ teaspoon dried onion flakes
½ teaspoon parsley flakes

Mix all ingredients well. Store in glass container overnight in refrigerator. Serve with plenty of fresh vegetables.

Judy Pulley

Vegetable Mousse

2 tomatoes, chopped
1 small white onion, chopped
1 cup celery, finely chopped
1 bell pepper, finely chopped
1 cucumber, finely chopped
1 envelope plain gelatin

¼ cup cold water
¼ cup boiling water
1 pint Kraft mayonnaise
1 teaspoon salt
Tabasco to taste
Lemon juice to taste

Finely chop all vegetables. Drain well on paper towels. Soften gelatin in cold water, then add hot water. Let cool. Fold in mayonnaise and seasonings. Add vegetables last. Refrigerate overnight. Serve as a dip with melba rounds. Can also be used to stuff tomatoes. Serves 20 to 30 as a dip.

Mrs. Sam Morse

Cocktail Cheese Log

8 ounces cream cheese
1 jar Kraft Old English cheese

1 small triangle Roquefort cheese
Chopped pecans

Bring 3 cheeses to room temperature. Put in mixer and first blend Philadelphia, then Old English, then Roquefort. With wet hands shape into a ball or log. Roll in chopped pecans on waxpaper. Wrap in same paper. twist ends and freeze overnight. Defrost 1 hour before serving. Serve with melba·toast or crackers.

Mrs. Hoshall Barrett

Cheese Crispies

1 cup flour
1 cup Rice Krispies
1 stick butter

4½ ounces sharp cheese
½ teaspoon salt .
½ teaspoon cayenne

Grate cheese, soften butter and add all ingredients and mix well with hands. Roll into balls, place on ungreased cookie sheet. Bake at 325⁰ for 20 minutes. Yields about 100 balls.

Mrs. Donnie Riley

Cheese Puffs

1 loaf unsliced bread (or bread
  sliced one inch thick)
3 ounces cream cheese
¼ pound sharp cheddar cheese

½ cup butter
2 egg whites, stiffly beaten

Trim crust and cut into one inch cubes. Melt cheeses and butter in top of double boiler. Remove from heat and add stiffly beaten egg whites. Dip cubes into mixture until well coated. Place on cookie sheet and refrigerate overnight. Bake at 400⁰ for 10 minutes until puffy but not brown.

Mrs. Charles McReynolds

Mexican Cheese Squares

1 pound mild Kraft cheddar cheese
1 pound Monterrey Jack cheese
1 can chopped green chilies or
  jalapenos chopped to taste

1 large can evaporated milk
2 eggs
1 cup flour

Crumble cheese in pan. Sprinkle chopped chilies or jalapenos on top. In blender mix milk, eggs, and flour. Pour over cheese mixture. Bake at 350⁰ for 30-40 minutes. Cool slightly before cutting.

Mrs. William E. Smallwood

Cheese Wafer Bites

³/₄ cup butter
¹/₂ cup shredded cheddar cheese
¹/₃ cup blue cheese
¹/₂ clove garlic, minced

1 teaspoon parsley
1 teaspoon chives
2 cups sifted flour

Cream butter and cheeses together. Add seasonings and work in flour. Shape into small rolls and chill. Place on greased cookie sheet and bake at 375° for 10-12 minutes or until firm and golden.

Janet Malcom

Spinach-Cheese Squares

2 tablespoons butter or oleo
3 eggs
1 cup flour
1 cup milk
1 teaspoon salt

1 teaspoon baking powder
¹/₂ pound cheddar cheese, shredded
¹/₂ pound shredded mozzarella cheese
2 packages frozen chopped spinach
*   thawed and drained*

Preheat oven to 350°. In a 9 x 13 baking pan melt the butter in the oven. Remove from oven. In a large mixing bowl beat the eggs. Add the flour, milk, salt and baking powder. Mix well. Add the cheese and spinach. Pour into the baking pan. Bake in a 350° oven for 35 minutes. Remove from oven and let cool for 45 minutes in order to set. Cut into bite-size squares. Makes 25 appetizers. To freeze: place squares on a cookie sheet and freeze. Transfer into plastic bags. Before serving remove from bags, place on cookie sheet and heat in 325° oven for 12 minutes.

Hope Goldin

Merry Cheese Ball

1 (8 ounce) package Philadelphia
*   cream cheese, softened*
1-2 tablespoons Heinz 57 bottled
*   steak sauce*

1 cup or a little more pecans chopped
1 clove garlic, minced
Few drops Tabasco sauce
Paprika

With beater or spoon combine the cream cheese, steak sauce, pecans, garlic and Tabasco. Form mixture into a ball. Wrap in waxed paper or food wrap. Chill for several hours. Unwrap and place on serving dish. Sprinkle lightly with paprika. Keep chilled. Take out 15 minutes ahead of serving. May be doubled, also freezes well.

Ardeth Bertucci

Cheese Crock

¼ pound blue cheese, crumbled
½ pound sharp cheddar cheese
¼ pound camembert (remove rind)

½ cup heavy cream
Tabasco sauce

Put cheese in double boiler over hot water. Add ½ cup heavy cream and Tabasco to taste. Heat gently and stir until smooth. Pour into crock and chill. Will keep for a long time in refrigerator.

Suzy Ellis

Holiday Pineapple-Cheese Ball

16 ounces cream cheese
2 tablespoons chopped green pepper
2 tablespoons chopped onion

¼ cup drained crushed pineapple
2 teaspoons seasoned salt
2 cups chopped pecans

Soften cream cheese. Add green pepper, onion, pineapple, seasoned salt and 1 cup pecans. Mix well. Shape into ball and roll in remaining pecans. Chill for several hours. Serve with crackers or fresh vegetables.

Mrs. R. E. Fairbank, Jr.

Quick Party Rounds

Mix: 4 tablespoons Parmesan cheese
      4 tablespoons mayonnaise
      1 teaspoon finely ground onion
      Party rye or pumpernickle bread

Spread mixture on bread and broil until bubbly.

Mrs. William M. Rainey

Roquefort Mousse

2 teaspoons gelatin
¼ cup cold water
2 cups sour cream
1 package Good Seasons Italian
   dressing mix (dry)

¼ cup Roquefort cheese, crumbled
1 cup creamed style cottage cheese
Parsley for garnish
Paprika for garnish
Waverly Wafers

Soften gelatin in cold water; place over boiling water, stirring until dissolved. Mix into sour cream. Add dry dressing mix, Roquefort cheese, and cottage cheese. Blend well with mixer. Pour into 3½ cup mold or small loaf pan. Chill until firm. Unmold and garnish with parsley and/or paprika. Serve on Waverly Wafers.

Mrs. John Morrow

Beef Roll-Ups

¼ pound dried beef in bag
  (or use corned beef)
6 ounces cream cheese
3 tablespoons grated onion

3 teaspoons prepared horseradish
1 dash Worcestershire sauce
2 tablespoons white wine
  (may need more)

Combine all ingredients except meat. Beat until creamy, adding more wine if needed. Place small amount of mixture on each slice of meat. Roll up and chill. Cut into one inch pieces to serve.

Mrs. Phyllis Perry

Hot Dried Beef Dip

8 ounces cream cheese
½ cup sour cream
2 teaspoons milk
2½ ounce jar dried beef,
  finely chopped

2 tablespoons minced onion
2 tablespoons green pepper,
  finely chopped
1/8 teaspoon pepper

Combine cream cheese and milk. Add dried beef, onion, green pepper and pepper. Fold in sour cream and spoon into a baking dish. Bake covered at 350° for 15 minutes. Stir once or twice to be sure it is heated through. Serve with crackers or raw vegetables.

Betty Bachkai
Mary Jane Helfrich

Hot Curried Cheese Dip, by Gay Graves, uses the same recipe but omits the minced onions. She adds 1½ teaspoons curry powder to the mixture and tops it with ⅓ cup chopped nuts before serving.

Chili Con Queso

1 (4 ounce) can green chilies,
  drained and chopped
¼ pound processed cheese,
  cut in small pieces

1 shake garlic salt
1 pinch sugar
1 tablespoon milk

Place pan on low heat. Drain can of chilies; chop them. Add cut cheese, milk, garlic powder, sugar. Stir until all cheese is melted. Do not let boil. Cook, refrigerate. Keeps well for days. Serve as a dip with corn chips or crackers. Also great as a spread for meat sandwiches. By adding a little more milk, you will have a thinner mixture which can be used as a sauce for squash or cauliflower instead of the regular cheese sauce. Mild or sharp cheddar may be used also.

Irma Spear

Hamburger Dip

1 pound ground beef
1 large onion, chopped
1 can tomatoes
2 jalapenos (hot chili pepper)
¾ cup diced pimento
1 can tomato paste

¾ cup slivered almonds
¼ teaspoon oregano
1 teaspoon salt
¼ teaspoon pepper
2 garlic buds

Brown meat with onions. Add other ingredients and simmer one hour. Serve hot with king-size corn chips.

Ame Deen

Party Meatballs

1½ pounds ground beef
1 pound ground veal
1 (4½ ounce) can deviled ham
1 small can evaporated milk
2 eggs
1 tablespoon grated onion
1 cup soft whole wheat bread
   crumbs (2 slices)

½ teaspoon salt
½ teaspoon allspice
¼ teaspoon pepper
¼ cup shortening
¼ cup water
Creamy dill sauce

Combine everything but water and shortening. Mix lightly with a fork. Shape into about 72 balls. Brown a few at a time in shortening in large pan. Drain any fat. Return meat balls to pan, add water and cover. Simmer 20 minutes, or until cooked. Can refrigerate after browning then reheat with water in frying pan just before serving. Spoon into chafing dish, cover with creamy dill sauce.

DILL SAUCE

2 tablespoons butter
2 teaspoons flour
½ teaspoon salt
1 cup water

1 cup sour cream
1 tablespoon catsup
1 tablespoon dill weed

Melt butter, blend in flour and salt, cook; stirring constantly until mixture bubbles. Stir in water slowly, cooking and stirring until sauce thickens. Add sour cream, catsup, and dill weed and heat to boiling. Pour over meatballs. Yields 2 cups sauce.

Margaret Swanson

Sweet and Sour Meatballs

MEATBALLS

1 pound ground pork (or beef
   or beef and pork together)
2 green onions, chopped
1 teaspoon chopped ginger
1 tablespoon soy sauce

½ tablespoon sherry
1 teaspoon salt
1 tablespoon cornstarch
1 egg

SAUCE

3 tablespoons vinegar
4 tablespoons sugar
4 tablespoons tomato catsup
1 cup water

3 teaspoons cornstarch
1½ teaspoon salt
1 teaspoon sesame oil (optional)
1 tablespoon soy sauce

GARNISH

Pineapple cubes
Water chestnut

Pearl onions
Cubed green pepper (blanched)

Mix all items to make meatballs and form into small balls. Place on a foil covered cookie sheet and bake in 350⁰ oven until done. This part can be done ahead and the meatballs frozen.

Mix items for sauce and put in a pan over medium heat and cook until thickened. If any or all of garnishes are to be added just put them in with the sauce when it is cooked. When thickened, add meatballs and serve in a chafing dish.

NOTE: The sweet and sour sauce may be used with pork, shrimp, or oven fried fish.

Mrs. Sidney Wong

Sweet and Sour Meatballs

1½ pounds ground chuck
1 medium onion, finely chopped
½ teaspoon garlic salt
½ teaspoon salt

½ teaspoon lemon pepper
1 (12 to 14 ounce) jar apricot
    preserves
1 (12 to 14 ounce) jar bar-b-que
    sauce

Mix first five ingredients and roll into bite size meatballs. Brown in small amount oil and drain. Mix preserves and barbeque sauce and simmer for 30 minutes. Add meatballs. Serve warm in chafing dish.

Jackie Craft

Soy Sauce Beef

2 pounds rump or sirloin
    tip roast
1 tablespoon oil
⅔ cup soy sauce
½ teaspoon salt
¼ cup dry sherry
2 scallions, cut in half

1½ cup water
1 tablespoon brown sugar,
    packed
4 slices fresh ginger or
¼ teaspoon ground ginger
1 star anise or ¼ teaspoon
    anise seeds

Rinse and wipe beef and cut into 4 pieces. Heat oil in wok or skillet and brown beef on all sides. Combine all other ingredients in medium saucepan and bring to boil. Add beef and cook over low heat for 45 minutes, turning occasionally. Slice and serve hot or cold. Can be prepared 2-3 days in advance. Refrigerate in sauce. Slice before serving.

Mrs. Victor T. Bazzone

Ripe Olive Spread

8 ounces cream cheese
2 (4¼ ounce) cans chopped ripe olives
½ cup chopped pecans
1 cup (or more) mayonnaise
2 teaspoons scraped onion

Tabasco
Worcestershire sauce
Garlic salt
Lemon juice

Mix cream cheese, olives, pecans and mayonnaise. Add 2 teaspoons scraped onion, 2 drops of Tabasco, 4 to 5 drops Worcestershire sauce, a little garlic salt, and approximately ½ teaspoon lemon juice. Adjust seasonings to taste. May make sandwiches the night before and place in a sealed container and refrigerate.

Kathy Russell

5 Layer Taco Dip

2 cans Ole El Paso refried beans with
    green chilies
3 ripe avocados
2 teaspoons lemon juice
Salt
Pepper
¼ cup mayonnaise

1 cup sour cream
1 package taco seasoning
2 bunches chopped green onions
1 large can chopped black olives
2 tomatoes chopped
1 cup grated cheddar cheese
1 cup grated Monterey Jack cheese

1st layer: 2 cans Ole El Paso refried beans with green chilies, stirred
2nd layer: avocados mashed with 2 teaspoons lemon juice, salt and pepper
3rd layer: mayonnaise, sour cream and taco seasoning mixed well.
4th layer: green onions, black olives and tomatoes, mixed well.
5th layer: grated cheddar cheese and Monterey Jack cheese.
The first 3 layers may be prepared ahead of time and refrigerated. Serve with favorite tostada chips.

Terri Easterling

Guacamole Dip

2 ripe avocados
1 teaspoon salt
1½ teaspoons lemon juice
1 clove garlic

1 teaspoon Worcestershire sauce
¼ teaspoon red pepper
1 teaspoon grated onion
3 dashes hot pepper sauce (optional)

Peel, mash avocados. Add salt and lemon juice. Stir in Worcestershire sauce, garlic, pepper, and onion. Add hot pepper, if desired, and onion seasoning to taste. Serve with crackers. Yields 1½ cups.

Mrs. William L. Seal

Deviled Ham and Onion Dip

1 pound country style cottage cheese
1 (4½ ounce) can deviled ham
½ package Fritos brand onion dip mix

Mix cheese in blender until smooth. Add deviled ham and onion dip mix and whip to dip consistency. Serve with corn chips.

Mrs. Gerald Phillips

Holiday Pate

8 ounces softened cream cheese
1 can corned beef
¼ cup chopped stuffed olives
2 tablespoons minced onion

2 teaspoons Worcestershire sauce
2 teaspoons lemon juice
Parsley and pimento for garnish

Mix cream cheese and corned beef until well blended. Add olives, onion, Worcestershire sauce and lemon juice. Mix well and place in a greased ring mold. Chill. Unmold and decorate with parsley and pimento to resemble a wreath. Serve with crackers.

Mrs. Richard Graves

Cocktail Hot Dogs

1 jar grape jelly
1 jar chili sauce
Chili powder

Cocktail hot dogs (or regular
cut into bite size pieces)

Heat jelly and chili sauce. Correct with chili powder to taste. May be used as barbeque sauce without hot dogs.

Mrs. Jerry Riley

Cheese N' Sausage Rolls

16 fresh pork sausage links
16 slices white bread
4 tablespoons softened butter
or margarine

1 cup (4 ounces) shredded
processed American cheese

Cook sausage links. Cut crust from the bread and roll each slice flat. Mix the cheese and butter together and spread on both sides of the bread. Roll sausage in each slice. Bake on greased baking sheet in 400° oven for 10 minutes. Cut into small pieces and serve hot. Will yield 5 dozen.

Mrs. Cragin Gilbert

Sweet and Sour Sausage Balls

2 pounds bulk sausage
2 eggs, slightly beaten
¾ cup soft bread crumbs
Salad oil

1½ cups catsup
6 tablespoons brown sugar
¼ cup wine vinegar
¼ cup soy sauce

Combine sausage, eggs, and bread crumbs; shape into teaspoon size balls. Makes about 100 small meatballs. Saute in oil until brown; drain. Combine remaining ingredients; pour over sausage balls, and simmer for 30 minutes. Serve hot. Sausage balls may be refrigerated or frozen in sauce. If refrigerated, bake at 350⁰ for 20 minutes to heat before serving.

Gay Graves

Crabmeat Hors d'Oeuvres

½ pound crabmeat
¼ cup mayonnaise
3 ounces cream cheese
1 egg yolk
1 tablespoon minced onion

¼ teaspoon mustard
Salt
8 English muffin halves, toasted
   and buttered (or bread rounds)

Combine crabmeat and mayonnaise. Combine softened cream cheese, egg yolk, onion, mustard, and a pinch of salt. On each English muffin half spread crabmeat mixture, then top with the cream cheese mixture. Place on cookie sheet and broil 5-6 inches from heat for 2-3 minutes. Slice into quarters and serve hot.

Gay Graves

Chutney Crabmeat Dip

1 can crabmeat
Lots of lemon juice
12 ounces cream cheese
¼ cup mayonnaise
1 cup sour cream
1 teaspoon curry powder

¼ bottle Major Greys Chutney
1 clove garlic
Crumbled bacon
Tabasco
Salt

Mix well and salt to taste. Serve with party crackers.

Mrs. Adron Swango

Fresh Crabmeat Dip

1 pound fresh crabmeat, flaked
1 cup sour cream
4 teaspoons horseradish
2 tablespoons Zesty Italian
   salad dressing

1 tablespoon chili sauce
Salt and pepper to taste

Stir together. Refrigerate at least one hour for flavors to blend.

Dayonne McGuire

Crabmeat Mornay

1 stick butter
1 small bunch green onions,
   chopped
½ cup finely chopped parsley
2 tablespoons flour
1 pint breakfast cream

½ pound grated Swiss cheese
1 tablespoon sherry wine
Red pepper to taste
Salt to taste
1 pound white crabmeat

Melt butter in heavy pot and saute onions and parsley. Blend in flour, cream and cheese until cheese is melted. Add other ingredients and gently fold in crabmeat. May be served in chafing dish with melba rounds or in patty shells.

Mrs. Annabelle Hilbert

Hot Party Crab Dip

8 ounces cream cheese, softened
1 tablespoon milk
1 pound crabmeat, fresh or frozen
2 tablespoons chopped onion

½ teaspoon horseradish
Salt and pepper to taste
Dash of Worcestershire sauce
2 ounces slivered almonds

Blend all ingredients but almonds. Put in baking dish, sprinkle almonds on top. Bake at 350° for 20 minutes. Serve with crackers.

Mrs. William L. Seal

Crab Puffs

1 cup crabmeat
2 cups Bisquick
¼ cup chopped green onion
¼ cup Parmesan cheese

Salt and white pepper to taste
½ teaspoon dillweed
1 or 2 eggs to hold batter
¼ cup milk

Mix all ingredients and drop by teaspoonful into deep fat fryer at 380°. Dip into Sweet and Sour Sauce or a hot mustard sauce to serve.

SWEET AND SOUR SAUCE:

12 tablespoons sugar
6 tablespoons catsup
1½ teaspoons cornstarch

12 tablespoons vinegar
6 tablespoons Worcestershire sauce

Cook together until thickened.

Jackie Craft

Marinated Crab Fingers

1 can crab claw fingers
6 ounces melted butter
2 teaspoons minced garlic
3 teaspoons parsley flakes

4 ounces white Chablis wine
Juice of ½ lemon
½ teaspoon garlic powder
Salt and white pepper to taste

Put 4 ounces of butter in pan and saute garlic lightly. Add parsley and garlic. Add Chablis and cook until wine is reduced to 2 ounces. Add rest of butter, lemon juice, salt and pepper. Place crab in hot mixture. Marinate for 15 minutes and serve.

Doris Harvey

Miss B's Hot Shrimp Dip

1 (8 ounce) package cream cheese
1 small can (4½ ounce) shrimp
2 tablespoons finely chopped
  green onion

1 can cream of potato soup
½ teaspoon garlic powder
Dash Tabasco to taste
6 ounces grated cheddar cheese

Mix all ingredients except cheddar cheese. Add salt and pepper to taste. Blend until smooth. Spread ½ of the mixture into bottom of buttered 8 x 8 Pyrex dish. Sprinkle with ½ grated cheese. Add remaining shrimp mixture and top with remaining cheese. Bake at 350° for about 20 minutes or until hot. Great with crackers or chips. Best when served hot.

Joann Bommer

Red & Green Shrimp Mold

2 (8 ounce) packages cream cheese,
  softened
4 tablespoons Worcestershire sauce
1 tablespoon Tabasco
2 teaspoons garlic powder
½ pound grated Mozzarella cheese

1 pound boiled-peeled shrimp, chopped
1 jar Heinz Cocktail Sauce
1 bunch chopped green onions
1 chopped tomato
1 chopped green pepper

Cream together cream cheese, Worcestershire sauce, Tabasco and garlic powder and set aside. Using a ring mold, layer grated Mozzarella cheese; chopped shrimp topped with cocktail sauce; cream cheese mixture. Chill over night. Unmold onto platter and top with chopped green onions, tomatoes and green pepper. Serve with Wheat Thins.

Cathey Riemann

Smoked Fish Mold

2 pounds fillet of speckled trout
1 cup mayonnaise
Juice of ½ lemon
1 tablespoon finely chopped onion
6 fresh basil leaves, chopped

1 small loaf Reising Bake and Serve
  French bread
Softened butter
Charcoal
Large hickory chip

I use a Mr. Smoker and smoke the trout about 45 minutes until it flakes. Mix mayonnaise, lemon juice, onion, and basil. Add enough of the mayonnaise mixture to moisten trout enough to pat into mold which has been rubbed with oil. Unmold and serve with remaining mayonnaise and toasted bread. Slice thinly the loaf of bread. Spread generously with butter. Bake in 350° oven about 20-30 minutes. Check for crispness. Should be lightly browned. I serve this as an hors d'oeuvre or a first course without the bread. This doesn't work without fresh basil and smoked fish, but it is well worth the effort to plant your own basil. I freeze basil leaves in water to use out of season.

Mrs. Ernest G. Martin, Jr.

Oyster Artichoke Dip I

1 cup chopped celery
3 cloves garlic, chopped
1 bunch shallots, chopped
1 bunch parsley, chopped
1 (8 ounce) bottle olive oil

Tabasco
2 cans artichoke hearts, drained and
  chopped (save liquid)
½ pint oysters, pureed in blender
Progresso bread crumbs

Saute celery, garlic, shallots, and parsley in olive oil until transparent. Add Tabasco, artichoke hearts, juice, and pureed oysters. Add as much of the crumbs as needed to acquire the proper consistency for dip, but be careful not to make it too dry. Place in Pyrex baking dish and bake in 350⁰ oven for 45 minutes. This will freeze, but it is not quite as good after it has been frozen.

Gay Graves

Oyster Artichoke Dip II

1 bunch green onions
1 stick butter
½ pound fresh mushrooms
2 pints drained oysters

1 can drained artichoke hearts
Sherry
Fresh parsley, minced

Saute chopped green onions in butter. Add oysters and mushrooms. Simmer until oysters curl. Place mixture in blender and add artichokes. Blend until desired consistency for dip. Add sherry to get proper consistency. Serve in chafing dish. Top with green onion tops and parsley. This may be served as an entree in large patty shells if blender is omitted and all ingredients are hand chopped.

Mrs. William E. Smallwood

Oyster Dip

1 stick margarine
1 medium onion, chopped
5 to 6 shallots with tops, chopped
1 pint oysters, drained and minced
4 tablespoons lemon juice
4 slices thin sliced white bread
* broken into small pieces*

3 hard cooked eggs, chopped
Salt, pepper, Tabasco and
* Worcestershire to taste*

Melt margarine in large saucepan. Add onions and shallots and cook until tender but do not brown. Add minced oysters and lemon juice. Cover and simmer for 10 minutes. Refrigerate. Thirty minutes before serving, add the bread pieces, chopped eggs, and seasonings to taste. Heat and serve in chafing dish with king-sized corn chips.

Mrs. Jim Nicholson

Oyster Loaf

16 ounces cream cheese
2 teaspoons Worcestershire sauce
Garlic powder to taste

2 tablespoons mayonnaise
2 cans smoked oysters, well
* drained and chopped*

Blend first 4 ingredients thoroughly by hand. Spray waxed paper with Pam. Spread mixed cream cheese mixture on waxed paper in rectangular shape about 8 inches long and 5-6 inches wide. Spread chopped oysters over cream cheese mixture. Roll as a jelly roll. May be made several days in advance or may be frozen and thawed at serving time. Serve with party crackers. There should be a definite garlic taste.

Mrs. Thomas Hunt, Ruston, Louisiana

Mock Oysters Rockefeller

2 packages frozen chopped broccoli
1 tube garlic cheese spread
1 large onion, chopped
1 bunch green onions, chopped
1 stick butter

1 pint oysters
1 can cream of mushroom soup
1 tablespoon anchovy paste
Bread crumbs
Parmesan cheese

Boil oysters in oyster liquor until edges curl; drain. Cook broccoli; drain. In a large pot, saute onions in butter until transparent. Add cheese, mushroom soup, and broccoli; fold in oysters. Add anchovy paste and put in a large casserole and sprinkle with bread crumbs and cheese. Bake at 325° for 30-35 minutes. Transfer to chafing dish and serve with crackers.

Gay Graves

Shrimp Relish

1½ pounds large fresh shrimp,
  cooked and cleaned
1 cup minced onion
1 cup snipped parsley

⅔ cup salad oil
⅓ cup vinegar
1 clove garlic, minced
1½ teaspoon salt
Dash of black pepper

In large bowl combine shrimp, onion, and parsley. In small bowl, mix oil, vinegar, garlic, salt, and pepper; beat well. Pour over shrimp. Refrigerate 1 hour or until served. At serving time heap shrimp in serving dish with a few on the rim. Yields about 30 shrimp.

Barbara Harvey

Marinated Shrimp

2 to 3 pounds shrimp,
  cooked and cleaned
1½ cups salad oil
¾ cup white vinegar
1½ teaspoons salt
2 teaspoons celery seed
3 tablespoons capers and juice
Dash of Tabasco

8 bay leaves
2 cups thinly sliced onion
1 cup thinly sliced oranges
2 cups bell pepper, thinly
  sliced in rings

In shallow dish alternate shrimp in layers with onions, oranges, bell pepper, and bay leaves. Combine in seperate bowl the salad oil, vinegar, salt, celery seed, capers with juice, and Tabasco. Mix well and pour over shrimp. Cover and refrigerate for 24 hours. Serve with toothpicks to spear shrimp. Beautiful for a buffet table. At Christmas time, use red and green bell peppers for a colorful, festive dish. Serves 12.

Mrs. Kent Lovelace, Jr.

Shrimp Mousse

1 can tomato soup
9 ounces cream cheese
2 envelopes gelatin
½ cups boiling water
1 pound cooked, deveined, and
  minced shrimp

½ cup finely chopped celery
½ cup finely chopped green pepper
½ teaspoon onion juice
1 cup mayonnaise
Worcestershire sauce, horseradish,
  and Tabasco to taste

Bring soup to boil. Dissolve cream cheese in soup. Melt gelatin in boiling water and add to soup mixture. Add shrimp. Add seasonings to taste. Add remaining ingredients. Mix well. Pour into mold. Refrigerate until congealed. Unmold on platter for serving.

Mrs. Sam Morse

Shrimp Pate

2 cans shrimp or ½ pound small
  shrimp, cooked
½ cup butter
2 tablespoons pale dry sherry
1 tablespoon lemon juice

1 tablespoon grated onion
¼ teaspoon nutmeg or mace
¼ teaspoon dry mustard
¼ teaspoon cayenne

Mince shrimp. (If canned shrimp are used, soak in cold water first and drain well.) Mix sherry and butter well. Add remaining ingredients. Pour into mold. Refrigerate. Serve with crackers.

Mrs. Alan O. Clark

Shrimp Squares

1 (4 ounce) can shrimp (or fresh)
10 ounces sharp cheddar cheese

6 medium eggs
Dash of salt

Drain shrimp and chop. Sprinkle chopped shrimp in bottom of 8 x 8 teflon coated pan. Grate cheese coarsely and sprinkle over shrimp. Beat 6 eggs slightly and add salt. Pour over cheese. Do not stir. Bake at 300° for 30 minutes. Cut into 1 inch squares. Crabmeat may be used.

Sue Smith

Saucy Shrimp and Eggplant Appetizers

1 young eggplant
Butter
2 large onions
3 or 4 green onions or shallots
½ cup celery
2 large cloves garlic
½ can cream of mushroom soup
½ cup fine French bread crumbs
½ pound cleaned raw shrimp, part
  of them minced

1 egg
3 bay leaves
½ teaspoon basil
1 tablespoon parsley
1/8 teaspoon thyme
¼ teaspoon Tabasco
1 teaspoon monosodium glutamate
White pepper
Rock salt, if served in oyster shells
Salt

Peel and cut up the eggplant and cook in a small amount of salted water. Mince and saute in butter the onions, green onions, celery, and garlic. Add eggplant and soup and simmer until vegetables soften. Add the bread crumbs and shrimp; then add the egg, beaten with a little water. Simmer until of good consistency, seasoning to taste with bay leaves, basil, parsley, thyme, Tabasco, MSG, pepper, and salt. Cook in large cleaned oyster shells (selected for attractiveness), small ramekins, or scallop shells. Bake in buttered shell at 350° for 25 minutes. If oyster shells are used, set in shallow pan of rock salt. This freezes well.

Margie Newman

Spicy Nuts

1 unbeaten eggs white
2 cups pecans or walnuts

¼ cup sugar
1 tablespoon cinnamon

Preheat oven to 300°. Coat nuts with combination of egg white, sugar, and cinnamon. Spread coated nuts on ungreased cookie sheet. Bake for 30 minutes.

Sarah Geil

Banana Milk Shake

Bananas
Milk
Vanilla

Use very ripe bananas with well-flecked skins. Put the bananas in the refrigerator with the skins on. When chilled, peel, place in a plastic bag and freeze. For each banana; cut in 1 inch cubes, add ½ cup milk and ½ teaspoon vanilla and place in blender. Blend covered at medium-high speed. This makes an excellent after-school snack and is a good way to save bananas that are getting too old.

Jamie and Amy Graves

Fruit Punch

1 large package strawberry gelatin
1 cup boiling water
5 small cans pink lemonade
5 lemonade cans water
1½ large cans frozen orange juice

1½ orange juice cans water
1 large can unsweetened pineapple
   juice
2 bottles ginger ale

Dissolve gelatin in boiling water. Combine all ingredients. Serve cold. Can use lime or orange gelatin to change color. Yields about 8 quarts (40-50 servings.)

Mrs. William H. Murdock, Jr.

Holiday Orange Egg Nog

6 eggs
¾ cup sugar
¼ teaspoon cinnamon
½ teaspoon nutmeg
1 cup chilled evaporated milk

1 cup cold milk
1 cup chilled fresh orange juice
Grated orange peel
Nutmeg

In large bowl beat eggs until light and fluffy; add sugar, cinnamon and nutmeg. Stir in milk, blending well. Gradually stir in orange juice. Serve in small mugs or cups; sprinkle each serving with a little grated orange peel and a dash of nutmeg. Yields 24 cups. When recipe is doubled use one small 3 ounce can of orange juice concentrate. This makes the drink a little richer.

Mrs. Cragin Gilbert

Pot of Gold Punch

1 can (46 ounces) unsweetened
    pineapple juice, chilled
1 can (46 ounces) orange juice,
    chilled

1 pint lemon sherbet
1 pint orange sherbet
1 pint raspberry sherbet
1 quart ginger ale, chilled

Combine pineapple and orange juices in a punch bowl. Scoop sherbet into balls and float on punch. Add ginger ale and serve at once. Serves 25.

Amanda Fairbank

Brides Punch

3 bottles white wine (Paul Masson
    Emerald Dry)
¼ cup fruit brandy (peach
    or apricot)

2 tablespoons sugar
1 quart carbonated water (soda water)
Orange slices

Chill wine and soda water. Mix wine, brandy and sugar well and add carbonated water last. Garnish with orange slices. Makes about 18 (6 ounce) servings.

Mrs. Sidney Wong

Coffee Rum Punch

12 tablespoons instant coffee
2 cups sugar
2 cups water
3 large cans evaporated milk
3 large cans whole milk

½ gallon coffee ice cream (softened)
2 large bottles soda water
½ bottle light rum
Whipped cream

Add sugar and coffee to water. Stir, heat, blend, remove from heat, and chill. Add remaining ingredients. Top with whipped cream and serve. Serves 30 cups. A big hit for a brunch or luncheon.

Mrs. Harry Redmon
New Orleans, Louisiana

Heirloom Egg Nog

14 egg yolks, creamed
14 egg whites, stiffly beaten
2 quarts milk
1 quart whipping cream
1 quart half-and-half cream

4 cups sugar
1 cup brandy
1 cup rum
1 cup bourbon

Beat egg yolks. Add brandy, rum, and bourbon to egg yolks. Mix sugar and milk together and add to yolks. Fold in egg whites and whipped cream. The amount of brandy, rum, and bourbon may vary according to an individual's taste. Yields about 40 servings. You may wish to half this recipe as it makes a large quantity.

Mrs. Robert Ashford Little

Sunshine Punch

1 (6 ounce) can frozen lemonade
1 (6 ounce) can frozen limeade
1 (6 ounce) can frozen orange juice

4 cups water
1 quart ginger ale
½ bottle light rum

Mix all ingredients and serve chilled. Serves about 15. This recipe doubled fills a standard size punch bowl and should serve 30.

Mrs. Margaret Besnick

Hot Spiced Punch

2 quarts water
3 cups sugar
4 tablespoons pickling spice
1 can (46 ounces) pineapple juice

1 can (46 ounces) apple juice or cider
1 large can frozen orange juice
1 cup fresh lemon juice

Boil water, sugar, and pickling spice tied in several small cloth bags 10 minutes. Add juices and simmer at least 30 minutes. Leave spices in juice and store in glass containers in the refrigerator. Will keep 6 to 8 weeks. Serve hot. Other favorite juices may be added to basic ones. Delicious when served with Christmas goodies. Yields 25-30 servings.

Mrs. Robert Tate

Mrs. Wade Creekmore of Jackson, Mississippi, omits the pickling spice and adds 1 whole stick cinnamon, 1 teaspoon whole cloves, and uses honey, rather than sugar to sweeten. Your house smells divine while this is simmering.

Spanish Spiced Tea

1 gallon boiling water
2 teaspoons tea (cover and let
   stand 10 minutes)
½ teaspoon all spice
½ teaspoon cinnamon

½ teaspoon cloves
Juice of 4 oranges
Juice of 2 lemons
1½ cups sugar (or more to taste)

Boil water in large pot. Add tea and spices (tied in cloth bag) and steep for 10 minutes. Add fruit juices and sugar. Simmer and serve hot. May be made ahead of time and reheated.

Mrs. E. L. Byrd
Yazoo City, Mississippi

Instant Russian Tea

½ cup instant tea
1½ cups sugar
2 (7 ounce) jars Tang
2 envelopes Wylers Lemonade Mix

1 tablespoon cinnamon
½ teaspoon ground cloves
½ teaspoon nutmeg

Mix ingredients well. Store in tightly covered jar. Use 2-3 teaspoons in cup of boiling water to serve.

Shirley Beckett
Auburn, Alabama

Red Reindeer

Cranberry juice
Vanilla ice cream

Ginger ale

Half fill a tall glass or parfait glass with cranberry juice. Add a scoop of vanilla ice cream and enough ginger ale to float the ice cream.

Debra and Bill Piper
Burke, Virginia

Red Rooster

1 large (32 ounce) jar cranberry
*   juice drink*
24 ounces vodka

1 small can frozen orange juice
*   concentrate*

Mix ingredients and freeze. Take out of freezer a few minutes before serving. Stir and spoon into glasses. May be served with a straw or spoon. Garnish with slices of orange or lime or sprigs of mint.

Mrs. Ernest Martin, Jr.

TULLIS MANOR
Tullis Manor was built for New Orleanian Christoval Sebastian Toledano in 1856 as a summer residence. Toledano, a cotton and sugar cane broker, died in 1869. Seventeen years later, the house was sold to his niece, after which it passed through a succession of owners including Garner H. Tullis, President of the New Orleans Cotton Exchange in 1939. Damaged by Hurricane Camille, it was bought by the city of Biloxi in 1975 and has been restored to its former beauty. Open to the public.
Photograph by Vernon Matthews, Gulf Publishing Company, Inc.

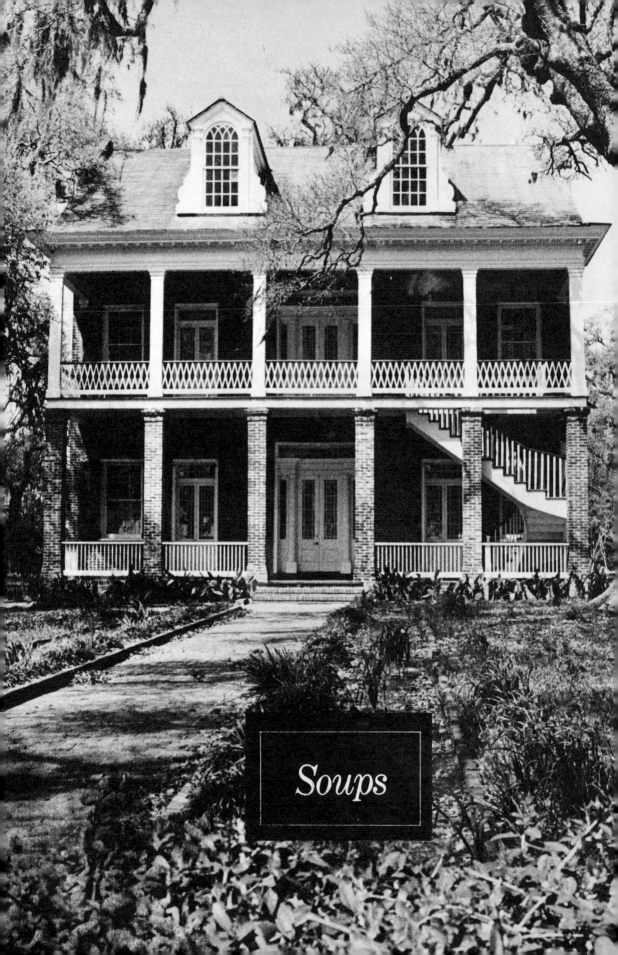

Soups

Soups

Cold Avocado Soup

3 ripe avocados (about 2 pounds)
2 (13 ounce) cans potato soup
2 cups light cream

1 cup chicken broth
¼ cup lemon juice
½ avocado for garnish

Peel avocados; slice. Blend half of all ingredients (except avocado for garnish) at high speed for 1 minute. Add other half of ingredients; blend until well mixed. Cover and refrigerate until well chilled, about 4 hours. Serve with avocado slice as garnish. Serves 6-8.

Mrs. Robert A. Mitchell

Okra Seafood Gumbo

¾ cup margarine
1 pound cut okra
2 cups chopped onions
2 cups chopped celery
2 cups chopped green pepper
4 tablespoons gumbo filé
   (ground sassafras leaves)
1 tablespoon Tabasco sauce
1 teaspoon minced garlic
1 teaspoon salt
¾ teaspoon red pepper
1 bay leaf crumbled fine

1½ teaspoons sweet paprika
½ teaspoon black pepper
½ teaspoon white pepper
½ teaspoon thyme and oregano
1¼ cups tomato sauce
5 cups seafood stock or good
   chicken stock
1 pound medium peeled shrimp
½ pound crabmeat
1 dozen oysters (optional)
1⅓ cups cooked rice

SEAFOOD STOCK

heads and shells of 1 pound shrimp
5 cups cold water
1 large cut up carrot
1 large quartered onion

1 stalk cut up celery
1 large clove garlic, unpeeled and
   quartered

Place stock ingredients in large pot. Simmer 4 hours. (Stock cooked for 20 minutes is better than water in the gumbo.) Add water as stock cooks down. Strain. May be frozen for 6 months.

In a heavy 4 quart soup pot melt margarine, fry okra over medium heat until tender. Stir frequently. Stir in onions, celery, and green peppers. Increase heat to high, add gumbo filé, Tabasco, garlic, and seasonings. Cook for 6 minutes stirring to prevent sticking. Reduce heat to medium; stir in tomato sauce. Cook for 5 minutes, scraping the bottom of the pan. Add stock; bring to a boil, then reduce heat and simmer covered for 50-60 minutes. Stir occasionally. Add seafood and rice. Cover and turn off heat. Allow to poach for a minimum of 10 minutes.

Serves 4 main courses or 8 appetizers. May be frozen before adding seafood. Thaw and bring to a boil before adding seafood and rice.

Dr. Gordon Stanfield

Corn Soup

1 can Pride of Illinois
   creamed corn
1 carton half-and-half cream

2 tablespoons whipped cream
Nutmeg for garnish

Use a sieve to remove all juice from corn. Discard corn. Add an equal amount of half and half cream. Refrigerate. Serves 2. Serve cold with one tablespoon whipped cream per serving. Garnish with nutmeg.

Mrs. Stanford Morse, Jr.

Cauliflower Soup

1/2 cup onion, chopped
1 tablespoon butter
1/2 teaspoon curry powder
6 cups chicken broth
1 1/2 cups cooked rice

1 cauliflower
1 cup heavy cream
1 teaspoon salt
1/2 teaspoon pepper

Saute onion in butter. Add curry powder and 2 cups of chicken broth. Simmer 15 minutes. Add rice to mixture and pour mixture into blender. Blend thoroughly. Wash cauliflower and break into flowerets. Cook in remaining 4 cups chicken broth for 15 minutes. Add mixture from blender to cauliflower mixture. Stir in cream; add salt and pepper. Serves 6.

Mrs. William S. Haynie

Crab Soup

1 can tomato soup
1 can green pea soup
2 cups half-and-half cream

1/2 cup sherry
8 ounces white or claw crab meat

Combine all ingredients in a 2 quart pot. Heat thoroughly but do not boil. Serves 8.

Mrs. J. Robbins Clower, Jr.

She-Crab Soup

1 pound white crab meat or Alaskan
   king crab
1 medium onion, chopped
4 teaspoons butter
3 teaspoons flour
1 quart whole milk

1 cup light cream
1/2 teaspoon white pepper
Salt to taste
1 teaspoon Hungarian paprika
Dry sherry

Saute onion in half the butter over low heat. Melt the rest of the butter in the top of a double boiler. Blend in the flour. Stir in onion and add milk gradually, stirring constantly. Add crab meat, pepper, and salt. Cook slowly for approximately 20 minutes. Add cream, paprika, and wine. Immediately remove from heat. Serve in heated bowls to which 1 teaspoon of sherry has been added. Serves 6 to 8.

Mrs. Charles Groover

Easy She-Crab Soup

1 can She-Crab soup
2 cans cream of celery soup
1 can cream of mushroom soup
1 package cream cheese, with
   chives if desired

1 can of milk to each can of soup
1 pound of white crab meat, washed and
   all shells removed
½ teaspoon Accent
1 cup dry sherry

Mix all ingredients in double boiler except sherry. Cook over low heat until thoroughly warmed and cheese is melted. Add sherry before serving. Serves 8-10. If there is left-over soup, save and refrigerate. Reheat and let it cook down very slowly. Mix with any seafood and use to fill crepes. Pour some of mixture over top. Great Sunday night supper served with green salad, French bread and glass of white wine.

Mrs. Robert A. Mitchell

Gazpacho

3 to 4 cups tomato juice
1 peeled cucumber
½ cup bell pepper
1 medium onion

2 tablespoons olive oil
1½ tablespoons vinegar
2 tablespoons sherry
Dash of Tabasco
1 clove garlic

Combine ingredients in blender. Blend 2-3 minutes. Chill several hours before serving.

CONDIMENTS:

1 tomato, diced
1 cucumber, diced
1½ cups celery, diced
1 cup croutons

½ cup toasted slivered almonds
½ cup crisp crumbled bacon
½ cup chopped black olives
½ cup chopped green onions

Mrs. James B. Roberts

Creole Gumbo

1 cup salad oil or bacon drippings
1 cup all-purpose flour
2 large onions, chopped
2 stalks celery, chopped
1 large green pepper, chopped
6 cloves garlic, minced
1 gallon warm water
2 beef bouillon cubes (optional)
4 cups sliced okra
3 tomatoes peeled and chopped,
   or 2 #2 cans of tomatoes

2 tablespoons salt
1 teaspoon red pepper
Black pepper to taste
1 pint oysters, undrained
1 pound crabmeat
1½ to 2 pounds fresh or frozen
   shrimp, peeled
½ cup chopped parsley
½ cup chopped green onion tops
Hot cooked rice
Gumbo file (optional)

Combine oil and flour in an iron pot over medium heat; cook stirring constantly until roux is the color of a copper penny, about 10-15 minutes. Add onion, celery, green pepper, and garlic to roux; cook stirring constantly until vegetables are tender. Do not let roux burn as it will ruin gumbo; reduce heat if necessary. Gradually add water, a little at a time; add okra and tomatoes. Bring to boil. Reduce heat and simmer, stirring occasionally, for 1-1½ hours. Stir in seafood. Add parsley and green onions; simmer 10 minutes. Serve over hot rice. Serves 12-14.

Jim Nicholson

Shrimp Gumbo

1 pound shrimp, peeled	3 tablespoons bacon drippings
1 can tomato sauce	½ teaspoon poultry seasoning
½ pound okra (either frozen, fresh, or ½ can canned)	¼ teaspoon pepper
	1 teaspoon salt
Few springs parsley (optional)	2 teaspoons Worcestershire sauce
½ cup chopped celery	3 tablespoons flour
1 medium onion	1 quart water

Chop onions, parsley, celery, and peel shrimp. Cut hard ends off okra. Put bacon drippings in skillet and saute onions until limp. Add flour and brown for roux. Add tomato sauce, okra, celery, and parsley stirring constantly until mixture is very thick. Have a quart of water boiling in large sauce pan. Pour contents from skillet into boiling water. Add seasonings and shrimp. Cook slowly for about 1 hour. Serve with cooked rice. More water may be added if it boils down too low. Crab meat may be added if desired. Serves 4.

Mrs. William Pettey

For taste variation, chicken broth can be used in place of water. Smoked sausage, chicken or ham may be added.

Mama Mavis' Seafood Gumbo

16 cups (4 quarts) water	2 cups chopped okra
1 tablespoon salt	1 (14 ounce) can tomatoes, mashed not drained
1 teaspoon black pepper	
1 teaspoon garlic powder	1 teaspoon McCormick's Seafood Seasoning
¾ cup oil	
1¼ cups flour	6 cups (approximately 3 pounds) peeled shrimp
1 cup chopped onions	
½ cup chopped green pepper	2 cans (6½ ounces each) crabmeat
½ cup chopped celery	

In 12 quart magnalite stock pot bring water to boil. Add salt, pepper, and garlic powder. In iron Dutch oven add oil and heat. Then add flour stirring constantly on low heat until golden dark brown. Do not burn. Add onions, green pepper and celery. Continue stirring until mixed. Add okra and mix. Add tomatoes and mix. Spoon roux to boiling water and cook on medium heat 1½ hours. Add seafood seasoning, shrimp and crabmeat or crabs. Cook 20 minutes longer. Season to taste. Serve over cooked rice. Serves 15.

Mavis Cospelich

If you like crabs, you can add fresh cleaned crabs and claws.

Onion Soup Gratinee

4 to 5 large onions (4 to 5 cups
  minced)
3 tablespoons butter or margarine
1/4 teaspoon peppercorns, coarsely
  crushed
1 tablespoon flour
3 cups water

3 (10 1/2 ounce) cans condensed
  beef broth
1 bay leaf
6 to 8 slices French bread, toasted
1/2 cup grated Swiss cheese

Slice and mince onions. Melt butter in heavy saucepan; add onions and peppercorns; cook stirring constantly until light brown. Sprinkle onions with flour; cook 1 minute stirring constantly. Add beef broth, water and bay leaf. Bring to boil; simmer 30-40 minutes. Discard bay leaf and correct seasoning. Pour into oven-proof tureen, top with toast slices, and sprinkle with cheese. Place under broiler until cheese turns golden. Serves 6-8. Great as a soup course or as a meal with a hearty salad, more French bread and crackers.

Mrs. William M. Rainey

Oyster Bisque

3 tablespoons butter
1 small onion, minced
1 small stalk celery, minced
1/4 teaspoon paprika
1 tablespoon flour

1 cup fresh oysters, drained and
  picked over
2 cups chicken broth, fresh or canned
1 cup milk (may use part cream)

In large heavy saucepan, saute onion, celery, and paprika in butter until transparent. Bring oysters to a boil in the chicken broth. Pour liquid into sauteed mixture. Add milk mixed with flour and heat until thickened; simmer slowly 5 minutes. Add oysters, and correct seasoning. This recipe may easily be doubled. Improves on standing and may be refrigerated for two or three days.

Louise Graves

Oyster Soup

1/2 cup butter
1 cup finely chopped celery
1 cup finely chopped shallots
1 tablespoon flour
1 teaspoon chopped garlic

Oyster water plus water to make 6 cups
2 dozen large oysters
2 bay leaves
Salt and pepper to taste

Melt butter in saucepan; saute celery and shallots until tender. Blend in flour and cook, stirring, over low heat for 5 additional minutes. Add remaining ingredients and simmer 20 minutes. Remove bay leaves and serve. Yields 1 1/2 quarts.

Barbara Harvey

Pumpkin Soup

2 tablespoons butter
½ cup chopped onion
1 teaspoon curry powder
1 tablespoon flour
2 cans chicken broth
1 cup milk or cream

1 can pumpkin
1 teaspoon brown sugar
1/8 teaspoon nutmeg
1/8 teaspoon pepper
¼ teaspoon salt

Saute onion in butter. Add curry, flour, and butter. Bring to bubble. Remove and gradually stir in broth. Add pumpkin, salt, sugar, nutmeg, and pepper. Bring to simmer and add milk. A special treat for a holiday party!

Mrs. George C. Lynde,
Muskogee, Oklahoma

Vichyssoise

8 large potatoes
1 onion, sliced
½ stalk celery, coarsely chopped
1 cup diced ham or small ham bone
½ cup shallots, finely chopped

4 cups milk
1 cup cream
1 tablespoon Worcestershire sauce
Dash of cayenne
Salt to taste

Peel potatoes and cut in quarters. Put in pot and cover with a liberal amount of water. Add ham, onions, and celery. Boil until potatoes fall to pieces. Add water if necessary. Remove from heat and add milk and cream gradually stirring constantly. Strain. Then add chopped shallots. Season and chill. Serve cold.

Barbara Hill

Hearty Beef Vegetable Chowder

1 pound ground beef
2 tablespoons butter
4 cups hot water
½ bay leaf
½ teaspoon Worcestershire sauce
1 (10 ounce) package frozen mixed
    garden vegetables

1 cup chopped onion
2 cups canned tomatoes
2 beef bouillon cubes
1/8 teaspoon pepper
1 cup sliced celery
1 cup uncooked noodles
¼ teaspoon thyme (optional)

Saute meat and onions in butter until well browned. Add tomatoes, water, bouillon cubes, salt, pepper, bay leaf, celery and Worcestershire sauce. Bring to a boil, cover and simmer for 30 minutes. Add noodles, mixed vegetables and thyme. Bring to a boil again and cook 15 minutes. Makes 6 to 8 servings. Freezes well.

Mrs. Don Ambrose
Monroe, North Carolina

Delicious Seafood Chowder

1 large potato, diced
1 onion, chopped
½ cup celery, chopped
1 pint oysters, drained
4 tablespoons melted butter
  or margarine
2 tablespoons flour
Dash of Tabasco
Milk or Water

Dash of Worcestershire
1 (8 ounce) can minced clams, drained
2 (4½ ounce) cans shrimp, drained and
  chopped or ½ pound shelled, cooked
  shrimp
Salt and pepper to taste
Chopped parsley
Chopped green onion tops

Place potato, onion, and celery in saucepan; cook in water to cover until tender. Drain. Cook oysters in butter over low heat until edges of oysters curl. Combine flour, salt and pepper, Worcestershire sauce, and Tabasco in large saucepan; blend until smooth. Add potatoes, onion, celery and remaining ingredients except parsley and green onion tops. Add milk or water to desired consistency. Cover and let stand 15 minutes. Heat, sprinkle top with parsley and green onion tops, and serve. Serves 6.

David Veal

Fresh Mushroom Soup

1 tablespoon butter
1 tablespoon olive oil
1 large onion, chopped
1 clove garlic, minced (or the
  equivalent of garlic powder)
1 pound sliced mushrooms (caps and stems)

3 tablespoons tomato paste
3 cups chicken broth
2 tablespoons sweet vermouth
Salt and pepper to taste
Accent

Melt butter, add olive oil and saute onion. Add garlic, saute and remove. Add mushrooms and saute slightly. Blend in tomato paste mixing well. Add chicken broth, vermouth, salt and pepper. Simmer 10 minutes. Garnish and serve immediately. Serves 4 to 6.

GARNISH

4 egg yolks
2 tablespoons finely chopped parsley
2½ or 3 tablespoons Parmesan cheese

4 to 6 slices French bread
Butter

Beat together first 3 ingredients. Toast buttered bread placing 1 slice in each serving bowl. Bring soup to a boil. Add egg yolk mixture to boiling soup and ladle onto bread slices. Soup may be prepared ahead and garnished at serving time.

T. Glover Roberts

CHURCH OF THE REDEEMER   Church of the Redeemer and the Ring in the Oak are two of the Mississippi Gulf Coast's interesting historical sites. Pictured is the Church of the Redeemer as it stood prior to Hurricane Camille. There now remains the 1891 bell tower with the original building of 1873-74 behind. In the churchyard is a curious open ring (photo - upper left) in the limb of a giant live oak tree that perpetuates one of the most charming of Gulf Coast Indian legends. The story is told that a Biloxi Indian maiden fell in love with the son of the Chieftan of the Pascagoulas, an enemy tribe. Her father, Chief of the Biloxi tribe, denied the suitor until a ring grew in the sapling oak. Soon after, its branches were twisted into a ring by a hurricane.

Photograph by Chauncey T. Hinman

Breads

Breads

Fantastic Apple Bread

⅔ cup margarine
1¼ cups sugar
4 eggs
⅓ cup buttermilk
2 cups peeled apples, grated
   or minced

4 cups flour
2 teaspoons baking powder
1 teaspoon each salt, soda,
   and cinnamon
¼ teaspoon mace
1 cup chopped walnuts

Cream margarine and sugar. Add eggs beating well after each. Stir in milk and apples. Mix dry ingredients and stir in. Add nuts. Pour into 2 greased loaf pans. Let stand 20 minutes. Bake at 350⁰ for 50-60 minutes. Turn out and cool on rack.

Mrs. Harry Simpkins III

Banana Bread

1 stick butter
1 cup sugar
2 eggs
2 cups sifted flour

1 teaspoon soda
½ teaspoon cinnamon (optional)
3 or 4 large ripe bananas
1 cup chopped nuts (optional)

Cream butter and sugar. Beat in eggs, one at a time. Mix in sifted dry ingredients. Beat in mashed bananas. Pour into greased and floured loaf pan. Bake 50-60 minutes at 325⁰-350⁰.

Mrs. Virgil Gillespie

Oatmeal Bread

1 cup old fashioned oatmeal
1 cup water
2 tablespoons butter
1½ teaspoons salt
5 tablespoons honey

½ cup warm milk
2 packages dry yeast
3 tablespoons hulled sunflower seeds
3 tablespoons chopped walnuts
1 cup plus 2¼ cups unbleached
   white flour

Cook oatmeal and water together in a double boiler for 30 minutes. Remove to mixing bowl and add butter, salt, and honey, mixing in well. Mix together milk and yeast and soak for 15 minutes. Combine yeast mixture and oatmeal mixture. Add sunflower seeds, walnuts, and 1 cup flour and mix in well. Add 2¼ cups flour and knead until correct consistency, about 10 minutes. Let rise to double the bulk; then shape into loaves and place in well greased loaf pans. Let rise again, but not too high as it will sink in the oven because of the oatmeal in the dough (not enough gluten in it). Bake at 375⁰ for 40 minutes. To decorate top of loaves, brush them with a mixture of egg white and a little water; then sprinkle with raw oats.

Joanne G. Kennedy

Homemade Bread

2 packages dry yeast
½ cup warm water
2 cups milk
2 eggs, beaten

⅔ cup sugar
½ tablespoon salt
⅔ cup oil
9 cups flour

Sprinkle yeast on warm water. Let stand 7-10 minutes or until dissolved. Add sugar, salt, and oil to milk and warm until sugar dissolves. Cool to lukewarm. Beat eggs and add to milk. Add dissolved yeast to other liquids. Place combined liquids in large mixing bowl and add flour a cup at a time stirring or beating well after each addition. As it becomes stiff, you may have to mix with hands. All the flour may not be needed if too stiff; or more flour may be added if too runny. Knead slightly when all flour is added. Grease a large bowl and place dough in it to rise. Cover with plastic and clean cloth. Place in a warm, draft-free place to rise until double, about 1 hour. Punch down and turn out on floured surface and knead until smooth. Shape into 3 or 4 loaves and place in greased loaf pans. May brush tops with melted butter. Cover again and let rise in warm, draft-free place until double, about 45-60 minutes. Bake in preheated oven at 350⁰-375⁰ for 30-40 minutes or until brown and loaf sounds hollow when tapped on bottom. Remove from pans and cool.

Mrs. Cecil Kilpatrick,
Mobile, Alabama

Swedish Flat Bread

2¾ cups unsifted, unbleached
    white flour
¼ cup sugar
½ teaspoon soda

½ teaspoon salt
½ cup butter or margarine
1 cup buttermilk

Blend flour, sugar, soda, and salt. Cut in butter until mixture resembles fine crumbs. Stir in buttermilk, using a fork, until mixture holds together adequately. Divide in half. Roll on floured board to ¼ inch thick. Cut in 2 x 3 inch pieces or any size of your choosing. Place on ungreased cookie sheet. Bake at 400⁰ for 5-8 minutes, depending upon degree of browness desired. Delicious served with honey.

Joanne G. Kennedy

Sour Cream Corn Bread

1 cup self-rising corn meal
3 eggs
½ cup corn oil
1 teaspoon baking powder

2 teaspoons sugar
1 (8 ounce) can cream style corn
1 cup sour cream

Mix all ingredients in the order in which they are given and beat well by hand. Pour into large greased iron skillet and bake in 350⁰ oven until brown on top. Serves 8-10.

Mrs. Leonard Blackwell

Russian Easter Bread

1½ cups milk
½ cup butter
½ cup white sugar
½ teaspoon salt
2 tablespoons brandy
1 teaspoon vanilla
1½ cups mixed glace fruits (pineapple, cherries, white raisins)

2 envelopes dry yeast
½ cup lukewarm water
2 beaten eggs
4 cups plus additional 4½ to 5 cups unbleached flour, sifted
½ cup slivered almonds

Scald milk. Add butter, sugar, salt, brandy, vanilla and stir. Cool to lukewarm. Dissolve yeast in water and add to milk mixture. Stir in eggs and 4 cups flour. Cover and let rise in warm place until doubled in bulk, about an hour. Add almonds and fruit to yeast mixture. Stir well. Place 4½-5 cups flour in a ring about the size of a dinner plate on board. Pour mixture into center. Knead flour into dough. Grease well 5 one pound coffee cans. Divide dough into five pieces and work well to form five smooth balls. Place dough in each can pressing down firmly. Let rise until about doubled. Bake at 375° for 30-35 minutes or until skewer inserted in center comes out clean. Top with confectioners sugar icing. Freezes well, but is less messy if iced after thawing.

Joanne G. Kennedy

Bagels

2 packages dry yeast
4½ cups sifted flour
1½ cups lukewarm water

3 tablespoons sugar
1 tablespoon salt

In large bowl, combine yeast and warm water. Let dissolve. Add sugar and salt. Mix. Add 1¾ cups flour and stir well. Stir in enough of remaining flour to make fairly stiff dough. Turn out on floured surface and knead about 10 minutes, or till dough is smooth. Add flour as necessary to keep from sticking to kneading surface. Cut into 15 to 16 pieces. Shape into balls and poke hole in center of each with floured finger. Pull gently to enlarge hole. Cover and let rise 20 minutes. In large pan, heat to simmering about 1 gallon of water and 1 tablespoon sugar. Cook 4 to 5 bagels at the time for 7 minutes, turning once. Drain. Put on ungreased baking sheet and bake at 375° for 30-35 minutes. The bagels should brown. They will be slightly chewy. May be frozen in large bags and reheated at 375° for 20 minutes.

Mrs. James Sheffield

Hush Puppies

2¼ cups Pioneer Self-rising Cornmeal Mix
1 white onion, finely chopped
½ green pepper, finely chopped
Salt to taste

1 egg
¾ cup beer
1 (8 ounce) can cream corn

Mix all together and drop by teaspoonsful into hot deep fat. Makes about 2 dozen.

Mrs. William Smallwood

Hush Puppies

¾ cup flour
½ cup corn meal
1 heaping tablespoon baking powder

Dash of salt
1 cup chopped onion
Just enough milk or water to moisten

Mix all ingredients together in bowl. Keep the batter stiff. Drop by teaspoonful into hot fat. Cook until brown. May be kept warm in oven until serving time.

Mrs. Frank Scott

Virginia Spoon Bread

1 cup corn meal
1⅓ cups boiling water
1⅓ cups milk
3 whole eggs

1 tablespoon baking powder
4 tablespoons butter
1½ teaspoons sugar
1½ teaspoons salt

Mix sugar and salt with cornmeal. Pour boiling water over corn meal mixture stirring constantly. Add butter, let stand and cool. Beat eggs until light. Add eggs and baking powder to mixture. Add milk and pour mixture in a 2 quart buttered baking dish. Place in a shallow pan of hot water in a 350⁰ oven. Bake about 35 minutes.

Mrs. Charles Groover

Battle Bread

1 cup milk
½ cup cornmeal
1 stick butter
1 cup cooked rice

2 eggs, well beaten
1 teaspoon salt
1 teaspoon baking powder

Cook milk, cornmeal and butter on top of stove until it thickens. Then add rice, eggs, salt and baking powder. Pour into greased 1 quart Pyrex dish. Bake at 350⁰ for 1 hour.

Mrs. Donnie Riley

Refrigerator Rolls

¾ cup Crisco
1 cup boiling water
2 beaten eggs
½ cup sugar
2 teaspoons salt

1 cup cold water
2 yeast cakes or 2 packages dry
½ cup lukewarm water
7½ cups flour, sifted

Combine Crisco and boiling water. Stir until Crisco melts. Mix eggs, sugar, and salt. Stir in cold water. Soften yeast in lukewarm water. Combine the 3 mixtures and add flour. Cover and chill overnight. Shape, let rise, and bake at 425⁰ until brown. Makes 3 dozen medium sized rolls. May be prebaked and frozen. Let thaw for a few minutes before heating.

Mrs. Jack VanLandingham

Hot Rolls

2 packages yeast
½ cup lukewarm water
1 cup smoothly mashed potatoes
½ cup hot water (may use water
    potatoes are cooked in)
½ cup hot milk

1 cup margarine
⅔ cup sugar
1 tablespoon salt
2 eggs, beaten
8 cups flour, sifted

Soften yeast in warm water and set aside. Combine hot mashed potatoes with water-milk mixture, margarine, sugar, and salt. Stir until margarine is melted. When this mixture is warm, add yeast and eggs; work in 4 cups flour, 1 cup at a time. When well mixed, work in more flour, saving about ½ cup for the board. Knead dough on well floured board. When smooth, shape in a ball and place in well greased bowl and set aside to rise. When double in bulk, punch down. Work dough one-fourth at a time. Roll ¼ inch thick on floured board and cut into circles. Fold over each for a parker-house roll or form into 3 small balls and place in greased muffin tin for cloverleaf. May make into loaves for bread. Brush with oil and set aside for rising. When double, bake rolls at 450⁰ for 10 minutes or until brown. Adjust baking temperature and time to individual oven. To freeze, bake until beginning to brown; cool and freeze.

Jane Joyner

Tiny Orange Muffins

½ cup butter or oleo
1 cup sugar
2 eggs
1 cup buttermilk

2 cups flour, unsifted
1 teaspoon soda
2 orange rinds, grated
1 cup raisins, finely chopped

Combine butter and sugar. Add eggs and milk. Add dry ingredients. Add orange rind and raisins, stir until moistened. Bake 15 minutes in 400⁰ oven in small greased tins. Dunk while hot in sauce made with 1 cup brown sugar and 1 cup orange juice boiled together.

Mrs. Paul C. Krass

Spicy Apple Muffins

1 cup soft margarine
2 cups sugar
2 eggs
2 cups all purpose flour
½ cup chopped nuts

3 teaspoons cinnamon
2 cups hot applesauce
2 teaspoons allspice
1 teaspoon ground cloves
2 teaspoons soda

Cream sugar and oleo. Add eggs, flour and other ingredients. Mix well. Spoon into small muffin tins. Bake at 350⁰ for 10 minutes or until done.

Mrs. Trent Lott,
Pascagoula, Mississippi

Special Bran Muffins

2 cups boiling water	4 eggs, beaten
2 cups 40% Bran Flakes	5 cups flour, sifted
3 cups sugar	5 teaspoons soda
1 cup oil	1 teaspoon salt
1 quart buttermilk	4 cups all bran

Pour boiling water over bran flakes. In another bowl, cream sugar and oil; add buttermilk and eggs; add hot bran mixture. Add flour, soda, salt, and all bran. Mix well. Bake in greased and lightly floured muffin pans at 400° for 10 minutes. Let cool slightly. Run knife around cup and ease out. Makes 6-8 dozen. Very moist after cooked. Reheat by wrapping in foil. Mixture will keep in glass jar in refrigerator about 2 weeks. Recipe easily halved.

Mrs. Liddell White

Mrs. William S. Haynie uses 100% bran and adds ½ pound raisins (optional). Sugar may be reduced, if desired, to as little as 1½ cups; and flour may be half and half combination of whole wheat and white.

English (White) Muffins

2 cups flour	½ teaspoon salt
2 teaspoons baking powder	2 tablespoons sugar
1 beaten egg	4 tablespoons melted butter
1 cup milk	

Put all ingredients in a mixing bowl. Mix until thoroughly blended. Bake in greased muffin tins at 325° about 25 minutes. Makes 18 muffins.

Mrs. E. C. Tutor,
Grenada, Mississippi

Angel Biscuits

2 packages yeast	1½ teaspoons salt
¼ cup lukewarm water	¼ cup sugar
5 cups flour	1 cup shortening
3 teaspoons baking powder	2 cups buttermilk
1 teaspoon soda	

Dissolve yeast in water. Sift dry ingredients, blend in shortening, add to milk, and mix well. Then add yeast. Knead well. Put in greased bowl in refrigerator. Roll out on floured surface. Cut with biscuit cutter and brush with melted butter. Fold in half. Bake at 400-450° for about 20 minutes.

Mrs. Virgil Gillespie

Yorkshire Pudding

1 cup sifted flour
1 teaspoon salt
1 cup milk

2 eggs, beaten
1 tablespoon melted fat from roast beef
Melted butter or roast drippings

Sift flour with salt. Add milk, eggs, and melted fat. Mix and beat well. Melt butter (or use roast drippings) and pour small amount into bottom of muffin tins. Fill tins with beaten mixture. Bake for 20 to 25 minutes at 400º-425º. Do not open oven. Makes 12 muffins. Serve with roast beef instead of rolls.

Louise Ellis

Cheese and Onion Hamburger Buns

5 to 7 cups unsifted flour
3 tablespoons sugar
1½ teaspoons salt
2 packages yeast

2 tablespoons butter, softened
2 cups very hot tap water
1½ cups grated cheddar cheese
¾ cup finely minced onion

Mix well 2 cups flour, sugar, salt, and undissolved yeast. Add butter. Gradually add water and beat 2 minutes at medium speed of electric mixer. Add 1 cup flour or enough for thick batter. Beat at high speed 2 minutes, scraping bowl occasionally. Stir in cheese, onions, and enough additional flour for a soft dough. Turn out on lightly floured board, kneading until smooth and elastic. Place in well greased bowl turning to grease top. Cover and let rise until doubled in bulk, about one hour. Punch dough down; turn out on lightly floured board. Divide into 20 equal pieces, forming each into a smooth ball. Place balls 1½ inches apart on greased baking sheets. Cover and let rise until doubled, about 45 minutes. Bake in hot 400º oven about 15 minutes or until done. Cool on wire racks.

Mrs. Harry Simpkins III

Bun Barbeque

1 package dry onion soup mix
2 pounds beef stew meat
1½ cups water
¼ cup vinegar
2 to 4 tablespoons sugar to taste
4 teaspoons mustard
2 teaspoons salt

¼ teaspoon red pepper
2 slices lemon
2 chopped onions
¼ cup butter (optional)
1 cup catsup
3 tablespoons Worcestershire sauce
½ cup ripe olives, sliced (optional)

Combine first 11 ingredients in heavy pot. Simmer until beef is falling apart, adding more water if necessary. Add catsup and Worcestershire sauce and simmer until very thick. Add ripe olives, if desired. Serve on buns or, even better, French bread. This recipe can also easily be adapted to use leftover roast beef or pork. If leftover meat is used, simmer all ingredients except meat, catsup, Worcestershire, and olives for 30 minutes; add meat, catsup, Worcestershire, and simmer until very thick and meat is falling apart. Add olives and serve. Freezes well. Serves 6-8.

Mrs. George Morse

Italian Popovers

2 eggs
½ cup milk
½ cup water
1 cup all purpose flour

1 teaspoon dry Italian salad dressing mix
¼ teaspoon salt
1 teaspoon cooking oil

In a bowl, combine eggs, milk, water, flour, dressing mix, and salt. Beat 1½ minutes at medium speed. Add oil. Beat 30 seconds more. Don't overbeat. Pour batter into 6 greased muffin cups, 6 ounces each. Bake at 475° for 15 minutes. Reduce temperature to 350° and bake an additional 25 minutes.

Mrs. William Seal

Cornmeal Hotcakes

2 eggs
1 cup buttermilk
½ teaspoon salt
¾ cup cornmeal

¼ cup plain flour
2 tablespoons melted butter
2 teaspoons baking powder

Beat eggs well, then stir in ingredients in order listed. Beat to smooth batter. Cook as you would regular pancakes. Makes 12 to 15 medium hotcakes.

Mrs. Watson Weatherly

Mrs. Tom Roberts adds 2 tablespoons miller's bran to batter and uses whole wheat flour in place of plain flour.

Pizza

2 packages dry yeast
1¼ cups lukewarm water
Pinch of sugar
3½ cups all-purpose flour
1 teaspoon salt

¼ cup olive oil (or cooking oil)
Corn meal
2 cups tomato and garlic sauce
1 pound mozzarella cheese, grated
½ cup Parmesan cheese

Sprinkle yeast and sugar into ¼ cup lukewarm water. In large bowl, sift flour and salt. Make a well in flour and pour in the yeast mixture. Add 1 cup lukewarm water and oil. Mix dough with fork or fingers. Form a ball and knead for 15 minutes. Set in dry place for 1½ hours or until it doubles in bulk. When dough is ready, preheat oven to 500°. Oil 2 large and 1 medium pizza pans and sprinkle with corn meal. Prepare pizza with tomato sauce and favorite topping. Cover with cheeses and bake for 25-30 minutes.

TOMATO AND GARLIC SAUCE

1 large can tomatoes
1 small can tomato sauce

Seasonings to taste as garlic, onion,
   parsley, oregano
1 tablespoon sugar

Mix all ingredients together. Cook in saucepan while dough is rising. Stir occasionally.

Jan Casey

Barbecue Sandwiches

1 can corned beef
½ cup catsup
1 cup barbeque sauce
1 tablespoon caraway seed

1 tablespoon Worcestershire sauce
Tabasco sauce to taste
1 cup sharp cheddar cheese, shredded
Buns

Mix all ingredients well. Spread on buns. Wrap in aluminum foil and bake at 450⁰ for 10-15 minutes. Sandwiches may be frozen by wrapping individually in aluminum foil and storing in a plastic bag. They need not be thawed before baking but will take longer to heat.

Gay Graves

Crab Omelet Sandwiches

1 bell pepper
1 onion
Butter or margarine
8 eggs, slightly beaten
1 pound crabmeat
Worcestershire sauce

Salt
Pepper
Very fresh bread
Mayonnaise
Tomatoes

Chop bell pepper and onion. Saute in butter until tender. Put eggs and crabmeat in bowl. Mix with Worcestershire sauce, salt, and pepper. Add sauteed vegetables. Cook like pancakes in small amount of butter. Make sandwiches with mayonnaise, sliced tomatoes, and crab omelets. Serves approximately 12-14.

Annie Pearl Waller
Ann Shelton

Hearthside Sandwich

Bread of choice
Sliced, cooked ham
Sliced Swiss cheese
Tomatoes (optional)
Butter or margarine as needed for grilling

Mayonnaise, mustard, as desired
1 egg, thinned with about 1 tablespoon
   milk, plus 1 teaspoon sugar per four
   sandwiches

Assemble sandwiches, then dip in egg, milk and sugar mixture. Melt butter in skillet and grill sandwiches. Serve immediately. May be frozen cooked by wrapping individually in foil. Reheat wrapped in oven. Do not freeze if tomatoes or mayonnaise used.

Mrs. William M. Rainey

Shrimp Sandwich

3 ounces Philadelphia Cream Cheese
2 tablespoons mayonnaise
1 tablespoon catsup
1 small can shrimp

¼ cup minced celery
1 teaspoon onion grated
Dash garlic powder (optional)

Mix all ingredients and spread on buttered bread.

Mrs. Tommy Roberts

Reuben Sandwiches

1/2 cup low-cal Thousand Island
   dressing
4 teaspoons Dijon mustard
2 teaspoons fresh horseradish
3 tablespoons softened margarine

Ryebread or Cocktail Ryebread
3/4 pound thinly sliced corned beef
1 cup sauerkraut drained well
12 ounces sliced swiss cheese
Pam

Combine dressing, mustard, horseradish and let marinate for 1 hour. Spread 1/2 teaspoon of margarine on each slide of bread. Place handful of corned beef on bread topping with 1 tablespoon of sauce, one tablespoon of sauerkraut and a slice of cheese. Top with bread slice and pan fry in Pam turning twice until golden brown on both sides. For Cocktail modification leave open-face and broil until cheese melts. Yield: 4 sandwiches

Note: Use Party Rye or Pumpernickle rounds for cocktail sandwiches.

Susan Oustalet

Baked Asparagus and Cheese Sandwiches

6 slices bread, thick, firm
   textured (Pepperidge Farm)
6 square slices Swiss cheese

24 to 30 asparagus spears,
   cooked and drained
1/2 cup shredded sharp cheese

CUSTARD TOPPING

4 eggs
2 cups milk
1 teaspoon salt

1/8 teaspoon pepper
1/4 teaspoon nutmeg
1 tablespoon onion, finely chopped

Trim crusts from bread and arrange in bottom of a 9 x 13 inch pan. Top each slice with Swiss cheese. Beat eggs slightly. Add milk, seasonings and onion. Pour over bread and bake in oven at 325° for 25 minutes. Remove from oven and top each bread slice with 4 or 5 asparagus spears. Sprinkle each "sandwich" with cheese and return to oven for 15 minutes or until custard is set and the top is golden. Let set 5 minutes after final baking time. Cut into 6 squares and serve hot.

Mrs. Harry Woodbury

Ed's Homemade Pimento Cheese

1 (4 ounce) jar chopped pimentos
1/2 pound grated cheddar cheese

1 teaspoon dry mustard
Mayonnaise to moisten

Drain pimentos and mix with grated cheese in a small saucepan. Add dry mustard. Over low to medium heat stir cheese mixture to soften and blend ingredients. Stir constantly to keep cheese from sticking to pan. This should take approximately one minute. Remove from heat and add enough mayonnaise to make it creamy. Serve warm or chilled.

Sherryl F. Decker

Debbie LaRose suggests spreading a small amount on a floured tortilla. Roll seam down and microwave a few seconds. Good warm.

Strawberry Fig Jam

2 cups peeled and mashed ripe figs
  (measure after mashing)
2 cups white sugar
2 small or 1 large strawberry gelatin

Combine figs, sugar, and gelatin in heavy saucepan. Bring to a boil and cook 5 minutes. Place jam in hot, sterile jars and seal. Store in dark, cool place. Best if used within a year.

Mrs. W. E. Bommer

Pear Preserves

6 cups pears (about 16)
3 cups sugar
1 lemon sliced thin

Peel and slice pears and cover with water. Add sugar and lemon. Cook slowly for 4 or 5 hours (until fruit is light colored). Makes 3 to 4 pints. Pack in jars and seal.

Mrs. George Schloegel

Banana Jam

12 cups sliced bananas (about 20
  medium bananas)
6 cups sugar
1½ cups orange juice
6 whole cloves

¾ cup lemon juice
3 strips orange peel
6 strips lemon peel
2 sticks cinnamon

Combine all ingredients in large kettle. Stir over moderate heat until sugar dissolves. Boil rapidly 10 minutes, reduce heat and simmer, stirring, until thickened, 15 to 20 minutes. When thick, remove from heat and ladle at once to sterilized jelly or canning jars, filling to within 1/8" of top. Screw caps on evenly and tightly. Invert a few seconds, then stand jars upright to cool. If jam is to be stored for a long time, set jars on rack in large kettle and cover with boiling water. Boil 10 to 15 minutes. Remove from water and cool. Makes about 5 pints.

SMALL-QUANITY BANANA JAM

Combine 1½ cups sliced bananas, ¾ cup sugar, 3 tablespoons orange juice, 5 teaspoons lemon juice, 1 small cinnamon stick and 1 whole clove in 2-quart saucepan. Stir over moderate heat until sugar dissolves. Boil rapidly 5 minutes, reduce heat and simmer, stirring, until thickened, about 10 minutes. Pour into small jars or other container, cool, then store in refrigerator. Makes about 1½ cups.

E. A. Myrick

Salads

Salads

New Orleans 1000 Island Salad Dressing

2 cloves garlic
1 cup mayonnaise
¼ cup chili sauce
¼ cup catsup
Juice of one onion, grated

1 teaspoon black pepper
1 teaspoon dry mustard
1 cup Wesson oil
Dash Tabasco
2 tablespoons water

Combine all ingredients in quart jar and store in refrigerator at least overnight. Shake before using.

Mrs. Virgil Gillespie

Oil and Vinegar Salad Dressing

2 tablespoons onion
½ cup olive oil
¾ teaspoon each of basil,
   oregano, sugar, Worcestershire,
   and dry mustard

2 teaspoons salt
2 teaspoons pepper
¼ cup red wine vinegar
1 tablespoon lemon juice

Place all ingredients except vinegar and lemon juice in blender and blend well. Then add vinegar and lemon juice and blend again. Makes one cup.

Mrs. Gordon Myrick

Roquefort Dressing

1 small egg
¾ cup salad oil
2 tablespoons red wine vinegar
½ teaspoon salt
½ teaspoon dry mustard

½ teaspoon sugar
1/8 teaspoon pepper
3 drops Worcestershire sauce
2 drops Tabasco sauce
1 ounce Louis Rigal roquefort,
   crumbled

In blender, whip egg; add oil slowly; after it thickens, add the other ingredients in order. Mixture will be thick; add water slowly until consistency of cream. Chill and use in any green or mixed vegetable salad. Keeps well in refrigerator.

Louise Graves

COAST RECREATION

Water sports on the Coast include sailing, fishing, and regattas. The Mississippi Deep Sea Fishing Rodeo is the largest of such events in the world with competition in spear, deep sea, and fresh water fishing. The Rodeo is a holiday carnival complete with record-setting catches and fireworks. Excurision and charter boats make it possible for visitors to travel to offshore islands such as Deer Island, pictured here in the background.

Photograph by Chauncey T. Hinman

Trilby's Salad Dressing

2 tablespoons salt
1 tablespoon dry mustard
1 teaspoon each oregano, marjoram,
   celery seed, and paprika
1 tablespoon pepper

1/3 quart superior quality olive
   oil
1/3 quart vegetable oil
1/3 quart wine vinegar

Mix the dry ingredients; add the oils and vinegar and shake well.

Trilby's Restaurant, a tradition in Ocean Springs since 1939, remains a favorite with local residents and tourists as it continues in the tradition of excellence in dining. This is the house dressing served on Trilby's salad, and is a highlight of a meal at Trilby's.

French Quarter Sauce for Shrimp

1 pint Creole mustard
1 pint French dressing (Kraft)
2 tablespoons paprika

2 tablespoons grated horseradish
1/2 cup chili sauce
1 tablespoon chopped parsley

In blender, combine ingredients and blend until smooth. Refrigerate. Serve over seasoned boiled shrimp on a bed of shredded lettuce.

Roger G. Weill

Lescari Dressing

1/2 pound Romano cheese,
   finely grated
1 pint salad oil

2 lemons, juice only
3 garlic cloves, juice only

Shake all ingredients in a quart jar. Dressing will keep indefinitely in refrigerator. Especially good on lettuce, watercress, and parsley mixed. Use salt and pepper to taste.

Verne Lanegrasse

Mayonnaise

2 egg yolks
1 tablespoon vinegar
Juice of 1 lemon (or 1/2 lemon
   if large
1 teaspoon prepared mustard

1/2 teaspoon salt
1/4 teaspoon sugar
2 cups Wesson oil

With a mixer on medium high speed beat all ingredients except oil. When well combined, add oil in a thin stream, beating constantly.

Mrs. Sam Morse

Spinach Salad Dressing

½ cup sugar
½ cup cider vinegar
2 tablespoons salad oil
2 to 3 small green onions,
    chopped

1 teaspoon Worcestershire
1 teaspoon salad mustard
Dash of black pepper

Combine all ingredients. Refrigerate before using.

Mrs. William H. Murdock, Jr.

Meemon's Sweet Fruit Dressing

½ cup sugar
1 teaspoon salt
1 teaspoon dry mustard
1 teaspoon celery salt

1 teaspoon paprika
1 teaspoon grated onion
1 cup salad oil
¼ cup vinegar

Mix dry ingredients. Add onion. Add oil, a small amount at a time, alternating with vinegar. Mix well and keep in refrigerator until chilled. Serve over fruit in lettuce bed. Pears and pineapple are especially good. Makes 1½ cups and keeps well.

Mrs. George W. Edwards

Cranberry Relish

1 small box lemon gelatin
1 small box cherry gelatin
2 cups boiling water
1 pound cranberries,
    ground but not too fine
1 large orange, finely ground
2 cups sugar

1 cup crushed pineapple
1 large apple, finely chopped
20 large marshmallows, cut up
1 cup celery, finely chopped
1 cup pecans, finely chopped

Dissolve gelatins in boiling water. Let cool. Combine all other ingredients. Pour cooled gelatin mixture over all. Put in mold and chill overnight. Serves 8-12.

Mrs. Ronald Brown

Frozen Fruit Salad

3 ounces cream cheese
2 tablespoons heavy cream
3 tablespoons mayonnaise
2 tablespoons lemon juice
1 cup pineapple chunks, drained
1 cup fresh cherries, halved and
    pitted, or canned cherries

1 cup seedless grapes
1 can mandarin orange sections
½ pint whipped cream
Pinch of salt
2 tablespoons sugar

Mix cheese with cream. Add mayonnaise, lemon juice, salt, sugar, and fruit. Fold in whipped cream. Freeze in 5 or 6 cup mold. Serves 8-10.

Mrs. Leonard Blackwell

Blueberry Salad

1 (15 ounce) can blueberries
1 (8¼ ounce) can crushed pineapple
2 (3 ounce) packages black
    raspberry gelatin
1 cup boiling water
8 ounces cream cheese, softened

1 (8 ounce) carton sour cream
½ cup sugar
1 teaspoon vanilla
1 cup chopped pecans (optional)

Drain blueberries and pineapple, reserving liquid. Dissolve gelatin in boiling water. Add enough water to reserved liquid to make 1¾ cups. Add to dissolved gelatin. Add fruit and pour into a 13" x 9" pan. Chill until firm. Combine cream cheese, sour cream, sugar, and vanilla. Beat until smooth. Spread over gelatin and sprinkle with pecans. Chill until set.

Mrs. James O. Dukes
Mrs. Mollie Morse

Salad Delight

1 large package apricot gelatin
2 cups hot water
¼ cup orange juice
1 large can crushed pineapple, drained

3 bananas, sliced
1 cup marshmallows, chopped
1½ cups cold water

Dissolve gelatin in hot water. Add remaining salad ingredients. Congeal.

TOPPING

3 tablespoons flour
½ cup sugar
Dash of salt
1 egg, beaten

Coconut
1 cup pineapple juice
2 tablespoons butter
2 packages dessert topping mix,
    prepared

Mix flour, sugar, salt and egg. Add pineapple juice. Cook until thick. Add butter. Cool. Fold in dessert topping mix. Spread on congealed gelatin. Sprinkle with coconut.

Mrs. John DeLuca

Melon Balls in Rum Sauce

1 cantaloupe
1 small honeydew melon
1/8 of a watermelon
⅔ cup sugar

1 tablespoon grated lime rind
6 tablespoons lime juice
½ cup light rum
⅓ cup water

Make melon balls, put in serving bowl, and chill. In small saucepan mix sugar and water. Bring to a boil and simmer 5 minutes; then add lime rind. Cool to room temperature. Stir in lime juice and rum. Pour over melon balls and chill several hours. Serves 8.

Mrs. John W. Puckett

Congealed Fruit Salad

1 package lemon gelatin
2 cups hot water
½ pound marshmallows
1 small can crushed pineapple,
    drained

9 ounces cream cheese
1 cup chopped pecans
1 cup salad dressing or mayonnaise
1 cup whipped cream

Dissolve the lemon gelatin in hot water. Cut up marshmallows and stir in the gelatin mixture while hot. Drain the pineapple and add to lemon gelatin mixture. Add remaining ingredients and cream all together, folding in whipped cream last. Pour into 8" x 12" pan and put in refrigerator until congealed. Then add following layer.

2 packages cherry gelatin
2 cups hot water
2 cups cold water

After lemon gelatin mixture has congealed, dissolve the cherry gelatin in hot water. Then add cold water. When cool, pour over lemon gelatin mixture. Return to refrigerator until congealed. Serves 20.

Mrs. C. H. Brandon

Molly's Salad

8 ounces cream cheese
1 (3 ounce) package lemon gelatin
1 large can crushed pineapple,
    drained (reserve liquid)

1 cup pecans, chopped
1 small can pimento, chopped
½ pint whipping cream, unwhipped
Olives

Mix cheese and pineapple. Add nuts, pimento, and whipping cream. Take juice of pineapple and water to make 1 cup. Bring to boil. Add gelatin and stir until dissolved. Add other ingredients and chill until set. Garnish with stuffed olives. Serve with crackers. Use 8" square pan or mold. Serves 6-8.

Mrs. Alben N. Hopkins

Pickled Peach Salad

1 envelope plain gelatin
½ cup cold water
1 large can pickled or spiced
    peaches
1 to 2 cans pineapple tidbits

1 package lemon gelatin
½ cup sliced stuffed olives
5 sweet gherkins, sliced
1 cup chopped pecans

Soften unflavored gelatin in cold water. Heat juice from fruit (should be 2 cups) to dissolve both gelatins. When cooled to consistency of raw egg whites add all other ingredients. Pour in slightly oiled mold and chill. Serve with homemade mayonnaise. Especially good with ham or turkey. Serves 8.

Mrs. George Morse

Minted Pear Mold

1 (29 ounce) can sliced pears,
   drained (reserve liquid)
1/3 cup green creme de menthe
2 envelopes unflavored gelatin

Water
1 cup sour cream
1/3 cup chopped pecans or
   sliced almonds

In a medium bowl, marinate pears in creme de menthe. In medium saucepan, sprinkle gelatin over 1 cup pear syrup. Stir over low heat until gelatin dissolves. Add water to remaining syrup to equal 1½ cups and add to gelatin mixture. Add sour cream. Chill, stirring occasionally, until mixture is consistency of unbeaten egg whites. Fold in pears with creme de menthe and pecans. Turn into a 5 cup mold and chill until firm or about 4 hours. Serves 8.

Mercedes Parks

Cranberry Waldorf Salad

2 cups cranberry or cranapple
   cocktail juice
1 (3 ounce) package lemon gelatin
1/4 teaspoon salt

1/2 cup chopped celery
1 cup diced unpared apple
1/4 cup chopped pecans or walnuts

Heat 1 cup juice to boiling, add gelatin. Dissolve gelatin. Add remaining juice and salt. Chill until partially set. Stir in celery, apple and nuts. Pour into 4 to 6 individual molds. Chill until firm. Unmold on lettuce leaf.

Mrs. James LaRose

Tangy Ambrosia D'Lite

1 pink grapefruit, peeled and sectioned
1 medium orange, peeled and sectioned
1/2 cup diced mango
1/2 cup sliced fresh pineapple

1/2 cup diced papaya
1/4 cup low-fat yogurt
2 packets Equal

Mix fruit together. Chill. Place onto individual serving dishes. Blend yogurt and Equal together. Top each serving of fruit with some of the yogurt mixture. Serve well chilled. You can double recipe and stir the yogurt mixture into the fruit and serve in large bowl. Serves 10 to 12.

Note: Canned fruit may be substituted, but be sure to use the kind packed in its own juice.

Dixie N. Boyd

Kidney Bean Salad

2 cans kidney beans, drained
1 small onion, chopped

2 hard boiled eggs, chopped
1 stick celery, chopped
Mayonnaise and horseradish mustard

Mix together with sufficient mayonnaise and horseradish mustard to serve as dressing. Serves 6.

Mrs. D. Lionberger

Marinated Snap Beans

1 pound fresh snap beans, cut
   diagonally (about 4 cups)
1/3 cup fresh lemon juice
1/4 cup chopped parsley
1 teaspoon salt

1 cup fresh carrots, sliced
2/3 cup olive oil
1 medium onion, thinly sliced
2 tablespoons chopped green pepper
1/8 teaspoon black pepper

Cover and cook green beans and carrots in small amount of boiling water for 5 minutes. Drain and cool. Combine all other ingredients in large bowl. Add cooled vegetable mixture. Refrigerate at least 4 hours turning occasionally. Serves 4-6.

Mrs. E. H. Currie, Jr.

Marinated Cucumbers

6 cucumbers, thickly sliced
1 cup white vinegar
1/2 cup sugar

1/2 teaspoon salt
1 tablespoon chives
1 tablespoon parsley, chopped

Combine last 5 ingredients and pour over cucumbers. Serves 10-12.

Mrs. Cot West

Jellied Consumme

2 cans consumme, undiluted
Tabasco sauce
Worcestershire sauce
Lemon juice

Celery salt
4 tablespoons sour cream
4 tablespoons watercress, chopped
2 avocados, halved (optional)

Heat consomme in a saucepan on low heat. Season to taste with Tabasco sauce, Worcestershire sauce, lemon juice, and celery salt. Remove from heat and pour into 4 individual small soup bowls or ramekins. Refrigerate until firm. When ready to serve spoon 1 tablespoon sour cream and 1 tablespoon chopped watercress on top of jellied consomme. The jellied consomme may also be served in avocado halves. Serves 4.

Nancy Mize Sneed

Asparagus Salad

1 large can asparagus, chilled
   and drained
Lettuce
1 egg yolk, boiled and mashed
1 teaspoon salad mustard
1 tablespoon salad oil

1 tablespoon cider vinegar
Salt and pepper
1 teaspoon lemon juice
1 egg white, boiled and chopped

Arrange asparagus spears on lettuce. Combine egg yolk, mustard, salad oil, vinegar, salt, pepper, and lemon juice. Beat well. Spoon over asparagus. Sprinkle chopped egg white over all. Serves 4.

Iona Page

Congealed Asparagus Salad

1 large can cut green asparagus
1 (3 ounce) box lime gelatin
1 cup liquid (asparagus juice
    and additional water to
    make liquid)
¼ teaspoon salt
1 cup mayonnaise

½ cup milk
½ cup grated sharp cheese
1 tablespoon grated onion
1 tablespoon wine vinegar
A few drops Tabasco

Dissolve gelatin in heated cup of liquid. Add salt and allow to cool until syrupy. Mix mayonnaise, milk, cheese, onion, vinegar and Tabasco. Fold into thickened gelatin; add asparagus. Turn into greased mold or 13" x 9" pan. Refrigerate until set. Serves 8 or 9. A big hit with the ladies for lunch.

Mrs. Carroll Kemp, Jr.

Congealed Broccoli Salad

1 package frozen chopped broccoli,
    cooked and drained
1 envelope gelatin, dissolved in
    ½ cup cold water
½ can beef consomme
8 ounces cream cheese
1 cup mayonnaise

1 small can chopped pimento
¾ teaspoon salt
¼ teaspoon black pepper
2 tablespoons lemon juice
2 tablespoons Worcestershire sauce
¼ teaspoon Tabasco
2 hard boiled eggs, chopped

Stir hot consomme into gelatin mixture. Cream together cream cheese and mayonnaise. Add broccoli, eggs, pimento, salt, pepper, lemon juice, Worcestershire, Tabasco, and gelatin-consomme mixture. Chill until firm. Serves 10.

Dodie Wright

Marinated Broccoli Supreme

1 teaspoon onion salt
1 teaspoon oregano
½ teaspoon thyme
1 teaspoon garlic salt
½ teaspoon pepper
½ teaspoon dry mustard
3 tablespoons white vinegar
⅔ cup salad oil

1 bunch fresh broccoli or 2 packages
    frozen broccoli spears, cooked
    and drained
2 hard cooked eggs, chopped
Lemon slices
Parsley

Combine first eight ingredients in a mixing bowl; beat 1 minute at medium speed of electric mixer. Place broccoli in an 8 inch square dish; add marinade. Cover and refrigerate overnight. Before serving, drain off marinade. Place broccoli in serving dish and sprinkle with chopped eggs. Garnish with lemon slices and parsley. Yields 6 servings.

Nancy Mize Sneed

Party Salad

4 or 5 medium tomatoes, sliced
2 medium avocados, sliced
9 or 10 fresh mushrooms, sliced
   (save crumbs)
1 can hearts of palm, drained and
   sliced vertically
4 green onions including tops,
   chopped

1 cup sour cream
1 cup mayonnaise
1 additional green onion with
   top, finely chopped
Paprika
Parsley

Place tomatoes around outside of a round platter. Then, working toward the center (save a place in the center of the platter for dressing) arrange in pinwheel fashion the avocados, mushrooms, and hearts of palm. Sprinkle chopped green onions over the above. Mix the sour cream and mayonnaise well and place in the center of the platter. Garnish the dressing with parsley and paprika. Sprinkle the mushroom crumbs and the finely chopped green onion on the dressing. May be prepared early in the day.

Mrs. Frederick Taul,
Mobile, Alabama

Company Tossed Salad

1 clove garlic, pressed
1 teaspoon salt
2 tablespoons lemon juice
1/4 teaspoon sugar
1/4 teaspoon coarse pepper
1/8 teaspoon celery seeds
1/2 teaspoon paprika
3/4 teaspoon dry mustard

5 tablespoons salad oil
1 medium head lettuce
1/2 small bunch romaine or 1 bunch
   watercress
1/2 cup slivered toasted almonds
1 cup tiny raw cauliflowerets
1/2 avocado, diced
1 tomato, cut in small wedges

Place first 9 ingredients in blender; blend well and refrigerate. Tear salad greens into bowl. Add tomatoes, avocado, cauliflowerets, almonds. Pour salad dressing over all and toss well. Serve immediately. Serves 6.

Mrs. Cleve Allen, Jr.

Mixed Vegetable Salad

1 can peas, drained
1 can shoe peg corn, drained
1 can French green beans, drained

1 green pepper, sliced
1 onion, sliced
1 jar pimento, chopped

Mix all ingredients together. Pour following dressing over all.

DRESSING

2/3 cup vinegar
1/3 cup Wesson oil

1 teaspoon salt
1/2 cup sugar

Marinate vegetables with dressing for several hours.

Mrs. Donnie Riley

Layered Salad

1 large head lettuce, shredded
½ cup celery, chopped
½ cup onion, chopped
1 (10 ounce) package frozen
English peas, cooked, drained,
and cooled

½ cup mayonnaise and ½ cup sour
cream, combined
2 tablespoons sugar
6 ounces grated cheese
8 strips bacon, cooked crisply
and crumbled

Use a large bowl and place ingredients in layers in the order given. Cover tightly and refrigerate at least 8 hours. Serves 12.

Ame Deen

Make Ahead Salad

1 head cauliflower,
washed and chopped
2 small boxes frozen
chopped broccoli,
thawed and drained.

½ medium onion, chopped (red is pretty)
1 cup mayonnaise
3 tablespoons sugar
5 tablespoons wine vinegar

Mix all ingredients. Refrigerate over night. Test before serving for additional salt and pepper. Serve on lettuce leaf. Keeps well for over a week. Serves 8.

Mrs. Frank Robertson,
Butler, Missouri

Spinach Salad

1 (10 ounce) package fresh spinach
½ cup sour cream
½ teaspoon horseradish
Herb vinegar, to taste

Salt and pepper
1 cup creamed cottage cheese
½ cup chopped walntus

Wash and tear fresh spinach into pieces. Drain well. Blend the sour cream, horse-radish, vinegar, salt and pepper. Toss this dressing with the spinach. Lightly toss with cottage cheese and walnuts.

Mrs. Leland Fisher,
Harlingen, Texas

Spinach and Mushroom Salad

1 pound fresh spinach
¼ pound sliced bacon
1 pound fresh mushrooms
2 or 3 green onions

3 ribs celery with leaves
Oil and vinegar dressing
Grey Poupon mustard
Salt and pepper

Wash, dry and devein spinach. Fry bacon until crisp and crumble coarsely. Wash mushrooms, trim, and slice. Chop green onions and celery. Combine these ingredients and dress with oil and vinegar with a little Grey Poupon mustard added. Correct seasoning and chill. Serves 6.

Joyce Bordelon

Twenty-four Hour Spinach Salad

1 pound fresh spinach, washed,
dried and torn
4 hard cooked eggs, sliced
1 pound bacon, cooked
and crumbled
1 small head iceberg lettuce,
shredded
12 ounces baby Swiss cheese, shredded

1 large bag frozen English peas
2 Bermuda onions, thinly sliced
½ cup mayonnaise
½ cup Miracle Whip
Salt and pepper to taste

Place spinach into a large glass salad bowl so that the layers may be seen. Sprinkle with salt and pepper. Add a layer of eggs, crumbled bacon, lettuce and another sprinkle of salt and pepper. Add a layer of onions and uncooked frozen peas. Repeat this process until the bowl is filled. Cover and refrigerate overnight. Early in the morning of the day the salad is to be used, mix mayonnaise and Miracle Whip and spoon over the top of the salad. This topping should penetrate through the salad. Sprinkle shredded Swiss cheese over top and refrigerate until serving time. Serves 12.

Shirley Haynie Bergfield

Okra Salad

Fresh okra pods
Vinaigrette dressing or Wishbone
Italian dressing

Boil okra in salted water in uncovered saucepan until barely done and still crisp. Drain and serve immediately on individual salad plates with dressing.

Mrs. Jack Thompson

Hors d'Oeuvre Jardiniere
(Garden Salad)

¾ cup mayonnaise or salad
dressing
3 ounces cooked or canned peas
1 large potato, cooked and
diced
4 ounces diced cooked ham
4 medium or large tomatoes

¼ cup breadcrumbs
¼ teaspoon chopped chervil
1 tablespoon chopped black olives
¼ cup milk
Lettuce and green peppers
2 hard boiled eggs

Slice off the tops of tomatoes and scoop out the seeds and pulp with a spoon. Mix the diced cooked potatoes, the cooked peas and mayonnaise together and add the diced ham. Fill the tomatoes with this mixture. Take shells off the hard boiled eggs, and slice in half. Remove the yolk. Soak the breadcrumbs in milk and mash yolks and breadcrumbs together. Add the chopped chervil and chopped black olives. With this mixture, stuff the white hollow halves of the eggs. Place one of the stuffed half eggs on top of each stuffed tomato as a lid. Cut lettuce and green pepper in thin strips and make a nest on which each tomato will be served. This salad, which contains meat, starch, and vegetable, may be used as a main dish.

Mrs. Paul Krass

Fresh Tomato Relish

1 pound fresh ripe tomatoes
   preferably from your garden
1 tablespoon onion, finely chopped
1 tablespoon lemon juice
Salt

Pepper
Shredded lettuce
Mayonnaise

Peel tomatoes and chop coarsely. Add lemon juice and onion; season to taste with salt and pepper. Refrigerate at least until chilled. Serve drained tomato mixture over shredded lettuce and top with mayonnaise thinned with some of the seasoned juice. This may also be served in a bowl to be passed at table or for buffets. Serves 4.

Helen Phillips

Vegetable Marinade

1 cup salad oil
1/3 cup wine vinegar
2 teaspoons oregano
1 teaspoon salt

1/2 teaspoon pepper
1/2 teaspoon dry mustard
2 garlic cloves, minced
1 medium onion, minced
1 teaspoon parsley

Mix well and pour over tomatoes and/or cucumbers. Marinate in refrigerator. Serve on lettuce leaf.

Mrs. Robert A. Mitchell

Marinated Cole Slaw

Large head of cabbage
2 large onions
1/4 cup sugar
1 teaspoon celery salt

1 1/2 teaspoons salt
1 cup salad oil
1 cup vinegar
1 tablespoon mustard

Shred cabbage. Slice onions. Layer cabbage and onion rings. Mix all other ingredients and bring to a boil. Pour over cabbage and onions. Cover. Let stand in refrigerator for 24 hours. Stir occasionally. The longer it marinates, the better it becomes.

Linda Lewald

Mrs. Robert G. Parker adds 1 chopped green pepper.

Sauerkraut Salad

2 cans sauerkraut
1 cup diced celery
1 cup diced green pepper
1 large jar pimento, chopped

2/3 cup vinegar
1/3 cup water
1/3 cup oil
1/4 cup sugar
1 small can water chestnuts

Heat vinegar, water, oil, and sugar. Stir until dissolved. Pour over remaining ingredients and chill.

Mrs. Virgil Gillespie

Potato-Slaw Salad

3 to 4 cups cooked potatoes, diced
1 1/2 cups coarsely shredded cabbage
1/2 cup raw grated carrot
2 tablespoons green pepper, finely
   chopped
1 teaspoon salt
1 teaspoon pepper
1 tablespoon mustard

2 tablespoons salad oil
1 tablespoon vinegar
2 tablespoons fresh onion, grated
1/2 cup dill pickle, chopped
2 tablespoons chopped pimento
2/3 cup mayonnaise
2 to 3 eggs, boiled and chopped

While potatoes are still warm, combine all ingredients in a large mixing bowl.
Chill. Serves 8-10.

Mrs. John Cotten

Anna's Potato Salad

4 medium boiled potatoes, peeled
1 tablespoon chopped bell pepper
1 tablespoon chopped onion
1 hard boiled egg, chopped
1 large dill pickle, grated

1 grated carrot
1/2 cup finely chopped celery
Salt and red pepper to taste
Mayonnaise to taste

Combine all ingredients except mayonnaise. Salt and red pepper to taste and refrigerate for 24 hours. Add mayonnaise to taste. Serves 4 to 6.

Anna Stanfield

Hazlehurst Cabbage Salad

1 large head cabbage, shredded
2 medium onions, thinly sliced, separated

1 green pepper, thinly sliced
1 medium jar pimento, drained

Layer ingredients in a large container. Do not stir!

DRESSING

1 cup oil
3/4 cup white vinegar
1 teaspoon celery seed

1 cup sugar
1 1/2 teaspoons salt

Mix together and boil for 2 minutes. Pour the hot dressing over the vegetables.
Cover tightly and refrigerate at least 4 hours before serving. Will keep indefinitely.
Good hot or cold. Serves 8 to 10.

Thelma Furlow
Hazlehurst, Mississippi

Tabooley
(Lebanese Salad)

1 small bunch green onions
1 large bunch parsley, leaves only
1 bunch fresh mint or 3 teaspoons
    dried mint
3 or 4 large tomatoes

¼ cup cracked wheat
½ cup olive oil or salad oil
Salt and pepper to taste
Lemon juice to taste

Finely chop all vegetables. Rinse wheat in cold water and soak about 10 minutes; squeeze dry. Add remaining ingredients, adding more seasoning if necessary. Chill before serving. I use a lot of lemon juice.

Mrs. Philip Hage

Corned Beef Salad

½ envelope unflavored gelatin
1 tablespoon cold water
1 package lemon gelatin
1 can beef bouillon
1 soup can water
½ green pepper, diced

3 hard boiled eggs, chopped
1 cup diced celery
1 can corned beef, flaked
¾ cup mayonnaise
1 small onion, grated

Dissolve unflavored gelatin in water. Warm bouillon and can of water; pour over lemon gelatin. Stir in gelatin to dissolve. Let cool to consistency of egg whites or stiffer. Add eggs, celery, beef, mayonnaise, onion and pepper. Mix well. Pour into oblong dish and chill overnight. Serve on lettuce in squares or slices. May be molded in egg containers or served on melba rounds as an appetizer. Serves 10-12 as salad or 20-24 as appetizer.

Mrs. Cleve Allen, Jr.

Sunshine Chicken Salad

4 pounds diced chicken
1 (6 ounce) can frozen orange
    juice, thawed and undiluted
¾ cup corn oil
¼ cup vinegar
3 tablespoons sugar
½ teaspoon dry mustard

¼ teaspoon salt
1/8 teaspoon red pepper sauce
1 cup celery, chopped
½ cup ripe olives, sliced
1 medium avocado, diced
¼ cup slivered almonds

Put undiluted orange juice concentrate, corn oil, vinegar, sugar, dry mustard, salt, and red pepper sauce in blender and blend at high speed until smooth. Cover and refrigerate. Place diced chicken, celery, olives, avocado, and almonds in salad bowl. Coat lightly with chilled dressing. Cover and chill salad at least 30 minutes before serving. Serves 4-6.

Judy VanLandingham

Molded Chicken Salad

2 cups chopped, cooked chicken
½ cup ripe olives
1 cup mayonnaise
2 tablespoons capers
3 tablespoons gelatin
½ cup cold water (over gelatin)

2 cups canned green peas
3 hard boiled eggs, mashed
1 cup celery
½ cup sliced almonds
1½ cups hot chicken broth

Add 1 cup mayonnaise to broth and add chicken. Add other ingredients and congeal in a mold or 8 inch square pan. Cut in squares and serve on lettuce. Serves 8.

Mrs. Wade Creekmore, Jr.
Jackson, Mississippi

Chicken Salad Bake

½ cup chopped onion
1 cup thinly sliced celery
¼ cup margarine
¾ cup mayonnaise
1 tablespoon lemon juice
1/8 teaspoon pepper

5 ounce can water chestnuts,
   drained and sliced
¾ cup light cream
½ teaspoon salt
3 cups cubed cooked chicken
¼ cup shredded cheddar cheese

Saute onion and celery in margarine until tender. Mix with all other ingredients. Put in casserole. Bake at 425⁰ for 30-35 minutes. Bake covered for first 15 minutes, then uncovered.

Mrs. H. Jerry Pettit,
Branson, Missouri

Chicken Salad

2 cups coarsely cup up
   cooked chicken
2 tablespoons lemon juice
½ teaspoon salt
1 cup seedless grapes

1 cup sliced celery
2 hard boiled eggs, chopped
½ cup mayonnaise
¼ cup toasted almonds

Mix the chicken, lemon juice, and salt; let stand overnight in the refrigerator. The following day add the remaining ingredients and mix well. Serves about 6.

Mrs. William Barrett

Marinated Shrimp Salad

5 pounds cooked and peeled shrimp
¾ cup chopped green onions
1 (8 ounce) jar Creole style mustard

1 cup finely chopped celery
1 quart mayonnaise
Juice of 4 lemons

Mix all ingredients and marinate for several hours. May be served with toothpicks as party food or on lettuce for luncheon dish.

Mrs. Holcomb Hector

Shrimp Remoulade

2 to 3 pounds shrimp
1/2 cup horseradish mustard
2 1/2 tablespoons paprika
1 teaspoon salt
1/2 cup salad oil
1/4 cup finely minced celery

2 cloves garlic, finely minced
2 tablespoons catsup
3/4 teaspoon red pepper
1/3 cup tarragon vinegar
1/2 cup chopped green onions and tops

Boil shrimp, peel, and marinate in sauce made with remaining ingredients. Serve in large bowl with marinade, using toothpicks to spear the shrimp. The flavor improves with marinating overnight. Serves 6-8. For a party increase the shrimp to ten pounds and triple the sauce.

Mrs. Jack Halliday

Red Remoulade Sauce for Shrimp

1 bunch chopped green onions, pureed
2 small ribs chopped celery, pureed
2 sprigs chopped fresh parsley, pureed
1 finely sliced green onion
2 teaspoons minced parsley
5 teaspoons paprika
1/2 teaspoon dried basil
1/4 teaspoon salt

1 teaspoon cayenne pepper
1/3 teaspoon pepper
1 celery rib finely sliced
4 tablespoons creole mustard
1/3 cup white vinegar
5 teaspoons fresh lemon juice
3/4 cup olive oil

Process onions, celery and parsley until almost a puree. Add dry ingredients and mix. Slowly add liquids and mix. Fold in sliced onions, celery and parsley, Place in covered storage jar. Refrigerate for 5 hours before serving. Keeps well. Serve over boiled shrimp, crayfish or crabmeat garnished with melons or avocados. This is an authentic creole sauce.

Mrs. John Edgar Johnson III

Mexican Chef Salad

1 head lettuce, torn
1 medium onion, chopped
4 fresh tomatoes, chopped
4 ounces cheddar cheese, grated
Italian dressing, bottle or mix
Hot sauce (optional)

1 large avocado, sliced (optional)
1 pound ground beef
1 (15 ounce) can kidney beans
1 teaspoon salt
1 (11 ounce) bag taco flavored
   tortilla chips

Toss together lettuce, tomatoes, onion and cheese. Add dressing and hot sauce, if desired. Crunch and add tortilla chips. Slice and add avocado, if desired. Brown ground beef in skillet. Add kidney beans and salt. Simmer 10 minutes. Mix into cold salad. Great topped with tomatoes and green chilies and/or avocado dip.

Mrs. James O. Dukes

Crab and Avocado Salad with Louis Dressing

3 large avocados
2½ pounds lump crabmeat
½ cup finely chopped celery
¼ cup lemon juice
4 tablespoons olive oil

¼ cup vinegar
¼ teaspoon cayenne
Salt to taste
3 tablespoons finely chopped shallots
½ cup thinly sliced radishes

Combine all ingredients except avocados an hour or two before serving. When ready to serve, cut the peeled avocados into medium sized cubes and toss with crabmeat mixture. Mound the salad on a serving dish and garnish with tomato wedges, boiled eggs, or whatever you like. Serves 12. Easily halved.

LOUIS DRESSING

1 cup mayonnaise (homemade or
   Hellman's)
2 tablespoons chopped parsley
¼ cup heavy cream, whipped

¼ cup chili sauce
1 tablespoon finely chopped chives
Dash of cayenne

Add other ingredients to mayonnaise. Fold in whipped cream last and serve with crabmeat.

Mrs. Sam Morse

West Indies Salad I

1 pound lump crabmeat
Large chopped onion
Salt and pepper
Celery seed
Capers

Bay leaves
4 ounces cider vinegar
3 ounces Wesson oil
3 ounces ice water

Layer crabmeat and onion; sprinkle with salt, pepper, celery seed, and capers; place a few bay leaves; add as many layers as you have crabmeat and onion. Stir up vinegar, oil and water with a fork and pour over the crabmeat mixture. Cover. Place in refrigerator. Will keep in refrigerator for two or three weeks. Improves with age. Let sit at least overnight before serving. Serves 4. Above proportions are for one pound of crabmeat; easily increased.

Mrs. Stanford Morse, Jr.

West Indies Salad II

2 cups crabmeat
1 large onion, finely chopped
½ cup oil
½ cup vinegar
1 tablespoon parsley

1 teaspoon Accent
Dash of Tabasco
1 tablespoon Worcestershire
Salt and pepper to taste
Shredded lettuce

Place crabmeat in a bowl. Cover with chopped onion. Add seasonings and pour the oil and vinegar over all. Toss to mix. Cover and refrigerate for at least 4 hours or overnight. Serve on shredded lettuce. Serves 6.

Sarah Ewing

White Cap's Shrimp Salad

5 pounds boiled peeled shrimp, chopped
1 small bunch green onions, chopped
5 boiled eggs, finely grated
3/4 cup dill relish
1 full stalk celery, chopped
1/4 cup green pepper, chopped

1/4 cup sweet relish
1-2 tablespoons horseradish
4 ounce Philadelphia cream cheese
2 cups Kraft heavy duty mayonnaise
Salt and pepper to taste

Mix ingredients except mayonnaise and cream cheese, a scoop or spoonful at a time and blending thoroughly, then mix a little of each ingredient again until all ingredients except mayonnaise and cream cheese are in salad. Blend 1 cup mayonnaise and cream cheese then add to salad. Add more mayonnaise until a creamy texture is attained. Salt and pepper to taste. Garnish with paprika, parsley and tomato wedges if desired. Serves 15 to 20.

Carl, Buck and Ray Lizana
White Cap Seafood Restaurant
Gulfport Yacht Harbor
Gulfport, Mississippi

Mardi Gras Pasta and Shrimp

2 cups garden style Ritoli
   (spinach and tomato pasta)
2 quarts water
1/2 cup choppd celery
2 tablespoons chopped pimento

1 small can sliced black olives
2 cups boiled peeled shrimp
   (boiled in crab boil)
Morton's Nature Seasons to taste
4-6 tablespoons Lite Ranch dressing

Boil pasta in water until tender (about 12 minutes). Do not over cook. Drain and let cool. Add celery, pimento, black olives and shrimp one ingredient at a time stirring after each addition. Season with Morton's Nature Seasons to taste, being careful not to use too much. Stir in dressing. Serve chilled. Serves 8 to 10.

Janet Miller

Beauvoir is the historic last home of Jefferson Davis, the only President of the Confederacy. The property on which Beauvoir stands was purchased in 1848 by James Brown, a Madison County planter. In 1852 he completed the present house of the finest native timbers, all whipsawed and hand dressed. The Brown family retained ownership of the property until 1873 when, after Mr. Brown's death, the house and property were sold to Mr. Frank Johnston, who soon sold it to Mrs. Sarah Anne Dorsey. She changed the name to Beauvoir, which means "beautiful view". At her death in 1879 she willed Beauvoir to Mr. Davis who lived there until his death. In 1904 it became a home for Confederate veterans and their wives or widows. In 1940 Beauvoir became a shrine and museum and is now open daily to tourists.

Photograph by Chauncey T. Hinman

Vegetables

Vegetables

Artichoke Casserole

6 to 8 fresh artichokes
1 onion
½ stick butter
1 can mushroom soup

1 small can sliced mushrooms
Salt, pepper, and celery salt
Seasoned bread crumbs

Boil artichokes until tender. Scrape the leaves and reserve the hearts. Mince the onion and saute it in the butter, add scraped portion of the artichoke, mushroom soup, and mushrooms. Add salt, pepper, and celery salt to taste. Mix well. Arrange artichoke hearts on bottom of greased casserole dish, pouring above mixture over all. Top with seasoned bread crumbs. Bake at 350⁰ approximately 30 minutes or until bubbly. Serves 4 to 6. (Fresh mushrooms may be substituted, boil first in a little water, then saute as above.)

Mrs. John Marquez

Mock Artichoke

2 (8 ounce) cans cut green beans,
   drained
3 to 4 slices bacon
2 large cloves garlic, chopped

1 cup Italian-style bread crumbs,
   plus 1 tablespoon
½ cup Parmesan cheese
Salt and pepper to taste

In large skillet fry bacon until crisp, drain on paper towel and crumble. In bacon drippings saute garlic until tender. Add drained green beans, 1 cup bread crumbs, Parmesan cheese, and crumbled bacon. Mix. Place in greased casserole, sprinkle with remaining 1 tablespoon bread crumbs. Bake at 350⁰ for 20 minutes until warm. Do not overbake. Serves 4.

Mrs. Dick Drown

Asparagus Make Ahead

3 eggs, beaten
1½ cups scalded milk
1 cup cut asparagus, drained
1 tablespoon minced onion

3 tablespoons butter, melted
½ cup cracker crumbs
Salt and pepper

Beat eggs, add milk, onion, asparagus, melted butter, and salt and pepper. Sprinkle crumbs on top, and add a dash of paprika if desired. Bake at 350⁰ for 45-60 minutes or until completely set. This can be made ahead and baked at serving time.

Mrs. John W. Puckett

Asparagus Casserole

2 tablespoons margarine
1 tablespoon flour
1 can cream of mushroom soup
1/4 teaspoon dry mustard
1 (15 1/2 ounce) can asparagus, drained

1 (17 ounce) can small English peas,
   drained
1 cup bread crumbs
1/4 cup grated cheese
4 hard-boiled eggs, sliced

Melt margarine in small pan. Add flour, soup (undiluted), and mustard. Cook until thick and bubbly. Put asparagus and peas in oven proof baking dish and cover with sauce. Saute crumbs in margarine until lightly browned. Place in casserole. Sprinkle with grated cheese. Bake at 300° for 30 minutes. Garnish top with sliced boiled eggs. Serves 6 to 8.

Susan Gray

Asparagus with Sour Cream Sauce

1 1/2 pounds fresh asparagus
1/2 cup sour cream

1/2 cup Parmesan cheese
2 tablespoons mayonnaise

Snap off tough ends of asparagus. Remove scales, if desired. Cook asparagus in boiling, salted water 8 to 10 minutes or until tender. Arrange in serving dish and keep warm. Combine sour cream, cheese and mayonnaise and heat. Serve over asparagus. Serves 4.

Susan McCormick

Baked Apricots

3 large cans apricot halves, drained
1 box brown sugar

1 box Ritz crackers, crushed
2 sticks butter

Layer half of apricots in greased baking dish. Cover with half of brown sugar and half of cracker crumbs. Dot heavily with 1 stick of butter. Repeat layers. Bake at 300° about 1 hour. Serves 10.

Mrs. James S. Murray, Jr.

Green Beans Almondine

2 (16 ounce) cans French style
   green beans, well drained
8 to 10 slices bacon
1/2 cup chopped onion

5 tablespoons vinegar
3 tablespoons slivered almonds
   browned in bacon drippings
Salt and pepper

Drain green beans and set aside. Fry bacon, crumble and reserve. Brown almonds and reserve. Brown onion in bacon drippings, adding beans, vinegar, salt and pepper. Heat thoroughly, then refrigerate all day. Before serving, place green bean mixture into a 1 1/2 quart casserole, then sprinkle almonds and bacon on the top. Heat thoroughly at 350° for approximately 20 to 25 minutes. Serves 4 to 6.

Mrs. Liddell White

Green Beans With Onions

2 (16 ounce) cans French style
   green beans
1/2 cup butter
1/2 cup slivered almonds
2 tablespoons brown sugar
2 teaspoons chopped garlic

3 tablespoons white wine
1/2 teaspoon salt
1/4 teaspoon pepper
1 large jar cocktail onions,
   drained

Cook beans according to directions. Drain. Melt butter in skillet. Stir in all remaining ingredients. Simmer 20 to 30 minutes with lid on securely. Coat onions well. Pour over hot beans. Serves 4 to 6.

Paula Alexander

Broccoli-Corn Bake

1 (16 ounce) can cream style corn
1 (10 ounce) package frozen chopped
   broccoli (cooked and drained)
1/2 cup cracker crumbs
2 tablespoons melted margarine

1 beaten egg
1 tablespoon minced onion
1/2 teaspoon salt
Dash of pepper

TOPPING

1/4 cup cracker crumbs

1 tablespoon melted margarine

Mix everything but topping and pour into casserole dish. Mix topping ingredients and sprinkle over other ingredients and bake at 350° for 35 to 40 minutes. Can be frozen. Serves 6.

Hope Goldin

Broccoli Elegant

2 (10 ounce) packages frozen
   broccoli, cooked
1/4 cup minced onion
6 tablespoons margarine
5 tablespoons flour
1 teaspoon dry mustard
3/4 teaspoon salt
1/8 teaspoon marjoram
1/8 teaspoon Accent

3 dashes hot pepper sauce
2 1/2 cups milk
2 chicken bouillon cubes
5 egg yolks, beaten
1 1/2 cups grated sharp cheese
1 (4 ounce) can sliced mushrooms
3 tablespoons slivered almonds
Dash of paprika

Arrange cooked broccoli in casserole. Saute onions in butter. Blend in flour and seasonings. Add milk and bouillon cubes. Cook over medium heat, stirring constantly until mixture thickens and comes to a boil. Add sauce to the eggs very slowly stirring. Add cheese, stir until blended. Add mushrooms. Pour approximately three cups of the sauce over broccoli. Sprinkle with almonds and paprika. Bake at 350° for 20 minutes or until brown. Serves 6 to 8.

Barbara Harvey

Broccoli-Cheese Casserole

¼ cup chopped onion
6 tablespoons margarine
2 tablespoons flour
½ cup water

1 (8 ounce) jar Cheese Whiz
2 packages frozen chopped broccoli,
   thawed and well drained
3 eggs, well beaten
½ cup soda cracker crumbs

Saute onions in 4 tablespoons margarine until soft. Stir in flour. Add water. Cook over low heat, stirring until mixture thickens and comes to a boil. Blend in cheese. Combine sauce and broccoli. Add eggs, mix gently until blended. Turn into greased 1½ quart casserole. Cover with crumbs. Dot with remaining butter. Bake at 325° for 30 minutes. Serves 8.

Mrs. Paul M. Newton

Cabbage Tamales

1 medium sized cabbage
½ cup rice, partially cooked
1 pound ground beef
1 medium onion, chopped
¾ stick butter

Juice of 3 lemons
3 or 4 cloves garlic
1 large can tomatoes
2 cups hot water
Salt and pepper to taste

Steam cabbage in boiling water until each leaf is separated. Trim out stem of each leaf. Brown beef in skillet with onion. Drain. Add rice, salt and pepper. Place small amount of meat mixture on a cabbage leaf and roll. Secure with toothpick. Line bottom of pot with leftover cabbage stems. Then add cabbage rolls. Sprinkle with salt and pepper and pour a can of tomatoes, hot water, lemon juice, butter and garlic cloves over rolls. Cook with lid on for 30 to 40 minutes. Serves 4 to 6.

Mrs. Watson Weatherly

Lowell Inn Red Cabbage

1 medium head red cabbage
1 medium yellow onion, diced
2 large apples, peeled and sliced
1 heaping tablespoon bacon grease
1 teaspoon salt
½ cup sugar

1½ cups water
1 bay leaf
2 whole allspice
2 cloves (heads removed)
6 peppercorns
1 cup vinegar (scant)

Remove outer leaves from head of cabbage. Wash, core and thinly slice. Dice onion and slice peeled apples. Toss cabbage, onion and apples together. Add remaining ingredients and simmer 1½ hours in a covered saucepan. Remove whole spices. Thicken slightly with about 2 tablespoons cornstarch blended with cold water. Especially good with game. Excellent reheated. White cabbage may be substituted. Serves 6.

Mrs. Joan Owen

Harvard Beets

1 can beets
1 tablespoon cornstarch
1/2 cup mild vinegar

1/2 cup sugar
1/2 teaspoon salt
2 tablespoons butter or margarine

In a saucepan combine all ingredients except beets. Stir well. Add beets and heat. Add 1 tablespoon orange marmalade for an unusual flavor if desired.

Mrs. Donnie D. Riley

Candied Carrots

10 carrots
1/2 cup cranberry jelly
1 teaspoon salt

1/2 cup margarine
4 tablespoons brown sugar

Cook whole carrots. Cut on diagonal about 1/2 inch thick. Melt margarine, add brown sugar, cranberry jelly, and salt. Put carrots in casserole. Pour cranberry mixture over carrots and heat covered in 350° oven until hot. Serves 6.

Mrs. William H. Murdock,
Greenwood, Mississippi

Carrots Supreme

4 cups cooked, sliced carrots
1 1/2 cups croutons
1 1/4 cups shredded sharp
   cheddar cheese
2 eggs, beaten

1/4 cup half-and-half or
   1/4 cup sour cream
1/4 cup margarine, melted
1 tablespoon Worcestershire
1 teaspoon salt

Place carrots in a buttered 1 1/2 quart casserole. Stir in croutons and cheese. Combine remaining ingredients and pour over carrot mixture. Bake uncovered at 400° for 20 minutes or until brown. Serves 6.

Mrs. William L. Seal

Carrots and Green Peppers

2 pounds carrots
1 stick margarine
1 large onion, sliced
1 large green pepper, sliced

1 tablespoon sugar
Additional sugar or artificial
   sweetener to sweeten to taste
Salt to taste

Peel carrots and cut on diagonal. Cook in small amount of water. Drain. Saute onion and green pepper in margarine. Add 1 tablespoon sugar. Add cooked carrots to green pepper mixture, stirring constantly to coat carrots. Salt to taste. Add additional sugar or artificial sweetener as desired to taste. Better made ahead and reheated in oven or on top of stove.

Mrs. H. Jerry Pettit,
Branson, Missouri

Cauliflower Vinaigrette

1 head cauliflower
White wine vinaigrette

Salt and pepper to taste
Parmesan or Romano cheese

Steam cauliflower whole until fork tender, about 15 minutes. Cool. Core cauliflower and break into flowerets. Toss with vinaigrette, salt and pepper and top with cheese.

VINAIGRETTE

¾ cup dry white wine
¼ cup white wine vinegar
½ teaspoon dry mustard

½ cup olive oil
1 teaspoon oregano
Salt/pepper to taste

Blend in blender or food processor or shake in jar. Refrigerate to store. Serves 8 to 10.

Betty Morse

Company Cauliflower

1 cauliflower, cut up
1 tablespoon butter
2 tablespoons flour

1 can cream of mushroom soup
1 cup sharp cheddar cheese, grated
Seasoned bread crumbs

Cook cauliflower in boiling salted water until tender. Place in greased casserole. In skillet or saucepan over low heat blend butter and flour. Add cream of mushroom soup and cook until thickened. Stir in cheese until melted. Pour over cauliflower. Sprinkle with bread crumbs. Bake at 325° until bubbly. *Julie Hatten*

Shoepeg Corn Casserole

2 (17 ounce) cans shoepeg corn
1 (5 ounce) can sliced water chestnuts
½ cup finely chopped onion
1 cup grated sharp cheddar cheese

1 cup sour cream
1 can cream of celery soup
1 stick melted butter or margarine
1½ cups crushed Ritz crackers

Layer shoepeg corn, water chestnuts, onion and cheese in buttered casserole. Mix sour cream and celery soup and pour over casserole. Melt butter, add crackers, toss and spread on top of casserole. Bake at 350° for 45 minutes to 1 hour. Serves 8 to 10.

Mrs. Lila Gould

Corn Pudding

¼ cup butter
¼ cup flour
2 teaspoons salt
2 tablespoons sugar

1¾ cups milk
3 cups fresh or frozen corn, chopped
3 eggs, well beaten

Melt butter in saucepan, stir in flour, salt, and sugar. Cook until bubbly, add milk and cook until thick. Stir in corn, either chopped or whole (chopped makes a smoother pudding). Stir in the eggs that have been beaten until frothy. Pour into well buttered 2 quart casserole and bake in a pan of hot water at 350° for 45 minutes. This recipe may be baked in buttered ramekins and cooked less time. Freezes well baked or unbaked. If canned corn is used, reduce sugar to 2 teaspoons and salt to taste. Serves 8. *Mrs. George P. Hopkins, Jr.*

Corn Souffle

1½ cups cheese cracker crumbs	1 teaspoon grated onion
⅓ cup butter	½ teaspoon Accent
1½ cups milk	½ cup slivered olives
2 cups fresh or frozen corn	2 tablespoons butter
2 tablespoons flour	2 eggs, beaten

Mix cheese cracker crumbs and ⅓ cup butter and line pie plate with them. Mix 1 cup milk, corn, onion, 2 tablespoons butter, and Accent in saucepan. Bring to boil. Cook 3 minutes, add 2 tablespoons flour and ½ cup milk (mixed to a paste consistency), and cook 2 more minutes. Add beaten eggs and slivered olives. Pour over crumbs. Bake 20 minutes at 400⁰. Put additional crumbs on top. Serves 6 to 8.

Mrs. H. C. Thompson

Corn Fritters

1 cup flour	½ cup milk
1 teaspoon baking powder	1 teaspoon vegetable oil
1 teaspoon salt	1 cup canned corn, drained
2 eggs, slightly beaten	

Mix dry ingredients, add eggs, milk and oil. Beat smooth. Stir in corn and drop by teaspoonfuls into hot grease. Serve hot with your favorite pancake syrup. Great with fried fish. Makes 10 to 12 fritters.

Mrs. Jerry Chaney,
Branson, Missouri

Best Ever Eggplant

1 large eggplant, diced (about 4 cups)	1 egg, slightly beaten
	½ cup chopped onion
⅓ cup milk	¾ cup seasoned bread crumbs
1 can cream of mushroom soup	

TOPPING:

½ cup seasoned bread crumbs	2 tablespoons melted butter
1 cup grated sharp American cheese	

Cook eggplant in boiling water until tender and drain. Stir milk into soup and blend into egg. Add eggplant, onion and bread crumbs. Toss slightly and pour into a greased baking pan. Toss ingredients for topping and sprinkle over top. Bake at 350⁰ for 20-30 minutes, or until hot and bubbly. Serves 6.

Willa V. Biggs

Fried Eggplant

1 eggplant, peeled
1 egg, plus 1 tablespoon milk,
  slightly beaten

2 parts plain bread crumbs to
  1 part Parmesan cheese
Salt and pepper to taste
Celery salt

Cut peeled eggplant into ½ inch to ¾ inch sticks. Soak in water for fifteen minutes. Combine egg and milk. Combine bread crumbs, Parmesan cheese, salt and pepper. Dip eggplant sticks into egg mixture, coat with bread crumbs and fry in hot grease until golden brown. Sprinkle with celery salt while draining.

Mrs. William H. Murdock, Jr.

Eggplant Fritters

1 medium eggplant
½ teaspoon salt
1/8 teaspoon black pepper

1 egg, slightly beaten
1 small onion
⅓ cup flour
2 tablespoons milk

Boil unpeeled eggplant until tender. When done, drain, peel and mash. Stir in the egg, onion, milk, salt and pepper. Add the flour. Drop batter by tablespoonsful into shallow hot fat and cook until brown on all sides. Drain on absorbent paper. Serves 4.

Mrs. W. H. Murdock,
Greenwood, Mississippi

Eggplant Puff

1 medium sized eggplant
1 onion, grated
1 green pepper, finely minced
1 egg
½ cup cream

3 slices bread, crumbled
3 tablespoons butter, melted
Salt to taste
¼ cup grated sharp cheddar cheese

Peel and cut up the eggplant and cook until tender in a small amount of salted water. Combine rest of ingredients except cheese and beat well. Pour into buttered deep baking dish, top with cheese and bake at 400° until well puffed. Serves 6.

Jean Conway

Grits and Sausage Casserole

1 cup grits
3 cups beef bouillon
½ teaspoon salt
1 pound ground sausage

2 sticks butter
1 cup milk
4 beaten eggs
½ cup grated cheddar cheese

Cook grits in bouillon. Add salt. Cook sausage until crumbly, drain on paper towel. Mix sausage with grits. Add butter, milk, eggs, ¼ cup grated cheese. Mix well. Top with remaining cheese. Bake at 350° for 30-45 minutes. This is great to make ahead. Keep refrigerated and pop into oven in the morning.

Dorrie Roney

Garlic Grits

1 cup raw grits	1 stick garlic cheese
4 cups salted water	Dash red pepper
2 eggs, slightly beaten	1 stick butter
(add enough milk to equal 1 cup	Parmesan cheese (optional)
egg mixture)	

Cook grits in salted water until tender. Add garlic cheese and butter. Stir until mixed. Add egg mixture and stir, add red pepper. Pour into greased dish and bake at 375° for 30 minutes or until lightly browned. This may be prepared early in the day. Parmesan cheese may be sprinkled on before baking. Excellent with ham and sausage for brunch. *Mrs. John H. Richards*

Hoppin' John Jambalaya

2 pounds smoked sausage, sliced and	1 pound salt pork, boiled 15 minutes,
sauteed (reserving grease)	cut into small pieces and sauteed
2 large chopped onions	1 pound black-eyed peas, boiled until
1 chopped green pepper	half cooked
1 cup chopped celery	6 cups chicken broth
1/4 cup dried parsley	3 cups rice
5 garlic cloves, chopped	Salt, pepper and hot sauce to taste
	1 bunch green onions, chopped

Heat about 3 tablespoons of sausage grease in large pot over medium heat. Add onion, green pepper, celery, parsley and garlic and saute about 10 minutes. Add sausage, salt pork, peas and chicken broth; bring to a boil. Add rice and return to a boil. Cover and simmer for about 45 minutes; DO NOT LIFT LID! Season to taste and add green onions, mixing well. Let stand 10 to 20 minutes before serving. Yield: 12 to 16 servings. Traditional New Year's Day dish. *Rush André*

Marinated Vegetables

1 head cauliflower, cut bite-size pieces	1 jar black olives, drained
1 green pepper, cut in oriental slices	1 jar green olives, drained
1 carrot, cut in oriental slices	1 jar pearl onions, drained
4 celery stalks, cut in oriental slices	2 cans mushrooms, drained
2 cans artichoke hearts, drained	2 garlic cloves, pressed

Wash all vegetables then mix in large plastic container. Add artichoke, black and green olives, pearl onions and mushrooms with the pressed garlic to vegetable mix. Make Marinade.

MARINADE

3/4 cup oil	2 teaspoons salt
1/2 cup wine vinegar	2 teaspoons oregano
1/3 cup sugar	1/2 teaspoon pepper
2 teaspoons prepared mustard	

In a large bowl, add oil, wine vinegar, sugar, prepared mustard, salt, oregano and pepper. Mix thoroughly with wire whisk. Pour over vegetables and marinate over night. Serves 10. *Debbie Lehman*

Marinade also very good on Shrimp and Crabmeat.

Stuffed Mushrooms

2 pints mushrooms
2 tablespoons onion, finely chopped
2 tablespoons butter
¼ cup soft bread crumbs
¼ cup toasted unblanched almonds, finely chopped

2 teaspoons lemon juice
½ teaspoon salt
¼ teaspoon Worcestershire sauce
½ cup light cream
½ cup shredded American cheese

Wash mushrooms and remove stems. Reserve caps. Chop stems; saute with onion in butter in small skillet for 5 minutes until tender. Add crumbs and almonds and cook 2 minutes longer. Stir in lemon juice and seasonings. Fill mushroom caps with stuffing. Place in baking dish. Pour cream around mushrooms. Bake at 400° for 15 minutes. Top with cheese. Bake 10 minutes longer, until cheese melts.

Mrs. Henry Thomas

Mixed Vegetable Casserole

1 package frozen green peas, cooked as directed
1 can bean sprouts, drained
1 small can water chestnuts, drained and diced

1 can mushroom soup
½ pound cheddar cheese
1 can fried onion rings
2 small cans mushroom pieces, drained

Place drained peas, bean sprouts, mushrooms, and diced water chestnuts into 9 inch casserole. Heat mushroom soup and pour over vegetable mixture. Grate ½ pound cheddar cheese and place on top of soup mixture. Bake at 350° for 30 minutes. Remove from oven and top with can of fried onion rings. Bake 15 minutes or until brown. Shrimp, chicken, turkey or ham can be added and make this into a main dish meal.

Mrs. Mack A. Bethea

Mixed Vegetables In Foil

1 (1¾ pound) can cut green beans (boiled with salt, pepper, bacon drippings, dash of sugar, celery and salt)
2 large sliced tomatoes
4 tablespoons melted margarine

¼ cup chopped onion
2 teaspoons prepared mustard
1 teaspoon prepared horseradish
1 tablespoon brown sugar
1 teaspoon salt
Dash of pepper

Beat the last seven ingredients, mixing thoroughly. Drain boiled beans and place either in a baking dish for the oven or thick foil for the grill. Place tomatoes on top of beans and dot with the mustard mixture. Cook 40 minutes on rack on grill or at 375° in oven. Serves 4.

Mrs. L. M. Chancellor,
Macon, Mississippi

French Onion Casserole

4 medium onions, sliced
3 tablespoons margarine or butter
2 tablespoons all-purpose flour
Dash pepper
¾ cup beef bouillon

¼ cup dry sherry
1½ cups plain croutons
2 tablespoons melted butter
2 ounces shredded Swiss cheese
3 tablespoons grated Parmesan cheese

Cook onions in butter until tender. Blend in flour and pepper. Add bouillon and sherry. Cook stirring until thick. Turn into 1 quart casserole. Toss croutons with 2 tablespoons melted butter. Spoon on top of onions. Sprinkle with Swiss and Parmesan cheeses. Place under broiler approximately 1 minute. Serves 4.

Jane Joyner

Onions Viennese

2½ pounds Bermuda onions
2 tablespoons sherry
½ cup chopped celery
1 cup mushrooms
½ cup chopped green pepper

½ teaspoon marjoram
Pinch of thyme
1 tablespoon seasoned salt
2 cups grated cheddar cheese
Cracker crumbs to cover casserole

CREAM SAUCE

½ stick margarine, melted
2 heaping tablespoons flour

½ cup cream
1 cup milk

Peel onions and quarter. Cover with cold water and bring to boil. Drain. Add wine, celery, mushrooms and other seasonings, making the "onion mixture". Prepare cream sauce using a heavy saucepan. Melt margarine and slowly blend in flour. Add the cream and milk and cook slowly over medium heat until sauce thickens. In buttered 9 x 12 inch casserole layer onion mixture, cream sauce, cracker crumbs, and cheese. Repeat. Sprinkle top with paprika. Bake for 1 hour at 325⁰. Serves 10.

Mrs. Alben N. Hopkins

Escalloped Pineapple Au Gratin

1 large can sliced pineapple,
   drained
2 tablespoons margarine or butter
2 tablespoons flour

1 cup milk
¼ pound grated American cheese
¼ cup slivered almonds
Salt to taste

Arrange drained pineapple slices in shallow baking dish. Melt butter or oleo in saucepan; add flour and stir to blend. Then add milk and stir until smooth and thickened. Blend in salt and stir in cheese until melted. Pour this cream sauce over pineapple in baking dish and top with almonds. Bake at 350⁰ for 15 minutes or until heated through and lightly browned. This is very good with ham or a pork roast. It is also good for a brunch. Serves 8.

Nancy Mize Sneed

Vrazel's Florentine Au Gratin

2 (8 ounce) packages frozen chopped
   spinach
1/2 stick butter or margarine
6-8 ounces cream cheese

Salt and pepper to taste
1 cup fresh bread crumbs
Parmesan cheese

Thaw spinach. Do not drain. In a sauce pan melt butter and cheese. Add undrained spinach and blend well. Make sure cream cheese is well mixed. Salt and pepper. Add fresh bread crumbs and mix well. Should be soggy. Place in casserole dish. Top with Parmesan cheese and bake at 350° until lightly brown and thoroughly hot.

Chef Bill Vrazel
Vrazel's
Fine Food Restaurant
Gulfport, Mississippi

Spaghetti Squash

1 spaghetti squash, 1 1/2-2 pounds
1 cup, or more Mozzarella cheese
1 cup or more cheddar cheese
1/2 diced green pepper

2 cups tomato sauce
1/2 teaspoon oregano
1/2 teaspoon garlic powder
1/2 cup grated Parmesan cheese

Cut squash in half lengthwise. Scoop out seeds. Place squash, cut side down, in 2 inches of simmering water; cover and cook 15 minutes. (Now call the kids to watch!) Holding the hot squash in a potholder, run the tines of a fork across its pulp and like magic there is your spaghetti! Mix the strands with the cheeses, green pepper, tomato sauce, oregano and garlic in a large bowl and scoop back into squash shells. Sprinkle tops with Parmesan and bake at 350° for 20 minutes. Kids love this. They think it smells and tastes a little like pizza. Freezes well.

Mrs. Joyce Youngblood

No Fuss Potatoes

6 medium potatoes, peeled and sliced
Salt and pepper
1 onion, minced

1 can cream of chicken soup
   slightly diluted with water
Mild cheddar cheese, sliced

Prepare potatoes and place in a buttered casserole. Sprinkle with onions and pour soup mixture over top. Bake 1 hour at 350°. Cover with sliced cheese and return to oven until cheese is melted. Serves 6 to 8.

Mrs. James Thomas

Potato Supreme

1 (2 pound) package frozen hash
   brown potatoes
½ stick melted butter
1 teaspoon salt
½ teaspoon pepper

½ cup chopped onion
1 can cream of chicken soup
10 ounces grated cheese
1 pint sour cream

Topping: ½ stick margarine, melted and 2 cups crushed cornflakes.

Mix all ingredients and put into large buttered casserole. Bake at 350° for 30 minutes. Top with topping mixture. Bake about 30 minutes. Serves 8.

Mrs. James Thomas

Sweet Potato Casserole

3 cups mashed sweet potatoes
   (3 or 4 medium potatoes)
2 eggs

1 cup sugar
¾ stick butter

TOPPING

1 cup brown sugar
¾ stick butter
½ cup chopped pecans

⅓ cup flour
1 teaspoon vanilla

Boil, drain, peel and mash the potatoes. Mix first four ingredients in blender or with electric mixer. Pour into a buttered 2 quart casserole dish. For topping, work ingredients with hands until crumbly and pour over potatoes. Bake uncovered at 350° (approximately 30 minutes) until thoroughly heated and brown on top. Serves 8. Delicious with ham or turkey.

Mrs. Kent Lovelace, Jr.

Ma's Sweet Potato Pone

3 cups mashed sweet potatoes
2 cups sugar
¼ cup milk
1½ cups flour
1 cup chopped dates or raisins

1 cup pecan pieces
1 tablespoon vanilla
1 stick butter
2 teaspoons baking powder

Preheat oven to 300°. Mix ingredients in bowl. Pour into a greased and floured pan and bake for 1 hour. Cut into serving pieces while hot. Serve hot for a vegetable. Serve cool with whipped cream for a dessert.

Linda Lewald

Rice Rutledge

1 stick margarine
2 small green peppers, chopped
2 medium onions, chopped
2 cans chicken and rice soup

1 small jar pimentos, chopped
1 can sliced mushrooms, with juice
1 cup Uncle Ben's rice

Saute chopped pepper and onions in margarine. Add all other ingredients. Bake in 1½ quart baking dish at 350° for 1 hour.

Mrs. J. Robbins Clower, Jr.

Chappy's Rice Pilaf

1 1/2 cups long grain rice
1/2 cup no cholesterol spread
1/2 cup white wine
1 bunch green onions, chopped

1 1/2 cups chopped mushrooms
1 cup blanched almonds
Garlic powder
White pepper

Cook rice in usual method. Saute the next 4 ingredients. Add the almonds. Combine the rice and sauteed mixture. Add the garlic powder and pepper to taste.

Chef John Chapman
Chappy's on the Beach
Long Beach, Mississippi

Brown Rice

1 stick margarine or butter
1 cup uncooked rice
Chopped onion or dried onion
    flakes, to taste
1 cup beef consomme or beef broth

1/2 small can sliced mushrooms,
    with juice
2/3 cup water
Parsley, optional

Melt margarine in skillet. Add rice and brown. Add onion and cook five minutes. Place in casserole, add soup, mushrooms and water. Bake in moderate 350° oven for 30 minutes until done. Garnish with parsley if desired. Serves 4.

Mrs. Ruth Stringfellow

Cold Rice Salad

1 box chicken flavor Rice-A-Roni (or
    herbed flavor may also be used)
1 small jar marinated artichoke hearts,
    drained (save juice)

1 small can chopped black olives
1/2 bunch chopped green onions
1/3 cup chopped green peppers
1/3 cup mayonnaise

Cook Rice-A-Roni according to package directions and let cool. Add all other ingredients except mayonnaise and juice from artichoke hearts. Whisk these together and stir into rice mixture. Chill. Serves 6.

Mrs. James S. Murray, Jr.

Green Rice

4 cups cooked white rice
2/3 cup sharp grated cheddar cheese
1 package frozen chopped spinach,
    thawed, uncooked
2 teaspoons salt
4 eggs

1 1/3 cups chicken broth
1/2 cup minced parsley
1/2 cup melted butter
1 1/2 teaspoons Worcestershire
2 teaspoons onion, grated

Combine all ingredients. Place in buttered casserole. Bake at 325° for 1 hour. Serves 10.

Mrs. Jerry Swetland

Dirty Rice

1 pound chicken livers, chopped
1 pound bulk sausage
½ cup margarine
1 package frozen chef's seasoning
    or chopped onion, celery and pepper
½ teaspoon thyme

½ teaspoon basil
3 cups cooked rice
Salt and pepper to taste
Hot sauce, to taste
1 can chicken broth

Saute chicken livers and sausage until browned. Remove from skillet and set aside. Melt margarine in large skillet, add chopped seasonings. Saute until tender. Add thyme, basil, rice, chicken livers, and sausage, mix well. Stir in salt, pepper, hot sauce, and chicken broth. Cook over medium heat until rice is hot, stirring often. Serves 8.

Mrs. Alton R. Perry, Jr.

Jackie's Wild Rice Dressing

½ pound bulk sausage
    (Tennessee Pride)
½ cup chopped onion
½ pound fresh mushrooms
¼ cup flour

1 box Uncle Ben's Long Grain
    and Wild Rice
1 cup sour cream
2 cups chicken broth
½ cup chopped pecans

Cook sausage until well done. Drain and reserve ¼ cup drippings. Saute onion and mushrooms in reserved drippings. Remove mushrooms and add flour. Cook rice as directed. When nearly done, add remaining ingredients. Bake at 425° for 30 minutes.

Mrs. William E. Smallwood

Spinach and Artichoke Casserole

4 (10 ounce) packages frozen, chopped
    spinach
1 (10½ ounce) can hearts of
    artichokes, halved
8 ounces cream cheese

1 can (5 or more ounces) sliced
    water chestnuts
Seasoned bread crumbs
1 stick butter

Cook spinach according to package directions. Drain. Melt cream cheese and butter in saucepan. Add spinach and blend well. Place artichokes and water chestnuts in bottom of a greased casserole 9 x 13 inches. Pour spinach over the top and sprinkle with seasoned bread crumbs. Bake in a 350° oven about 20 minutes or until bubbly. Unseasoned bread crumbs may be substituted. Serves 10 to 12.

Mrs. Allen Kerr

Spinach Madeline

3 packages frozen chopped spinach
4 tablespoons butter
2 tablespoons flour
2 tablespoons chopped onion
½ cup evaporated milk
½ cup vegetable liquor
1 teaspoon Worcestershire sauce
¾ teaspoon celery salt
¾ teaspoon garlic salt
½ teaspoon salt
1 (6 ounce) roll jalapeno cheese
½ teaspoon red pepper
½ teaspoon black pepper
Buttered bread crumbs, optional

Cook spinach according to directions on package. Drain and save ½ cup of liquor. Melt butter in saucepan over low heat. Add flour stirring until smooth. Add onion and cook until soft, then add liquid slowly, stirring constantly. Cook until smooth and thick. Add seasonings and chopped cheese. Stir until melted. Add cooked spinach. Pour into serving dish and top with bread crumbs. May be frozen or refrigerated overnight. May be served with crackers as an hors d' oeuvre.

Mrs. John H. Richards

Spinach Quiche

3 ounces cream cheese
1 cup half-and-half
½ cup bread crumbs
¼ cup shredded Parmesan cheese
2 eggs
1 cup chopped spinach, cooked
  and drained
4 tablespoons butter
1 onion, finely chopped
½ pound fresh mushrooms,
  chopped
1 teaspoon tarragon, optional
Pastry shell, unbaked
Salt to taste

Mix first five ingredients. Add spinach. Melt butter and cook onions and mushrooms. Add with tarragon to spinach mixture. Salt to taste. Pour into unbaked pastry shell. Bake in 400° oven for 25 minutes. Remove and let stand 10 minutes. Cut and serve.

Mrs. H. G. McCall,
New Orleans, Louisiana

Spinach-Broccoli Buffet

2 (10 ounce) packages frozen
  chopped spinach
2 (10 ounce) packages frozen chopped
  broccoli
2 cups sour cream
1 package dry onion soup mix
Salt to taste
½ cup grated cheddar cheese

Cook spinach and broccoli according to package directions, drain well. Combine sour cream and soup and add to vegetables. Mix well. Season with salt and pour into baking dish. Bake, covered at 325° for 40 minutes. Remove from oven, top with cheese and serve. Serves 10.

Mrs. R. E. Fairbank, Jr.

Spinach Pies

12 canned biscuits

FILLING

2 boxes frozen chopped spinach,
* thawed and drained*
1 onion, minced
3 tablespoons lemon juice

4 tablespoons olive oil
1½ teaspoons salt
¾ teaspoon pepper

Roll out each biscuit round (or pat thin). Squeeze out remaining water from spinach and mix with other filling ingredients. Place a heaping tablespoon of mixture in center of each round and bring edges together in center to form a triangle. Press to seal. Place on ungreased cookie sheet and bake at 400° until brown. May also be used as an appetizer.

Mrs. Mitchell Salloum

Summer Squash and Carrot Bake

2 pounds yellow summer squash, sliced
* (approximately 6 cups)*
½ cup chopped onion
1 can cream of chicken soup
1 cup sour cream

1 cup shredded carrots
1 (8 ounce) package herb seasoned
* stuffing mix*
½ cup margarine or butter, melted

Cook sliced squash and chopped onion in boiling salted water for 5 minutes. Drain. Combine soup and sour cream. Stir in carrots. Fold in drained squash and onions. Combine stuffing mix and margarine. Spread half of stuffing mixture in bottom of greased casserole. Spoon vegetable mixture on top. Sprinkle remaining stuffing mix on vegetables. Bake at 350° for 25-30 minutes or until thoroughly heated.

Mrs. Stewart Brumfield

Mrs. W. W. Warren of Birmingham, Alabama, makes the above casserole but includes 1 can chopped pimento and 1 can sliced water chestnuts in the vegetable mixture.

Summer Squash

3 pounds yellow squash
½ cup chopped onions
½ cup cracker meal or bread crumbs
2 eggs

1 stick butter
1 tablespoon sugar
1 teaspoon salt
½ teaspoon black pepper

Wash, cut and boil squash. When tender, drain thoroughly and mash. Using only ½ of the stick of butter, add all ingredients to the hot, mashed squash. Pour mixture into a 2 quart casserole. Melt remaining ½ stick margarine and pour over squash. Sprinkle with cracker meal or bread crumbs. Bake 45 minutes at 375°. Serves 8.

Mrs. John Stringer

Golden Squash

2½ pounds squash, cooked,
    drained and mashed
2 cups chopped onions
2 cups chopped celery
1 cup chopped green pepper
1 stick margarine

6 eggs, beaten
3 cups milk
1½ cups raw oatmeal
Salt and pepper to taste
Crumbs for topping

Cook, drain, and mash squash. Saute onions, celery and green pepper in margarine. Add to squash. Add beaten eggs, milk and oatmeal. Season to taste. Pour into a greased casserole, top with crumbs and bake in preheated oven at 350⁰ for 45 minutes. To test doneness, insert knife. If not set, bake a few more minutes. A shallow baking dish works best. Serves 12 to 15. This recipe divides nicely for fewer servings.

Mrs. Sherman Muths, Jr.

White Squash Casserole

3 cups sliced white squash
½ cup water
1 medium onion
2 eggs
1 small carton sour cream
    or 3 ounces cream cheese

1 cup grated cheddar cheese
1 tablespoon Worcestershire sauce
  (or more)
Salt and pepper to taste
Progresso bread crumbs
Butter

Cook squash and onion in salted water until tender. Drain. Beat eggs, blend with other ingredients and add to squash. Mix well. Pour into buttered dish, cover with bread crumbs. Dot with butter and bake at 350⁰ for 30 minutes. Serves 8.

Mrs. Robert A. Mitchell

Stuffed Squash

6 to 8 yellow squash
2 large, firm tomatoes, chopped
1 large onion, chopped
1 large green pepper, chopped

½ cup grated sharp cheddar cheese
2 tablespoons bacon bits
Progresso bread crumbs
Salt and pepper to taste

Boil whole squash until tender. Drain and cut in half lengthwise. Scoop out seeds and discard. Mix tomatoes, pepper, onion, cheese, and bacon bits. Place in shells. Sprinkle with crumbs, dot with butter. Bake in 350⁰ oven for 15-20 minutes. Serves 6 to 8.

Mrs. Robert A. Mitchell

Huevos Rancheros

3 tablespoons oleo
2 cloves garlic, chopped
1 green pepper, sliced
2 medium onions, sliced
1/8 teaspoon cumin
1/8 teaspoon marjoram

½ teaspoon basil
Ground pepper and salt, to taste
16 ounces canned tomatoes
2 teaspoons chili powder
4 eggs
¼ pound shredded cheddar cheese

Saute garlic, green pepper, onions in oleo till crisp tender. Add cumin, marjoram, basil, ground pepper, salt, tomatoes, and chili powder. Stir to mix well. Scoop out 4 places, putting a raw egg in each hollow. Cover with cheese. Bake at 425° for 8 to 10 minutes or till egg is cooked to your preference. Serve for breakfast, brunch, or supper. This recipe served with Mexican cornbread and beer serves 4 people or 2 very hungry ones. It can be used as the main course in a Mexican dinner, or as one of the dishes in a buffet. It can easily be doubled and more. It can be made ahead, adding the eggs and cheese when ready to bake.

Mrs. William J. Demoran

Zucchini Bake

3 or 4 zucchini squash
1 cup spaghetti sauce (meatless)
4 ounces cheddar cheese, grated

Grated Parmesan cheese
Salt and pepper to taste
Margarine

Cut zucchini in ¼ inch crosswise slices. Place alternate layers of zucchini, salt, pepper, spaghetti sauce and cheddar cheese in a 2 quart casserole, finishing the layering with cheddar cheese. Top with Parmesan and dot with margarine. Bake at 350° for 25 minutes or until bubbling and lightly browned. Spaghetti sauce freezes well so I always make extra and freeze in 1 cup containers. Serves 4.

Anne Graham

Cheese Pudding Side Dish

8 slices white bread
1/3 cup margarine, melted
2 cups sharp cheese, grated

3 cups milk
4 eggs, beaten
1/3 teaspoon salt
½ teaspoon dry mustard

Spread the bread with melted butter and cut each slice into quarters. Alternate layers of bread and cheese in a 1½ quart, deep baking dish, ending with cheese on top. Combine milk, eggs, salt and mustard. Pour over cheese and bread. Store covered in refrigerator overnight. Bake uncovered at 325° for 40 minutes. Serves 6 to 8.

Mrs. Harry Woodbury

Elegant Stuffed Tomatoes

8 medium tomatoes
⅓ to ½ medium sized
  head cabbage, shredded
½ pound sharp cheese, grated
¼ cup mayonnaise

1 teaspoon Worcestershire sauce
  (more if desired)
Lemon pepper to taste
Garlic salt to taste
Stuffed olives

Peel tomatoes by dipping in boiling water on end of fork, removing "jackets". Mix shredded cabbage, grated cheese, mayonnaise, Worcestershire sauce, garlic salt and lemon pepper in mixing bowl. After coring tomatoes, stuff them with the cabbage and cheese mixture. Garnish with pimento-stuffed olive. Serves 8.

Mrs. George P. Hopkins, Jr.

Baked Tomatoes

3 medium tomatoes
Italian bread crumbs

Salt and pepper to taste
Butter

Halve tomatoes. Place in casserole. Season with salt and pepper. Top with bread crumbs. Dot with butter. Add a small amount of water in bottom of casserole to prevent sticking. Bake at 350⁰ for 20 minutes. A colorful addition to meat or poultry.

Julie Pigott

Jiffy Tomato Stack Ups

3 large tomatoes
Salt
4 ounces Swiss cheese, shredded

1 (10 ounce) package frozen chopped
  broccoli, cooked and drained
¼ cup chopped onion

Cut tomatoes into slices ¾ inch thick and sprinkle with salt. Set aside 2 tablespoons of shredded cheese. Combine remaining cheese, broccoli, and onion. Place tomato slices on greased baking sheet and spoon broccoli mixture on top, dividing mixture evenly between slices. Sprinkle with reserved cheese and broil 7 or 8 inches from heat for 10 to 12 minutes. Serves 6.

Gay Graves

Bread and Butter Pickles

4 quarts cucumbers, thinly sliced
4 to 6 medium onions, thinly sliced
3 cloves garlic, thinly sliced
1 green pepper, thinly sliced
1 red pepper, thinly sliced
⅓ cup salt

3 cups white vinegar
5 cups sugar
1½ tablespoons tumeric
1½ tablespoons celery seed
2 tablespoons mustard seed
3 or 4 trays of ice cubes

Slice vegetables as directed and mix together. Add salt. Cover with ice cubes. Let stand 3 hours. Drain. Combine vinegar, sugar, and spices. Pour over cucumber mixture. Heat to a boil. Pack in sterilized jars and seal. Yields 8 pints.

Gloria Mauldin

Green Tomato Relish

6½ cups bell peppers (red, green
   or mixed)
4 cups green tomatoes

2 cucumbers
4 cups onions
½ cup pickling salt

Chop vegetables coarsely in food processor. Place in large bowl; sprinkle with salt; refrigerate overnight. Rinse to remove salt, drain and squeeze to remove moisture.

SYRUP

6 cups sugar
2 tablespoons dry mustard
1 tablespoon celery seed

4 cups cider vinegar
2 cups water
1½ teaspoons tumeric

Mix syrup ingredients in large pot (not aluminum). Add vegetables; boil for 5 minutes. Place in sterile canning jars; seal; process for 5 minutes.

Lucy Quarles

Lindbergh Relish

1 medium head cabbage
4 medium carrots
2 bell peppers

4 red or green hot peppers
1 medium onion

Grind all vegetables in food chopper. Add ¼ cup salt and let stand 2 hours. Drain and mix with 3 cups cider vinegar, 2½ cups sugar and ½ teaspoon each of mustard seed and celery seed. This relish requires no cooking. Can be sealed if to be kept for long period of time by putting in hot, sterile jars and sealing.

Mrs. D. Lyle Robertson

Sweet Pepper Relish

12 red sweet peppers
12 green sweet peppers
1 hot pepper
9 onions

1 cup sugar
1 tablespoon salt
2 cups cider vinegar
1 tablespoon mixed pickling spices,
   tied in cloth bag

Put peppers and onions through food chopper. Cover with boiling water. Let stand 5 minutes and then drain. Cover again with boiling water and let stand 10 minutes and then drain. Add sugar, salt, vinegar and spices. Cook 15 minutes. Remove bag of spices. Pack into hot jars and seal.

Mrs. D. Lyle Robertson

Pickled Okra

5 pint jars
Fresh tender okra
1 clove garlic to each jar
1 hot pepper to each jar

1 teaspoon dill seed to each jar
1 quart white vinegar
1 cup water
½ cup salt

Place garlic and hot pepper in bottom of clean hot pint jars. Pack firmly with young clean okra. Add dill seed. Bring vinegar, water and salt to a boil. Simmer 5 minutes, and pour, boiling hot, over the okra. Seal at once.

Mrs. George Schloegel

Squash Pickle

10 small yellow squash, thinly sliced
2 cups onions, thinly sliced
1 large jar pimento
2 green peppers, thinly sliced

3 cups sugar
2 cups vinegar
2 tablespoons mustard seed
2 tablespoons celery seed

Soak squash in ⅔ cup salt and 3 quarts water for 1 hour. Pour off water. Do not rinse. Mix sugar, vinegar, mustard seed, and celery seed in a saucepan and bring to a boil. Do not cook. Add drained vegetables. Bring to a boil once more, but do not cook. Put in sterile jars. Seal. Makes 4 pints. Good with vegetables.

Mrs. Virgil Gillespie

Hot Curried Fruit

1 large can peach halves
1 large can pineapple chunks

1 large can pear halves
1 small jar cherries

Drain fruit well. Mix ⅓ cup oleo, ¾ cup brown sugar and 4 teaspoons curry powder. Add to fruit and heat in oven. (Add a few pecans if you like).

Mrs. Holcomb Hector

Baked Orange Cups

6 medium oranges
6 medium apples, peeled and chopped
1 small can crushed pineapple

½ cup sugar
½ cup chopped pecans
Butter

Cut oranges in half, zig-zag top to make orange cup. Hollow out pulp from each half, reserve pulp and juice. Combine orange juice and pulp, apples, pineapple, and sugar. Cook until very thick. Fill orange cups with mixture. Cover bottom of shallow baking dish with ½ inch water and place orange cups in dish. Sprinkle with pecans and pats of butter. Bake at 300⁰ for 30 minutes. Excellent with game.

Mrs. Sam Morse

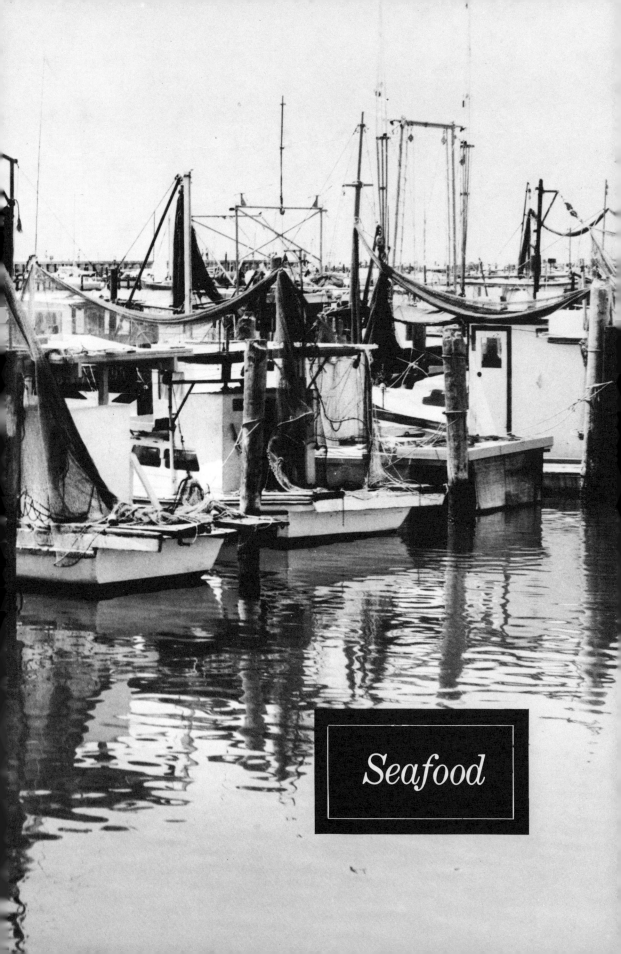

Seafood

Seafood

Grilled Shrimp

¼ pound butter (not margarine)
1 teaspoon Worcestershire
¼ teaspoon Cavenders seasoned salt
Garlic salt

Juice of one lemon
1 pound jumbo shrimp,
  deheaded and peeled
Lemon pepper
Cooked rice

Peel raw shrimp, thread onto skewers, and sprinkle with salt 30 minutes before grilling: then squeeze lemon over all. Make sauce of butter, Worcestershire, Cavenders, and lemon pepper. Seer shrimp on hot covered barbeque grill after basting with sauce once. Cook 3 minutes on each side. Heat remaining sauce to pour over shrimp on bed of rice before serving. Recommended with Mouton-Cadet Blanc Sec. Complete with green salad.

Donnie Riley

Shrimp Scampi

5 pounds jumbo shrimp, peeled
  and deveined
6 to 8 buds sliced garlic

1 stick butter
Salt to taste

Saute garlic in butter in heavy skillet for a few minutes. Add shrimp and saute 4 to 5 minutes. May be served with rice or French bread.

J. W. "Red" Reeves
Spring Bayou
Talullah, Louisiana

Shrimp boats are a familiar scene on the Coast where commercial fishing is a vital industry. Each June, Biloxi hosts the unique and colorful Blessing of the Fleet, a religious ceremony which originated more than three hundred years ago in countries bordering the Adriatic Sea. Although the purpose of the festival is to insure a bountiful catch and the safety of the fisherman, the ceremony, festivities, and revelry are for all.

Photograph by John Galloway

Broiled Shrimp With Cheese

Shrimp
Salt and pepper
Lemon juice

Butter
Cheddar cheese, grated

Peel and devein shrimp. Place in broiler pan without rack. Salt and pepper shrimp, dot with butter, and squeeze lemon juice over all. Place under broiler until shrimp are pink. Remove from broiler and sprinkle with grated cheese. Return to broiler until cheese bubbles. Serve immediately. Easy and delicious.

Patti Bannister

Shrimp in Beer

2 pounds fresh shrimp
1 medium onion, chopped
1 clove garlic, crushed
3 tablespoons oil
1 tablespoon salt

2 tablespoons parsley, chopped
1 bay leaf
A few celery leaves
½ teaspoon black pepper
1 pint beer

Wash shrimp but do not peel. Saute the onion and garlic in the oil for 2 minutes. Add shrimp and all other ingredients and simmer gently for 12 minutes. Let shrimp stand in the broth for 1 to 2 hours before serving. Serve with your favorite sauce.

Mrs. Jack Van Landingham

Baked Shrimp

5 pounds of unpeeled shrimp
2 cloves chopped garlic
1 teaspoon Worcestershire sauce
Juice of 2 lemons
1 chopped onion

Sprinkle of red pepper
Sprinkle of Italian seasoning
1 cup white or red port wine
1 cup olive oil
Salt to taste

Layer shrimp in ovenproof dish. Mix remaining ingredients and pour over shrimp. Let stand 1 to 3 hours. Bake at 350° for 20 minutes. Add salt if needed.

Mrs. J. W. Reeves
Ruston, Louisiana

Lucy's Shrimp

2 pounds shrimp, peeled and
    drained
½ stick butter
6 tablespoons olive oil
¾ teaspoon rosemary (crushed)
¾ teaspoon Italian seasoning

2 cloves garlic, crushed
¾ cup sauterne wine
1 lemon (juice and grated rind)
Salt and pepper

Place shrimp in a shallow baking dish in which the butter has been melted. Mix together remaining ingredients and add to shrimp. Bake at 350° for 45 minutes.

Mrs. Sam Mavar

Bar-B-Q Shrimp

3 pounds large shrimp, unpeeled
2 sticks butter or margarine
1/4 cup olive oil
Garlic salt
Celery salt

Lemon
1/2 cup Bar-B-Q sauce
Black pepper
1/2 cup rum

Cover bottom of shallow pan with half of melted butter. Place unpeeled shrimp in pan. Pour remaining melted butter on shrimp. Spinkle olive oil, garlic salt, celery salt, lemon, and Bar-B-Q sauce on shrimp. Sprinkle very heavily with black pepper. Place shrimp under broiler (put pan on center or lower rack) for about 5 minutes. Turn shrimp and broil other side for 5 more minutes. Remove from oven. Sprinkle shrimp with rum. Put back under broiler for one more minute. Serve with French bread (delicious dipped in butter sauce).

Mrs. Gibran B. Werby

Shrimp en Brochette

3 pounds uncooked shrimp,
   shelled and deveined
1 to 2 cloves garlic
1/2 cup cooking oil
1 teaspoon salt
1 teaspoon coarsely ground pepper

3 tablespoons chili sauce
1 tablespoon Worcestershire sauce
3 tablespoons vinegar
1/4 cup chopped parsley
Dash hot pepper sauce

Rinse shrimp, drain and arrange on 8 skewers. Place in large oblong pan. Make sauce by crushing garlic cloves, blend with the cooking oil. Add remaining ingredients. Brush shrimp with sauce. Cover with plastic wrap and let stand overnight or at least 4 hours in refrigerator. When ready to use, broil 10 minutes, turning often and brushing with marinade. Serve with rice and garnish with chicory, tiny skewers of orange sections, olives, pickles. Serves 8.

Mrs. William Seal

Quick Jambalaya

1 package brown and serve
   sausage links
2 cups uncooked instant rice
2 cups water
1/2 cup frozen green pepper
1 (16 ounce) can stewed tomatoes
1 (12 ounce) package cleaned,
   raw shrimp
1/4 teaspoon thyme

2 tablespoons instant minced
   onion
2 teaspoons instant chicken
   bouillon or 2 cubes
1 teaspoon salt
1/8 teaspoon cayenne pepper
1/4 teaspoon chili powder

Cut sausage links into one inch diagonal slices. Place in large skillet. Brown as directed on package. Add remaining ingredients except green pepper. Heat to boiling, stirring occasionally. Reduce heat; simmer uncovered for 10 minutes stirring occasionally. Stir in green pepper and heat through. Serve. Serves 6-7.

Mrs. Bob Monette

Baked Herbed Shrimp

5 pounds shrimp, unpeeled with
    heads on
1 pound oleo or butter

Handful of combination of oregano,
    rosemary, basil, and black pepper
    (mixed in palm of hand)

Place shrimp in casserole. Spoon on whipped oleo. Add herbs. Cover and bake at 400° for 20 minutes. Remove from oven and stir well. Cover and return to oven and cook 20 minutes longer. Serve with French bread to dip in sauce.

Captain Robert Engram, USN (Ret.)

Parmesan Stuffed Shrimp

1 cup round buttery cracker crumbs
1/4 cup grated Parmesan cheese
1 teaspoon fresh lemon juice
1/2 cup butter or margarine, melted

1 1/2 tablespoons sherry
1/4 teaspoon garlic powder
16 jumbo shrimp, butterflied
Paprika

Combine first six ingredients. Fill each shrimp with mixture. Bake in shallow pan at 250° for 25 minutes. Broil 1 minute or until lightly browned. Sprinkle with paprika and serve.

Walton Moore

Golden Fried Shrimp Batter

1 egg
1/2 cup milk
2 tablespoons melted butter or oleo
1/2 cup self rising flour

Salt and pepper to taste
Morton's Nature's Seasons seasoning
    blend to taste
Extra flour to roll shrimp in

Separate egg. Put yolk in small mixing bowl and put egg white in separate bowl. Beat egg yolk, 1/4 cup milk and melted butter in mixing bowl. Add flour and rest of milk and beat well. Beat egg white until stiff and fold in batter. Dip shrimp in batter then roll in flour. Fry in hot grease until golden. This batter can also be used for fried onion rings. If you like spicy shrimp, add a teaspoon of liquid crab boil to grease.

Janet Miller

Shrimp Curried Eggs

8 hard boiled eggs
1/3 cup mayonnaise
1/2 teaspoon salt

1/2 teaspoon paprika
1/2 teaspoon curry powder
1/4 teaspoon dry mustard

Cut eggs in half lengthwise. Remove yellow and combine yellow with remaining ingredients. Place mixture in egg whites. Place in shallow baking dish. Top with following sauce.

SAUCE

2 tablespoons butter
2 tablespoons all-purpose flour
1 can cream of shrimp soup

1 soup can of milk
1/2 cup sharp cheddar cheese
1 cup cooked shrimp (optional)

Stir all ingredients except cheese over heat until thick. Add cheese and stir till melted. Pour over eggs. Sprinkle with bread crumbs. Bake 15-20 minutes at 350°.

Mrs. James O. Dukes

Shrimp Creole

¼ cup flour
¼ cup oil
2 cups chopped onions
½ cup chopped green onions, and tops
2 buds garlic, minced
1 cup chopped green pepper
1 cup chopped celery, with leaves
2 bay leaves
3 teaspoons salt
½ teaspoon pepper
6 ounces tomato paste

1 (16 ounce) can tomatoes
8 ounces tomato sauce
1 cup water
5 pounds raw shrimp,
    peeled and deveined
Dash of Tabasco
½ cup chopped parsley
Juice of ½ lemon

In a Dutch oven or large heavy pot, make a roux of flour and oil. Add onions, green onions, garlic, green pepper, celery, bay leaves, salt, and pepper. Saute, uncovered, over medium heat until onions are transparent and soft. Add tomato paste and saute 3 minutes. Add tomatoes, tomato sauce, and water. Simmer for 45 minutes to 1 hour, stirring occasionally. Add shrimp and cook until shrimp are just done, about 5 minutes. Add Tabasco, parsley, and lemon juice. Stir, cover and remove from heat. This is best prepared several hours before serving. Let stand so seasonings and flavors can blend. Heat, but do not boil, and serve over rice. Serves 10.

Mrs. Walter Vick

Shrimp in Beer Creole

½ cup sliced almonds
1 tablespoon butter
1 tablespoon oil
2 pounds shelled shrimp
½ stick butter
Salt and pepper to taste
2 tablespoons butter

¼ cup green onions, chopped
1 green pepper cut into strips
½ pound small mushrooms
1 tablespoon sweet Hungarian
    paprika
1 teaspoon tomato paste
1 cup light beer
¾ cup heavy cream combined with
    ¼ cup sour cream

Saute almonds in 1 tablespoon butter and oil until golden. Drain on paper, salt and reserve. In skillet cook shrimp in ½ stick butter until they just turn pink. Transfer the shrimp and pan juices to a bowl and reserve. Then add 2 tablespoons more butter to pan and in it saute the green onion and green pepper until tender. Add mushrooms, Hungarian paprika, salt and pepper to taste and cook until mushrooms are tender. Stir in tomato paste, light beer, the reserved pan juices and reduce the liquid over high heat to ½ cup. Reduce heat to low, add heavy cream combined with sour cream and the reserved shrimp. Simmer until hot. Serve over brown or white rice seasoned with butter and freshly grated Parmesan cheese. Top with toasted almonds. Serves 4.

Mrs. William E. Smallwood

Shrimp Etouffe

3 pounds peeled, deveined shrimp
Salt, pepper, cayenne
1 large onion, chopped
3 stalks celery with leaves, chopped
1 stick butter or oleo

1 heaping teaspoon tomato paste
1 tablespoon corn starch, dissolved
  in 1/2 cup water
3 green onions and tops, chopped
1/4 cup minced parsley

Peel and devein shrimp. Salt and pepper shrimp and set aside. Saute onions and celery in butter or oleo until vegetables are soft. Add shrimp, tomato paste and corn starch. Simmer 10 minutes. Add green onions and parsley. Simmer a few more minutes. Serve over rice.

Betsy Matthews

Shrimp Ocean Springs

3 pounds boiled, peeled shrimp
1 pound fresh mushrooms, halved
3 tablespoons butter
Salt and pepper to taste
2 tablespoons flour

2 cartons sour cream
2 tablespoons imported soy sauce
6 tablespoons butter, softened
1 cup fresh Parmesan cheese, grated
Sweet Hungarian paprika

Place shrimp in shallow casserole. Salt and pepper if needed. Saute mushrooms in butter. Drain and toss with flour. Combine sour cream, softened butter and soy sauce. Stir into mushrooms. Spread mixture over shrimp in casserole. Top with grated cheese and sprinkle with paprika. Bake at 400° for 10 minutes or until bubbly. Serves 6-8.

Mrs. William E. Smallwood

Dr. Gordon Stanfield adds 1/4 teaspoon each: salt, white pepper, cayenne pepper, black pepper and garlic powder, and 5 whole sliced green onions to the sour cream mixture. He bakes the shrimp mixture in small patty shells for appetizers or in large puff pastry for dinner servings and bakes at 350° until bubbling.

Shrimp Over Rice

1 stick oleo
1 large onion, chopped
1 1/2 pounds shrimp
2 tablespoons butter
2 tablespoons flour
1 can chicken broth
Rice

1/2 teaspoon Kitchen bouquet
  (optional)
1 teaspoon catsup
1 large can mushrooms
1 1/2 teaspoons sherry
1 tablespoon capers
Parsley
Dash of tumeric

Saute onion in 1 stick oleo. Remove onion. Saute shrimp in this butter 5 to 6 minutes. Remove. In another skillet melt 2 tablespoons butter and add flour. Add chicken broth. Cook and thicken. Season with kitchen bouquet, catsup, mushrooms with juice, sherry, capers, parsley and tumeric. Add onion. Let shrimp stand in this sauce several hours. Serve over hot rice.

Mrs. H. C. Thompson

Shrimp and Artichoke Casserole

1 can cream of shrimp soup,
  undiluted
1 cup milk
2 tablespoons butter
2 tablespoons flour
2 pounds cleaned, raw shrimp
4 ounce can of whole mushrooms,
  drained
1 package artichoke hearts, cooked
  with a pinch of oregano

1 bunch of fresh parsley,
  chopped
Sherry or vermouth to taste
White pepper to taste
Salt to taste
Grated Parmesan cheese
Cooked rice or Chinese noodles
Worcestershire sauce to taste

In a small saucepan mix the shrimp soup, milk, butter, and flour. Transfer to a large skillet. Add the shrimp, mushrooms, artichoke hearts, and parsley. Mix well. Then add the wine, Worcestershire sauce, salt, and white pepper. Mix. Place the mixture in a casserole dish and top with Parmesan cheese. Bake in a moderate oven until it bubbles. Serve over hot, cooked rice, or heated Chinese noodles. This can be prepared the day before or frozen. If frozen, add the artichoke hearts when reheating.

James Poole
Little Rock, Arkansas

Shrimp and Green Noodles

1 (8 ounce) package green
  (spinach) noodles
3 or 4 diced green onions,
  including tops
2 to 3 pounds boiled, peeled
  shrimp
1 can cream of mushroom soup
1 cup sour cream

1 cup mayonnaise
Dash prepared mustard
2 to 3 tablespoons sherry or
  dry white wine
Grated cheese

Boil green noodles in boiling water until just tender, about 10 minutes. Add a little oil to prevent sticking. Drain and add diced green onions. Place in buttered 9" x 13" casserole dish and spread shrimp over top. Mix together soup, sour cream, mayonnaise, mustard, and wine, and pour over shrimp. Top with grated cheese, and bake in 350° oven 20-30 minutes or until bubbly. Cubed chicken may be substituted for the shrimp, in which case cream of chicken soup should be substituted for the mushroom soup. Serves 8-10.

Mrs. Allen Kerr

Spinach and Shrimp

3 packages frozen spinach
Garlic
1 stick butter
1 tablespoon Worcestershire sauce

1½ teaspoons salt
2 teaspoons anchovy paste
½ teaspoon hot sauce
2 pounds cooked shrimp
Bread crumbs

WHITE SAUCE

3 tablespoons butter   1½ cups milk
3 tablespoons flour   3 tablespoons Parmesan cheese

Cook spinach with garlic to taste and drain well. Melt 1 stick butter, add Worcestershire sauce, salt, anchovy paste, and hot sauce. Mix in spinach. Make a white sauce and add cheese. Layer shrimp, spinach mixture, and sauce in buttered casserole. Top with bread crumbs and bake at 350⁰ for 20 minutes.

Hazel Portwood

Shrimp Stuffed Peppers

1 teaspoon salt   2 tablespoons butter
3 cloves garlic   1 tablespoon chopped parsley
6 medium green peppers   1 cup grated Swiss cheese
½ cup raw rice   6 pats of butter
1 can mushroom soup   Paprika
Juice of 1 lemon   Black pepper to taste
1 small onion grated   1 pound (or more) small shrimp,
                                       cooked and cleaned

Clean peppers and boil in 2 quarts boiling water with salt and garlic cloves for 10 minutes. Boil rice till done and drain before adding to stuffing. Mix together mushroom soup, lemon juice, black pepper, grated onion, and 2 tablespoons butter. Place over low heat and cook stirring constantly until butter melts. Add cooked rice, cleaned shrimp and parsley to the sauce. Cook about 5 minutes. Stuff peppers with this mixture to 1 inch from top. Pack grated Swiss cheese to top. Place a pat of butter on each and sprinkle with paprika. Place peppers in large rectangular baking dish with a tiny bit of water at the bottom. Bake at 350⁰ for about 40 minutes. If your prefer a firmer bell pepper, do not precook before baking.

Mrs. G. W. Costello

Shrimp Patties

1 pound boiled peeled shrimp   ½ green pepper
2 small potatoes, cooked   1 egg
    and mashed   1 rib celery
4 crushed crackers   ½ cup olive oil
1 small onion   Salt and pepper
6 stems parsley

Chop onions, parsley, celery, green pepper and fry in olive oil until light brown. Add to mashed potatoes and shrimp ground in blender or food processor. Add egg and crackers. Mix and form into small patties. Roll in flour. Fry in deep fat until golden brown. Makes 15 patties.

Mrs. Matre G. Pitalo

Scalloped Squash Stuffed with Shrimp

6 young white squash (5" diameter)
1/4 cup bacon fat
3 onions
2 cloves garlic
3 ribs celery with leaves
1 bay leaf

Salt and pepper
3 slices toast
1 pound boiled shrimp (seasoned)
3 tablespoons cracker meal
2 tablespoons butter

Cover whole squash with boiling, lightly salted water and simmer until easily pierced with a fork. Lift out into a colander. Reserve liquid. Run cold water over them, let drain and cool until you can handle. Carefully cut a circle in the top, leaving at least 1/2" at the edge. Scoop out the squash leaving skin 1/4" thick. Place shells in buttered baking dish. Chop onions, celery and garlic and saute in bacon fat until lightly browned. Add bay leaf, toast soaked in cooking liquid and squash pulp. Cook covered for about 15 minutes. Add peeled shrimp, cut up if large, and cook uncovered, stirring frequently to prevent scorching, until excess liquid has evaporated. Season to taste and fill squash shells, rounding tops. Sprinkle with cracker meal and dot with butter. Bake at 350° for 30 minutes, running under broiler to brown. Serves 6.

Elizabeth Swan

Stuffed Mirlitons or Eggplants

3 mirlitons or 2 eggplants
1 large onion
1 clove garlic (optional)
1 tablespoon butter or margarine
1 tomato, chopped
1 sprig parsley, chopped

1 sprig thyme, minced
1 bay leaf, minced
1 1/2 dozen cooked shrimp (ham may be substituted)
3/4 cup bread crumbs
Salt and pepper to taste

Cut mirlitons or eggplants in half lengthwise and put into boiling salted water. Boil until tender, remove and cool. Scoop out pulp, remove seeds, mash and leave shell in good condition. Brown onion and garlic in butter, add tomato, parsley, thyme, and bay leaf, salt and pepper to taste. Add mirliton or eggplant and crumbs which have been soaked in cooking liquid, squeezed, and seasoned well. Mix with shrimp and fill the shells with the stuffing. Place additional crumbs over the top and dot each shell with butter. Place in 350° oven and bake for about 15 minutes or until golden brown.

Mrs. Edmund H. Crane, Jr.

Shrimp Stuffed Mirlitons

5 medium mirlitons
1/3 cup minced onions
2/3 cup chopped green onions
3 cloves garlic, minced
1/4 cup chopped parsley
3/4 cup melted bacon grease

3/4 cup fresh bread crumbs
1 teaspoon salt
1/2 teaspoon pepper
2 dashes Tabasco
1 egg, beaten
1 cup chopped raw shrimp

Cover mirlitons with water and boil until tender, about 1 hour. Cool and cut in half lengthwise. Scoop out tender pulp and reserve. Discard seeds and set aside shells for stuffing. Saute onions, green onions, garlic and parsley in ½ cup grease for 5 minutes or until onions are transparent. Add shrimp and cook, stirring for 5 minutes. Add mirliton pulp, ½ bread crumbs, salt, pepper, Tabasco and cook 10 minutes while stirring. Add ¼ cup grease if mixture is dry. Turn off fire and stir thoroughly. Add egg, return to heat, and cook 1 minute. Fill 8 shells and sprinkle with remaining bread crumbs. Bake in 375⁰ oven for 10-15 minutes, or until bread crumbs have browned.

Mrs. George P. Hopkins, Jr.

Pineapple Shrimp Curry

2 pounds boiled and peeled shrimp
4 tablespoons butter
4 tablespoons flour
2 cups milk
½ teaspoon salt
¼ cup butter
½ cup chopped onions
½ cup diced apples
1 teaspoon whole cloves

2 teaspoons curry powder
¼ teaspoon allspice
¼ teaspoon nutmeg
1 cup chunk pineapple with juice
½ cup sauterne
1 tablespoon lemon juice
2 tablespoons sugar
Salt to taste

Cook together 4 tablespoons butter, flour, milk and salt to form sauce. In another pan cook ¼ cup butter, chopped onions, diced apples and whole cloves until apples are soft. Add to apple mixture the curry powder, allspice, nutmeg, and chunk pineapple with juice. Add cream sauce mixture and stir in sauterne, lemon juice, sugar, and salt to taste. Add shrimp, heat thoroughly and serve over rice.

Mrs. Richard Sliz

Shrimp Spaghetti

2 cloves garlic, chopped
½ medium onion, chopped
1 green pepper, chopped
¼ cup oil
1 (16 ounce) can tomatoes
2½ teaspoons salt
Pepper to taste
½ teaspoon basil
1 (4 ounce) can mushrooms
   and juice

1 (6 ounce) can tomato paste
1 teaspoon dried oregano
1 bay leaf
3 teaspoons chopped parsley
½ pound or about 6 dozen small raw
   shrimp, shelled and deveined
   (weigh after cleaning)
½ teaspoon garlic salt
1 teaspoon prepared horseradish
8 ounces spaghetti, cooked
Grated Parmesan cheese

Saute garlic, onion, green pepper in oil till tender. Add tomatoes, salt, pepper, basil, and mushrooms with juice. Simmer uncovered 30 minutes. Add tomato paste, oregano, bay leaf, parsley, and shrimp. Simmer 15 minutes longer. Add garlic salt and horseradish. Serve over spaghetti with Parmesan cheese. Serves 4.

Mrs. William J. Demoran

Sweet and Sour Shrimp

1 pound cooked, peeled,
  deveined shrimp
1½ cups apple juice
½ cup sugar
½ cup vinegar
¼ cup catsup
2 tablespoons cornstarch

¼ teaspoon salt
2 tablespoons liquid margarine
  or oil
1 tablespoon soy sauce
½ cup sliced carrots
½ cup cubed bell pepper
¼ cup chopped green onions

Dissolve cornstarch in ¼ cup apple juice, set aside. Combine remaining apple juice, vinegar, sugar, catsup, margarine, soy sauce and salt. Bring to boil. Add carrots and cook 15 minutes. Add onions and pepper and cook for 5 minutes. Add diluted cornstarch gradually to hot sauce and cook stirring constantly until thickened. Add shrimp and heat. Serve over rice made crunchy with slivered almonds.

Lois McAlister

Shrimp Quiche

1 deep dish pie crust
  (Mrs. Smith's ideal)
8 to 9 ounces boiled shrimp
1½ cups Swiss cheese, grated
¼ cup onion, finely chopped
2 eggs, beaten

1 tablespoon lemon juice
1 teaspoon chives
¾ teaspoon garlic salt
½ teaspoon salt
1/8 teaspoon pepper
1 cup evaporated milk

Preheat oven to 450°. Thaw pie crust as package directs. Prick bottom and sides with fork. Bake on cookie sheet about 5 minutes. Remove from oven. Distribute shrimp over bottom of pastry shell. Sprinkle cheese and onions over shrimp. Beat together eggs, milk, lemon juice and seasonings. Pour over shrimp mixture. Bake on cookie sheet 15 minutes. Reduce oven to 350° and bake and additional 12-15 minutes, or until top is golden brown. Serves 6. For variety, use tuna or crabmeat. A popular dish.

Mrs. Gerald Phillips

Shrimp Wiggle

1 cup cooked shrimp
4 tablespoons butter or oleo
4 tablespoons flour
2 cups milk

1 teaspoon salt
Dash black pepper
1 cup cooked English peas, drained
Toast cups or pastry shells

In a large saucepan, melt butter or oleo. Remove from heat and stir in the flour until well blended. Gradually add the milk, stirring until smooth. Return to stove and cook until thickened. Add salt, pepper, shrimp, and peas. Continue cooking until heated through. Serve hot in toast cups or pastry shells. Serves 4-6. This mixture may be prepared in advance and refrigerated. When ready to serve, heat and put into toast cups or hot pastry shells.

Mrs. Gerald Phillips

Boiled Shrimp or Crabs

3 dozen live crabs or 10 pounds
    shrimp
2 to 3 gallons water
2 to 3 bags crab boil
2 tablespoons liquid crab boil

1 tablespoon McCormick's Seafood
    Seasoning
1 garlic, chopped
1 onion, chopped
1 cup salt

In a large pot, add crab boil, seasonings, garlic, onion, and salt. Boil for 15 to 20 minutes. Add seafood. Crabs must be alive when added to water. Return water to a boil and cook 8 to 10 minutes. Remove from heat. Let stand 5 minutes. Sample shrimp or crab and add additional salt if needed. Let stand 15 minutes longer before draining.

For a complete boiled dinner, whole small potatoes and/or corn on the cob may be boiled with the seafood. The potatoes and corn should be added to the pot immediately before the shrimp or crabs. Additional water may need to be added to cover seafood and vegetables. Continue to cook as directed for boiled shrimp or crabs.

Russell Necaise

Seafood Casserole

1 large onion, chopped
1 can mushrooms
4 tablespoons butter
4 tablespoons flour
1 can chicken broth
2 tablespoons lemon juice

½ cup cream
¼ cup dry sherry
1 pound peeled, cooked shrimp
1 pound white crabmeat
Bread crumbs
Cheese (optional)

Saute onion and mushrooms in butter. Add flour and chicken broth, stirring till thick. Then add lemon juice, cream, sherry, shrimp and crabmeat. Place in large greased casserole. Top with bread crumbs and cheese. Bake 25-30 minutes at 400°. Let stand a few minutes before serving. May be used in ramekins.

Mrs. Robert A. Mitchell

Seafood Pie

1 cup milk
2 tablespoons flour
1 stick butter
1 can or package English peas
Fresh mushrooms, sliced
½ bell pepper, chopped

1 onion, chopped
5 ribs of celery, chopped
1 pound of seafood (shrimp, crab,
    or oyster-may use mixture
    or only one kind)
1 small can pimentos, chopped
Pastry strips

Saute seafood (if oysters or shrimp) in ½ stick butter. Add pepper, onion, and celery. Cook until tender. Add mushrooms and set aside. Melt ½ stick butter, add flour, and milk. Stir over low heat until thick. Add other sauteed ingredients and pimento. Pour into casserole and top with pastry strips. Bake at 350° for 45 minutes.

Richard Jayner
Charlotte, North Carolina

Seafood Lasagna

6 to 8 lasagna noodles
1 cup chopped onion
2 tablespoons butter
8 ounces cream cheese
1½ cups cottage cheese
1 beaten egg
1½ teaspoons salt
1/8 teaspoon pepper

2 cans cream of mushroom soup
⅓ cup milk
⅓ cup dry white wine
1 (7½ ounce) can crabmeat
   (or fresh)
1 pound shrimp
¼ cup Parmesan cheese
½ cup grated sharp cheese

Boil and peel shrimp. Cook noodles and drain. Arrange 3 to 4 noodles in bottom of greased baking dish. Saute onion in butter, blend in cream cheese, cottage cheese, egg, salt, and pepper. Spread half of mixture on top of noodles. Combine soup, milk, wine; stir in shrimp and crabmeat. Spread ½ mixture over cheese layer. Repeat lasagna noodles. Repeat layers. Sprinkle with Parmesan cheese. Bake uncovered in 350⁰ oven for 45 minutes. Top with cheese. Bake 2-3 minutes. Let stand 15 minutes before serving. Serves 12.

Mrs. William Watson

Seafood Loaf

6 (4-inch) round French rolls
1 stick softened butter
1 bunch green onions, chopped
2½ pounds shrimp, sauteed in butter
½ pound fresh crabmeat
1 package frozen chopped spinach,
   cooked and drained

3 eggs, beaten
¾ cup mayonnaise
½ teaspoon grated whole nutmeg
1 teaspoon salt
Ground pepper to taste
6 slices peeled tomatoes
½ cup grated Swiss cheese

Slice small top off rolls and butter under side. Hollow out rolls and butter inside. Saute onions in butter and divide among rolls. Divide crab and shrimp among rolls. Mix eggs, spinach, mayonnaise, nutmeg, salt and pepper and put into rolls. Top with tomato slices, then cheese and put top on roll. Cook 30 minutes at 350⁰. Take top off and cook 10 minutes. Serve with top on. Serves 6. Oysters may be used instead of crab and shrimp. Be certain the spinach is thoroughly drained.

Celia Martin

Hot Seafood Salad

1 cup crabmeat
1 cup cooked and peeled shrimp
1 cup mayonnaise
Salt if needed
¾ cup green pepper, chopped

1 cup celery, chopped
1 cup Velveeta cheese, grated
Worcestershire sauce to taste
Bread crumbs
Pepperidge Farm pastry shells,
   baked

Toss lightly first 8 ingredients. Spoon into baking dish. Top with bread crumbs and bake at 350⁰ for 30 minutes. When done, spoon into baked pastry shells and then serve. Serves 4 to 5.

Mrs. Bob Monette

Seafood Ala Vrazel

12 ounces butter
1 teaspoon minced garlic
1 teaspoon parsley
16 shrimp
16 scallops

16 ounces crabmeat
Salt and pepper to taste
4 ounces white wine
8 ounces thin spaghetti, cooked
Endive and lemon wedge

Place butter, garlic and parsley in saute pan, add shrimp and scallops and cook till done. Add crabmeat, salt and pepper, white wine, bring to boil and serve on spaghetti. May garnish with endive and lemon wedge.

Chef Bill Vrazel
Vrazel's
Fine Food Restaurant
Gulfport, Mississippi

French House Shrimp

1 cup chopped onion
1 cup chopped celery
2 sticks butter or margarine
2 pounds medium peeled shrimp

1/2 pint sour cream
2 tablespoons Sherry
Cooked green noodles or rice
Chives

Saute onion and celery in butter until tender. Add shrimp and cook 10 minutes. Add sour cream and stir well, then add Sherry and let simmer 10 minutes. Serve on bed of green noodles or rice. Sprinkle with chives. Serves 4.

Mrs. Robert Smith

Amber Soft-Shell Crabs

2 large or 4 small soft-shell crabs
1 large chopped green onion
Garlic salt to taste
2 teaspoons sesame seeds
1 tablespoon butter or margarine

1 teaspoon celery flakes
1 1/2 teaspoons lemon pepper
1 tablespoon Sauterne wine
2 teaspoons Worcestershire sauce

Put cleaned crabs on square of heavy foil. Add remaining ingredients except Sauterne and Worcestershire. Fold foil up enough to hold last two ingredients and then add Sauterne and Worcestershire. Complete fold and cook 20 minutes on grill. Pour amber liquid over crabs before serving. Serves 2.

Walton Moore

Crabmeat Imperial

1 green pepper, minced
1 tablespoon dry mustard
1 tablespoon prepared mustard
1 teaspoon salt
1 teaspoon sugar

1 raw egg
1/8 teaspoon black pepper
Dash of Tabasco
3/4 cup mayonnaise
2 pounds crabmeat

Mix all ingredients together, adding crabmeat last. Place in buttered shells. Cover with bread crumbs. Bake at 375° for 30-35 minutes. Serves 10-12.

Mrs. D. Knox White

Easy Seafood Au Gratin

1 can cheddar cheese soup,
    undiluted
¼ cup milk
2 cups cooked seafood (shrimp, crab-
    meat, lobster, or a combination of all
    the seafood)

1 teaspoon parsley, chopped
Salt and pepper
¼ cup buttered bread crumbs

In a mixing bowl, stir soup until smooth. Gradually add milk and stir well. Add salt and pepper to taste. Mix in seafood and parsley. Place in a casserole dish or 4 individual ramekins. Top with buttered bread crumbs. Bake in 400° oven for 30 minutes. Serve with green salad and dessert. Serves 4.

Mrs. George W. Edwards

Shrimp or Crabmeat Au Gratin

3 tablespoons onion
1 (4 ounce) can drained
    mushrooms (or fresh)
3 tablespoons butter
¼ cup flour
¼ teaspoon dry mustard
½ teaspoon salt
Italian bread crumbs
1/8 teaspoon pepper

1½ cups milk
1 cup grated cheddar cheese
Dash celery salt
1½ teaspoons parsley flakes
1 pound cooked and peeled
    shrimp or 1 pound crabmeat
    or comination

Cook mushrooms and onions in butter until tender. Add flour and seasonings, blending together. Gradually add milk and cook until thick, stirring constantly. Add ¾ cup cheese and stir until melted. Add seafood and pour into well greased casserole or individual ramekins. Combine remaining cheese and crumbs and sprinkle over top. Bake 10 minutes at 400°. May be made before and refrigerated. Cook longer if refrigerated.

Mrs. William J. Hough

Crabmeat Au Gratin

3 tablespoons butter
½ green pepper, minced
½ onion, chopped
3 tablespoons flour
2 cups milk

2 cups crabmeat
½ teaspoon salt
Dash ground nutmeg
½ cup shredded cheese
Buttered bread crumbs

Melt butter in skillet; add pepper and onion, and cook for 5 minutes. Add flour and milk, then crabmeat, salt, and nutmeg. Cook 10 minutes. Pour in shallow buttered baking dish or crab shells. Sprinkle with shredded cheese and buttered bread crumbs and bake at 350° until cheese is brown.

Mrs. Carroll Malone

Acorn Squash and Crabmeat

3 acorn squash, cut in half
1 pound lump crabmeat
1 stick butter
¾ cup cream sherry

1 teaspoon lemon pepper
   marinade
½ cup chopped green onions
½ pound mushrooms, sliced

Melt butter slowly in skillet. Wash and cut squash. Pour small amount of butter in each squash half and swish around. Bake at 350⁰ in a shallow pan, cut side down, for 20 minutes. Saute green onions and mushrooms in remaining butter. Add ¼ cup cream sherry, all the crabmeat and lemon pepper marinade. Mix gently and turn off the heat. Turn squash right side up, pour remaining ½ cup cream sherry evenly into each squash. Bake 20 minutes more. Add crab mixture and bake 10 minutes more. Serve hot. Serves 6.

The Rev. James B. Roberts

Crabmeat Puget

1 can cream of shrimp soup
   (frozen or Campbell's)
⅔ cup milk
¼ cup grated New York cheddar
   sharp cheese
½ cup mayonnaise
1 pound crabmeat

2 cups raw thin noodles
1 cup water chestnuts, sliced
1 can fried onion rings

Heat soup with milk, cheese, mayonnaise, crab and noodles. Mix until smooth, add water chestnuts. Place in greased casserole. Cover and bake at 350⁰ for 30 minutes. Uncover and top with 1 can of crushed fried onion rings. Bake 10 more minutes. Serves 10-12.

Mrs. Cleve Allen, Jr.

Mother's Crabmeat and Mushrooms in Wine

1 pound lump crabmeat
1 (4 ounce) can mushrooms,
   drained
2 tablespoons butter
2 tablespoons flour
½ cup milk

½ cup white wine
1 small onion, grated
½ teaspoon salt
¼ teaspoon curry powder
Buttered bread crumbs

Pick through crabmeat for cartilage. Melt butter. Blend in flour. Gradually add milk and wine. Stir until smooth and well blended. Add seasonings. Cook over low heat, stirring constantly about two minutes. Add crabmeat and mushrooms. Place in greased, individual casseroles. Sprinkle top with bread crumbs. Dot with butter. Bake at 350⁰ about 30 minutes or until bubbly. Serves 4.

Mrs. Paul M. Newton

Crab Mornay Florentine

3 packages frozen leaf spinach
1 clove garlic
2 tablespoons grated onion
6 tablespoons butter
4 tablespoons flour
3 cups milk
1 cup Swiss cheese, grated

1 cup light cream
2 teaspoons lemon juice
Pinch of garlic powder
Dash of nutmeg
Salt and cayenne to taste
2 pounds crabmeat
1 cup fresh bread crumbs

Cook spinach with whole garlic and grated onion. Drain, remove garlic, and finely chop the spinach. Transfer to a buttered flat dish or 8 ovenproof shells. Preheat broiler. Melt 4 tablespoons butter in saucepan, stir in flour until smooth. Gradually add milk, stirring constantly until smooth and thickened. Add cheese along with cream and seasonings. Cook over low heat until thick, about 10 minutes. Remove from heat and carefully fold in crabmeat. Pour mixture over spinach, sprinkle with bread crumbs and dot with remaining 2 tablespoons butter. Broil about 5 minutes or until browned. Brunch suggestion: Layer hard boiled eggs, halved, on spinach; then top with sauce.

Barbara Harvey

Baked Stuffed Crab Kenneth

1 small onion, chopped
1 scallion, chopped
1 clove garlic, chopped
¼ pound butter
4 tablespoons flour

3 cups milk
1 teaspoon mustard
2 teaspoons Worcestershire sauce
1 pound crabmeat
¼ cup grated Parmesan cheese

Saute onion, scallion and garlic in butter for 5 minutes. Blend in flour; gradually add the milk, stirring constantly to the boiling point. Add mustard and Worcestershire sauce, then crabmeat. Allow to cool. Divide mixture into 6 ramekins or crab shells. Sprinkle with cheese. Bake at 400° for 15 minutes or until browned. Serves 6.

Mrs. Sidney Wong

Stuffed Crabs

1 pound crabmeat
⅔ loaf French bread
Water
⅔ cup cooking oil
3 stalks celery, minced
1 bell pepper, minced

½ to 1 bunch green onions
   and tops, minced
2 eggs, beaten
Salt and pepper to taste
Bread crumbs

Pick crabmeat for cartilage. Slice bread and lightly toast in oven. Soak bread in water for 2 minutes. Press water out of bread. Saute minced vegetables in cooking oil for a very few minutes. Vegetables should remain slightly crisp. Do not overcook. Remove from heat. Add crabmeat to vegetables. Add bread and eggs. Salt and pepper to taste. Mix well. Mixture may be placed in shells or formed into patties or loaf. Top with bread crumbs. Bake at 400° until lightly browned. Serves 6.

Russell Necaise

Mrs. George Poole's Stuffed Crabs

1 quart milk
6 eggs, well beaten
1 teaspoon salt
1 teaspoon black pepper
Dash of cayenne pepper
1 teaspoon prepared mustard
Cracker crumbs

Juice of 1 lemon
¼ pound butter
1 tablespoon bacon drippings
1 white onion, minced
1 cup celery, finely chopped
2 pounds lump or white
   crabmeat

Heat milk in a double boiler. When hot, pour slowly over the well-beaten eggs. Return to double boiler and cook slowly until it becomes a golden cream sauce. Add salt, black pepper, cayenne, mustard, lemon juice, butter, and beat until perfectly smooth. Place bacon drippings, onions and celery in skillet. Cook until done but not brown. Add ¼ cup water and simmer on low heat until very tender. Add cooked onion and celery to the cream sauce and enough cracker crumbs to make the mixture easy to handle. Add the crabmeat. Stuff crab shells or place in ramekins. Sprinkle cracker crumbs over the top of each. Put a lump of butter on each and broil until brown on top. Garnish with lemon and parsley. Will freeze. Will make enough for about 24 ramekins or crab shells. This was a favorite recipe of my grandmother, Mrs. George Crittenden Poole.

Nancy Mize Sneed

Sauteed Soft Shell Crabs

Allow 2 to 4 crabs per person

Clean soft shell crabs as usual with one exception; also remove the back shell. Season 2 cups milk with 1 pressed garlic clove, 1 teaspoon chopped parsley, 1 teaspoon salt, ¼ teaspoon black pepper, ¼ teaspoon thyme, ¼ teaspoon tarragon, ¼ teaspoon nutmeg. Marinate crabs in milk mixture in refrigerator for about 1 hour. Gently lift crabs out of milk mixture and coat with flour, salt and pepper. Saute in margarine until golden brown turning once, about 3 to 5 minutes total.

Karen Anne Graham

Soft Shell Crab Delight

6 soft shell crabs
1½ sticks butter
1 tablespoon chopped parsley
1 tablespoon chopped green onions

Juice of ½ lemon
¼ to ½ cup white wine (optional)
1 cup chopped pecans

Clean and drain soft shell crabs. Season with salt. Melt butter in a heavy skillet and brown the crabs first on the shell side, then the other side. Keep the crabs warm while the sauce is made. To the butter in the skillet, add chopped parsley, green onions, juice of half a lemon and white wine. Add chopped pecans and saute about 5 minutes. Pour over crabs. Serve at once.

Mrs. George Schloegel

Crab Stew

1 cup cooking oil
2 large cans tomato sauce
1 large can tomato paste
4 ribs celery, chopped
1 bunch green onions with tops,
    chopped
1 bell pepper, chopped

6 cups water (approximately)
Salt to taste
2 to 3 dozen whole crabs,
    cleaned and shells removed
1 pound crabmeat (if desired)
Cooked rice

In large heavy pot heat oil, add tomato sauce and tomato paste. Cook mixture over medium low heat for 30 minutes, or until oil separates from tomato sauce. Add chopped vegetables and cook for 5 minutes. Add seasonings and water. Add whole, cleaned crabs and bring to a boil. At this point add crabmeat if using additional crabmeat. Reduce heat to medium and cook crabs for 25 to 30 minutes. Serve over rice.

Russell Necaise

Teresa's Crab Casserole

1 pound crabmeat (fresh or canned)
½ pound cooked shrimp, shelled
    and deveined
½ pound fresh mushrooms, sliced
Salt and pepper
1/8 pound butter, gently melted
½ tablespoon dry mustard
1 tablespoon chopped bell pepper
2¼ teaspoons chopped onion or just
    a bit of onion juice

2 teaspoons lemon juice
3 or 4 tablespoons flour
1½ teaspoons Worcestershire
1 pint milk
¼ pound cheddar cheese
Buttered bread crumbs
Parmesan cheese

In skillet, saute mushrooms, pepper, and onion in melted butter. Combine all except cheddar cheese, bread crumbs, and Parmesan cheese. Take off fire and melt in cheddar cheese. Place in casserole dish. Sprinkle top with buttered bread crumbs, Parmesan cheese, paprika, salt and pepper. Bake 30-45 minutes at 350⁰. Serves 6-8.

Mrs. Jesse Adams,
New Orleans, Louisiana

The Landings Broiled Oysters

Oysters in shell
Butter
Fresh lemon juice

Worcestershire sauce
Salt and pepper

Open oysters in normal way (watch fingers!). Leave oyster on half of shell. Prepare lemon-butter sauce and add salt and pepper to taste. Baste each oyster with sauce. Add a drop or two of Worcestershire to each oyster. Place oysters on cookie sheet. Run under broiler. Watch carefully, and as soon as oysters begin to curl remove from oven. Serve at once. Simple, but tricky - do not overcook.

Tom Simmons, The Landing
Harbor Square, Gulfport

Minced Oysters

1 large bunch parsley,
  finely minced
1 large bunch shallots,
  finely minced
1 stick butter (not oleo)
1 quart oysters

¼ small dill pickle, minced
  (about 1 teaspoon)
Worcestershire sauce
Cracker crumbs, finely crushed
Salt
Pepper

Mince parsley and shallots (use tops). Cook in butter over medium heat in heavy skillet. Add to this finely minced oysters, dill pickle, and a dash of Worcestershire sauce. Cook for another 5-10 minutes. Add cracker crumbs to take up liquid. Salt and pepper to taste. Serve in chafing dish with pastry shells. May also be served in casserole or shells which have been lightly greased with butter. Heat thoroughly in oven. Garnish with slice of lemon and sprig of parsley. Freezes well.

Mrs. Jerry O'Keefe

Oysters Pierre

½ pound mushrooms,
  thinly sliced
1 stick butter
3 tablespoons flour
2 small garlic cloves, minced
3 tablespoons finely chopped
  green onions
3 tablespoons minced parsley

Dash cayenne pepper
1 teaspoon salt
⅓ cup dry sherry
4 dozen small oysters,
  well drained
½ cup bread crumbs

Saute mushrooms in 2 tablespoons butter and set aside. Melt 4 tablespoons butter and add flour. Cook, stirring constantly, until light brown. Add garlic, green onions, parsley, and cook 5 minutes. Add cayenne pepper, salt, and sherry. Add oysters, mushrooms, and simmer 5 minutes. Serve in individual ramekins. Top with bread crumbs and dot with butter. Heat in 350° oven until warm, about 15 minutes. Serves 8.

Mrs. Robert A. Little

Oysters King Harry

4 dozen small oysters, drained
  (reserve liquid)
¾ pound mushrooms, sliced
½ pound butter
4 tablespoons flour
2 garlic cloves, minced
4 tablespoons white onion,
  finely chopped
4 tablespoons green onion, finely
  chopped
4 tablespoons parsley, finely
  chopped

Cayenne
2 teaspoons salt
1 teaspoon white pepper
Dash of Tabasco
½ cup dry sherry
½ cup oyster water, from oysters
1 cup Italian bread crumbs

Drain oysters well. Reserve liquid. Saute mushrooms in 4 tablespoons butter and set aside. In a heavy skillet melt 6 tablespoons butter; add flour, and stir constantly on low heat until roux is light brown. Add garlic, onion, green onions and parsley and cook for 5 minutes. Add cayenne, salt, pepper, and Tabasco. Blend in sherry and ½ cup oyster water. Add drained oysters and mushrooms and cook for 5 minutes. Add Italian bread crumbs as needed to tighten the mixture so it is not runny. Divide mixture into 8 ramekins, top with Italian bread crumbs and butter. Bake until bubbly in 350° oven approximately 12 minutes.

Jane Kemp
from Blaize D'Antoni, Cafe Brulot
New Orleans, Louisiana

This recipe was created by Blaize D'Antoni in honor of Mrs. Kemp's father, Harry Bettes, when he was King of Bards of Bohemia during Mardi Gras in 1974. The recipe won a grand prize in the New Orleans Food Festival.

Ellen's Oyster Pie

2 jars oysters, drained
  (more if desired)
Butter
½ bunch green onions, chopped
½ bell pepper, chopped
2 teaspoons parsley, chopped
2 stalks celery, chopped
2 hard-boiled eggs, chopped

½ cup white sauce
1 egg yolk
1 teaspoon bacon grease
1 tablespoon Worcestershire
Dash of Tabasco
Salt and pepper to taste
2 tablespoons sherry
Pie shell

Brown oysters in a skillet with a little butter. Pour off most of liquid. Remove oysters and saute vegetables in the bacon grease. Make white sauce and add slightly beaten egg yolk to this. Add oysters, chopped hard-boiled eggs, and seasonings. Add sherry and heat mixture for 2 to 3 minutes. Pour mixture into 8" to 9" pie shell and put a lattice pie crust on top. Bake at 350° for 30 minutes or until crust is golden brown.

Mrs. Ernest L. Shelton III

Oysters Patricia

¼ cup butter
½ cup very finely chopped shallots
1 cup very finely chopped celery
1 teaspoon finely chopped parsley
2 (12 ounce) jars oysters, cut into
    quarters
2 (4 ounce) cans mushrooms, drained
    (or fresh mushrooms, sliced and
    sauteed in butter)

1 cup seasoned bread crumbs
1 teaspoon soy sauce
1½ tablespoons Worcestershire
½ teaspoon Tabasco (more,
    if desired)
1 teaspoon Accent
½ teaspoon salt
½ teaspoon pepper
3 beaten eggs

Melt butter in frying pan, add shallots, celery, and parsley. Cook over gentle heat until tender. Add oysters to cooked vegetables and set aside. When mixture is cool, add mushrooms, soy sauce, Worcestershire, Tabasco, Accent, salt, pepper, eggs, and seasoned bread crumbs. Mix well then cook over low heat, stirring often, until thick. Do not overcook; it must remain moist. Place mixture in individual baking shells and cover with seasoned bread crumbs, dot with butter. Bake at 350° for 20 minutes. Serve immediately. Serves 4.

Mrs. Dick Drown

Happy Gal III Oyster Spaghetti

1 stick butter (not oleo)
1 clove garlic, minced
3 shallots, chopped, tops
    and bottoms
White pepper to taste
Freshly ground black pepper
    to taste
Salt to taste

2 pints oysters, drained
    (reserve liquid)
½ bunch fresh parsley, chopped
3 tablespoons oyster liquid
Juice from ½ lemon
Parmesan cheese, grated
1 package thin spaghetti
    (spaghettini)

In a large iron skillet slowly melt butter. Add minced garlic and chopped shallots. Add white pepper, freshly ground black pepper and salt. When the onions are tender, add drained oysters and 3 tablespoons of the oyster juice. Sprinkle with fresh parsley. While the above mixture is cooking very slowly, cook 1 package of thin spaghetti (spaghettini) using the remainder of the oyster liquid and water. Drain the spaghettini in a colander. Rinse in cold water. Put the colander of spaghettini over a pan of boiling water. Sprinkle generously with freshly grated Parmesan cheese. Cover the colander with 2 paper towels. When oysters in the skillet have curled and the mixture has cooked down, add juice from ½ lemon. When the cheese has melted on the spaghettini and soaked through, spoon portions of the oyster sauce on top of a portion of the spaghettini. Serve immediately.

Chunn Sneed

Oyster Chowder

2 large potatoes, diced small
2 carrots chopped coarsely
1/2 cup butter or margarine
2 stalks celery, finely chopped
1/3 cup minced green onions
1/2 cup flour
1 1/2 quarts milk, warmed
1/2-1 teaspoon salt

1/2 teaspoon savory
1 quart oysters
1/2 cup oyster liquor
2 tablespoons parsley, minced
1/4 teaspoon white pepper
Tabasco to taste
Worcestershire to taste (about 1
   tablespoon)

Boil potatoes and carrots in enough water to barely cover until just tender. Drain water. Melt butter in Dutch oven and saute celery and onions until just transparent, not brown. Add flour and mix until well moistened. Add milk. While stirring add potatoes, carrots, salt and savory. Cook stirring until heated well. Simmer oysters in the 1/2 cup oyster liquor until barely curled. Add oyster (large oysters may be cut in half) mixture to milk mixture. Add parsley, pepper, Tabasco and Worcestershire. Heat and stir until oyster flavor blends with the milk. Adjust seasoning to taste.

Liz Turner

Oyster and Eggplant Casserole

1 medium eggplant
1/4 cup butter
3/4 cup chopped onion
1/2 cup Italian bread crumbs
1/2 teaspoon salt

1/8 teaspoon black pepper
1 1/2 pints fresh oysters and juice
1/2 cup light cream
1/4 cup sharp cheddar cheese, grated

Bake eggplant at 350° for 50 minutes or until fork pierces easily. Peel and cut in 1" cubes. Set aside. Saute onion in butter until yellow, not brown. Add bread crumbs, salt, pepper and mix well. Remove from heat. In heavy saucepan heat oysters in own juice until edges curl, about 4 to 5 minutes. Remove from heat. Butter a 2-3 quart casserole. Place layer of 1/2 of eggplant at bottom of casserole and sprinkle with 1/4 of onion and bread crumb mixture. Next make a layer of 1/2 of oysters and sprinkle with 1/4 of onion and bread crumb mixture. Repeat with 1/2 eggplant, 1/4 onion and bread crumb mixture, 1/2 oysters, 1/4 onion and bread crumb mixture. Pour cream evenly over top. Cover with grated cheese. Bake uncovered in preheated oven 350° for 15 minutes until brown on top.

Mrs. Suell Grimm

Oyster Jambalaya

2 tablespoons olive oil
2 large onions, chopped
Small amount ham, salt meat, and
   bacon, crisped
1 pod garlic, minced
3 cups oyster liquid

1 1/2 cups raw rice
4 green onions and tops, chopped
1/4 cup minced parsley
2 dozen or more oysters
Salt to taste

Fry onions in olive oil until lightly browned. Add crisped meat, 3 cups oyster liquid, and rice. Boil briskly about 5 minutes. Add oysters and garlic. Cover and simmer until rice is tender. Add green onions and tops. Season to taste.

Mrs. G. L. Douglas

Oysters and Spinach

2 packages frozen chopped spinach
4 tablespoons butter
2 tablespoons flour
½ cup green onion, chopped
1 clove garlic, chopped
½ cup evaporated milk
½ cup vegetable liquor
(optional)

½ teaspoon black pepper
¾ teaspoon celery salt
Salt to taste
6 ounce roll of Jalapeno cheese
1 teaspoon Worcestershire sauce
Red pepper to taste
2 pints oysters, drained

Cook spinach; drain and reserve liquor. Melt butter in saucepan over low heat. Add flour, stirring until blended and smooth. Add onion and garlic and cook until soft. Add liquid slowly, stirring constantly. Cook until smooth and thick. Add seasonings and cheese which has been cut into small pieces. Stir until melted. Combine with cooked spinach. Fold in drained oysters. Put in casserole and top with buttered bread crumbs. Cook at 350⁰ until bubbly or until oysters are done.

Mrs. Ben Stone

Stuffed Oysters

2 tablespoons ham fat
2 tablespoons flour
1 small onion, chopped
⅓ cup cooked ham, ground
4 pints oysters, cut fairly
small (reserve liquid)
1½ cups bread (softened in the oyster
liquid)
1 egg, beaten

1 tablespoon bell pepper, chopped
1 tablespoon parsley, minced
1 tablespoon butter
Freshly ground black pepper to taste
Bread crumbs to cover
Lemon slices for garnish
Parsley for garnish

Using a large skillet, brown the flour in the ham fat, stirring constantly. Add the chopped onion and brown; then add the ground ham and the cut-up oysters. Cook about 5 minutes. After the bread has been softened in the oyster water, squeeze dry, measure, and add to the mixture. Then add the egg, bell pepper, parsley, butter, pepper, and cook a few minutes longer. Remove from heat and fill 8 ramekins with the oyster mixture. Top with bread crumbs, parsley, and lemon slies. Bake until heated through.

Nancy Mize Sneed

Stuffed Flounder I

1 cup minced onions
½ cup minced shallots
1½ cups minced celery
3 cloves garlic, minced
2 tablespoons chopped parsley
½ pound margarine
2 tablespoons flour
1 cup milk

1 cup dry white wine
½ cup boiled shrimp, chopped
1 cup lump crabmeat
2½ cups bread crumbs
Salt and pepper to taste
6 1-pound flounders
12 boiled shrimp, peeled

Saute onion, shallots, celery, garlic and parsley in margarine. Add flour and blend in well. Gradually stir in milk and wine, cooking until thickened. Add shrimp and crabmeat and thicken further with bread crumbs. Season to taste. Split each flounder and fill with dressing. Top each fish with 2 whole shrimp and cook under broiler about 20 minutes, or until fish is cooked through. Serves 6.

Mrs. Leo Seal, Jr.

Stuffed Flounder II

1 bunch green onions, chopped finely
1 small bell pepper, chopped finely
2 stalks celery, chopped finely
1 clove garlic, chopped finely
¼ cup minced parsley
Salt and pepper
Sherry or 1 egg, beaten
Lemon Juice

½ pound (or 1 cup) crabmeat
   (lump or white)
1 pound raw shrimp, peeled
1½ sticks butter
¾ cup Reising or Pepperidge Farm
   bread crumbs
4 1-pound flounders, salted to taste
Paprika

Saute vegetables in ½ stick butter until soft. Add crabmeat and shrimp. Stir and saute until shrimp turns pink. Then add bread crumbs, 1 teaspoon salt and ½ teaspoon pepper (or to taste). Moisten to correct consistency with cooking sherry or beaten egg. Make a slit in fish large enough to hold a generous amount of stuffing. Stuff fish with above mixture and place in greased pan (stuffed side up). Sprinkle with lemon juice and paprika. Dot with remaining butter. Bake at 350°, uncovered, for 30 minutes or until fish flakes easily.

Mrs. William Weatherly

Broiled Fillets of Fish

Fillets of speckled trout or flounder,
   about ½ inch thick
1 or more lemons, thinly sliced
Butter

1 onion, thinly sliced
Salt
Pepper

Melt butter in foil-lined pan. Roll fillets in the melted butter, arrange close together skin side down and season with salt and pepper. Arrange slices of lemon and onion over fish, nearly covering them. Broil without turning until cooked through. Remove any charred onion or lemon slices before serving. The fish must not be too thick nor the broiler too hot for this method. Very good.

Joyce Bordelon

Tricia's Catfish Casserole

1 package frozen, chopped spinach
Salt and pepper to taste
6 small catfish fillets

1 tablespoon butter
¼ pound of sliced mushrooms
1 small chopped onion

In the bottom of a buttered casserole dish, put one package of frozen chopped spinach, thawed. Blot it slightly to absorb extra water. Add salt and pepper to taste. On top of the spinach put a layer of 6 small catfish fillets (you can substitute flounder or sole). Saute in 1 tablespoon of butter, sliced mushrooms and onion. Pour this over the fish layer.

WHITE SAUCE

3 tablespoons butter
2 tablespoons flour
1 cup milk

¼ cup white wine (optional)
¼ cup grated Parmesan cheese

Melt 3 tablespoons of butter in a saucepan and add 2 tablespoons of flour. Slowly add 1 cup of milk. Add ¼ cup white wine. Heat until thick and add ¼ cup grated Parmesan cheese. Pour over the casserole. Bake at 375° for 20-25 minutes, or until it bubbles.

Mrs. Trent Lott
Pascagoula, Mississippi

Chappy's Grilled Red Snapper

MARINADE:

1 cup tamari (soy sauce)
Juice of 2 lemons
6 fillets (red snapper, trout, tuna,
  catfish or chicken)

½ cup no cholesterol margarine
Dash of Tabasco
Barbecue spice

Combine all ingredients, except barbecue spice, for marinade. Place fish in marinade for 2 minutes. Remove fish from marinade and place on an open grill for 3 to 5 minutes then flip fillets to other side. Sprinkle with barbecue spice and cook until done.

Chef John Chapman
Chappy's on the Beach
Long Beach, Mississippi

Trout Almandine

8 large trout fillets
1 beaten egg
¼ cup milk

Salt and pepper
Flour
Toasted slivered almonds

SAUCE

Dash nutmeg
Dash cayenne
1 tablespoon minced parsley

¼ cup sherry
1 can brown beef gravy
½ cup melted butter

Dip trout fillets in mixture of egg, milk, and pinch of salt and pepper. Coat well in flour and fry in hot oil until brown and drain. Place in baking dish, cover and refrigerate. (May be prepared up to this stage the night before serving.) Before serving, pour sauce over fillets, cover with almonds, and heat uncovered in 350° oven about 30 minutes or until bubbly.

Mrs. Jack Halliday

A.V.'s Fish Dish

8 serving size trout fillets
1 (13 ounce) can evaporated milk
¼ teaspoon Tabasco
1½ teaspoons salt
½ teaspoon pepper

1 cup fine dry bread crumbs
¼ pound butter
½ cup pretoasted slivered almonds
Lemon juice

Add ¾ teaspoon of the salt and the Tabasco to the evaporated milk. Place fish in mixing bowl, add milk mixture, cover with a plastic wrap and refrigerate for at least ½ hour, or overnight if convenient. When ready to cook, preheat oven at hottest setting. Remove fillets from milk, drain and roll in bread crumbs and remaining ¾ teaspoon salt and pepper. Set aside momentarily. Place butter in baking pan, melt in oven. Watch carefully, do not brown. Remove pan and tilt so that butter forms a pool at lower end of pan. Dip each fillet in butter, coating one side; then place, unbuttered side down, in top end of pan. Repeat until all fillets are buttered and evenly spaced in pan. Place pan on middle rack of oven, cook until slightly browned and fillets flake. DO NOT OVERCOOK. Sprinkle with the pretoasted almonds, spoon on sauce and lemon juice and serve.

SAUCE

Remove cooked fillets to warm platter. Sprinkle about 2 teaspoons flour over butter in pan. Place over 2 burners on stove, heat over low heat. Mix well. Add ¼ cup dry white wine, ½ cup fish stock or juice, ½ clove pressed garlic, parsley, salt and pepper. Spoon over fish.

Arthur V. Hays

Fried Trout and Bream

Use trout fillets cut into 3 inch pieces or small whole bream (or larger bream halved lengthwise). Rinse in cold water and leave damp. Salt generously. Pepper to taste. Combine mixture of half white corn meal and half flour. Roll fish in this mixture until thoroughly covered and drop in deep fat fryer with corn oil heated to 375⁰. Cook until golden brown and crisp. Serve with hush puppies and cole slaw.

Mrs. Ben H. Stone

Trout Marguery

2½ pounds trout
1 tablespoon oil
1 cup water
2 egg yolks, beaten
Juice of 1 lemon, strained
2 sticks butter or margarine

Salt and pepper to taste
Cayenne
½ cup crabmeat
12 shrimp
½ cup oysters
½ can mushrooms
2 truffles (optional)

Skin and fillet trout. Place folded fillets in a pan with oil and water. Bake in hot oven for 15 minutes. To make sauce, put beaten egg yolks and lemon juice in double boiler over hot water. Gradually add melted butter stirring continuously until thickened. Add seasoning, crab, shrimp, oysters, truffles and mushrooms. Pour over fish and serve. The sauce cannot be kept warm over 5-10 minutes before serving because the ingredients tend to separate as they become overcooked.

Mrs. Jack Van Landingham

Trout Meuniere

4 medium or large fillets, skinned   Tabasco
1½ sticks butter   Salt
Juice of 1 lemon   Milk
2 tablespoons oil   Flour
¼ cup minced fresh parsley

Soak fillets in milk to cover, seasoned with 1 teaspoon salt and a few drops of Tabasco. Keep in refrigerator until ready to cook. Soak at least one hour. Dry trout on paper towel and roll in flour. Melt 1 stick butter and 2 tablespoons oil in skillet, heated to 350°. When butter bubbles and is hot, but not browned, add trout and cook until done, turning two or three times. Keep fish in warm oven, pour butter out. Add ½ cup butter to pan, scraping up brown particles. Add lemon juice and parsley, stirring to mix well. Pour over warm fish and serve immediately.

Mrs. Sam Morse

Trout in Mushroom Sauce

2 (4 ounce) cans mushrooms   2 cups half and half
   (stems and pieces)   1 cup grated Swiss cheese
4 tablespoons butter   8 trout fillets
4 tablespoons sherry   Salt and pepper to taste
4 tablespoons flour   ½ teaspoon dry mustard

Saute drained mushrooms in butter and sherry for 5 minutes. Add flour and mustard, blend until smooth. Gradually stir in cream and cook, stirring constantly, until mixture thickens slightly. Add grated cheese and stir until cheese is melted. Place fish fillets in oblong pan, pour mushroom mixture over fish and bake at 375° until fish flakes easily.

Sue Smith

Trout Walter

4 green onions and tops, chopped   Worcestershire sauce
1 green pepper, chopped   1 cup dry white wine
4 tablespoons butter or margarine   Salt
8 medium trout fillets   Lemon juice
Soy sauce

Saute in skillet the onion and pepper in margarine until soft. Place trout in baking dish, sprinkle lightly with salt, soy sauce, Worcestershire and lemon juice. Turn fillets over and repeat sprinkles of salt, soy sauce, and Worcestershire and lemon juice. Pour butter, onion, and pepper mixture over fish. Pour white wine over all. Bake 30-40 minutes at 350° or until done.

Mrs. Jack Halliday

Biloxi Bacon (Mullet)

Make sure your mullet is fresh. Salt fish. Dip fish in egg wash. Roll fish in yellow corn flour and fry in deep fat or hot grease. Cook at 400° for about 3 minutes. Fast cooking keeps the fish juicy.

Bobby Baricev

Grilled-Smoked Red Fish

1 whole red fish, 8 to 18 pounds

Cut head off red fish. Clean fish thoroughly, but do not scale. Cut fish from inside down backbone to butterfly fish, but do not cut through skin. Spread fish and clean again, remove rib bones, wash again, and dry with paper towel.

For cooking, use a rectangular charcoal grill. Place coals in opposite corners in ends of grill and ignite, leaving center area of grill without fire. Place damp hickory chips in center area.

Mix 1 cup olive oil with 4 to 5 pressed garlic cloves, salt and pepper, and heat over low heat. Coat fish well with olive oil mixture, and sprinkle with salt and coarsley ground black pepper. Place fish, skin side down, on center area of grill. Fire should not be under fish. Pour a little olive oil over fire to cause smoke. Close cover to grill. Smoke and cook fish until it flakes easily with a fork.

Baste occasionally during cooking with olive oil mixture. To serve, scoop meat out from fish skin, and place on heated platter. Heat remaining olive oil, sprinkled with fresh chopped parsley. Pour oil in gravy boat to serve with fish.

Walter James Phillips

Smoked Fish

*2 pounds Spanish mackerel, mullet
fillets or other fish fillets
(approximately ½-inch thick)*

*1 gallon water
1 cup salt
¼ cup cooking oil*

Combine water and salt and stir until salt is dissolved. Marinate fish in brine for 30 minutes in the refrigerator. Remove fish from brine and dry fish. To smoke the fish, soak 1 pound hickory or other hardwood chips in 2 quarts of water until thoroughly soaked (at least 5 hours). Use a hooded or covered electric, gas or charcoal grill. The heat must be kept low. If using charcoal, fewer briquets than with an average broiling fire are needed. Cover charcoal or ceramic briquets with ⅓ of the wet chips. The wet chips provide lower temperatures and smoke which flavors the fish. Place fish on a well-greased grill, skin side down, about 4 to 6 inches from the smoking coals. Baste fish well with oil at beginning and frequently during cooking. Close hood and smoke fish for 1 hour at 150°-175°F., or for 30 minutes at 200°F. Fish is done when surface is golden brown and flesh flakes easily when tested with a fork. Add remaining wet chips as needed to keep the fire smoking. Makes 6 servings.

* Smoke more fish than you will use at one meal and freeze it to use in other recipes. To freeze smoked fish, loosely wrap and cool completely in the refrigerator. Wrap fish in freezer paper and store at 0°F. for one to six months. If smoked fish is to be used as bites, salads, in dips or spreads which will not be heated, it is recommended that thawed smoked fish be wrapped tightly in aluminum foil and heated at 300°F. for 15 to 20 minutes.

*Dr. David Veal,
Sea Grant Advisory Service*

Fish with Lump Crabmeat Hollandaise

Fresh fish fillets
1 pound lump crabmeat
2 cups blender Hollandaise sauce
  (use your favorite recipe)

Butter
Flour
Lemon

In skillet melt 2 tablespoons butter. Add crabmeat and cook 5 minutes. Remove and set aside. Prepare Hollandaise sauce and set container in warm water until needed. Coat fish lightly with flour and saute in butter or margarine until cooked. Squeeze lemon juice over fish after cooked. Put fish on platter. Place crabmeat on top of each piece of fish, then cover each portion with Hollandaise sauce. Serve immediately.

Mrs. Kaleel Salloum

Courtbouillon

5 pounds fish
1 cup water
1 large onion, chopped
6 stalks celery
1 cup dry wine
¼ cup Worcestershire sauce
6 bay leaves
Good sized pinch sweet basil
Salt, black pepper, red pepper to taste

Salt and pepper
1 cup bacon grease
1 bell pepper, chopped
1 can tomato paste
1 can water
Small bunch green onions, chopped
Small bunch parsley, chopped
¼ teaspoon oregano

There is not a fancy name on this recipe because it is really a very basic dish, except that it is not widely circulated. If you want to impress your friends, tell them you are serving an old New England dish called court bouillon (the proper pronunciation is COO-be-yon). But don't tell them you are serving a fish stew, which is what it boils down to.

As listed above, this recipe will feed a family of four (minimum of two helpings each). For a party, I normally triple the recipe and use a bull redfish weighing about 25-30 pounds before cleaning. Cut the meat into two-inch squares and set aside. Cook the remainder of the meat on the bones in the water seasoned with salt and pepper. I use a very large pot such as those used in cafeterias and cook the meat until it falls off the bones, then remove the bones and pour the broth into another container to save. In the same pot, saute the onions, celery and bell pepper in bacon grease very, very slowly until the vegetables are congealed but not brown. For a large serving, expect this to take several hours. Add the tomato paste, water, fish broth, wine and the rest of the seasonings. Cook this very slowly for at least two hours, adding more water as necessary to maintain level. You don't want it too thick, just keep it the consistency it was when you added the last ingredients. About 20 minutes before serving, add the fish meat and increase the temperature. Serve over rice in a large bowl (that saves trips back to the kitchen) with a simple salad, garlic bread and white wine.

Figure at least seven to eight hours to prepare, during most of which the atmosphere of your kitchen and house and neighborhood will be permeated with a delicious aroma. But the effort will make finicky eaters get down to it.

Richard Glaczier

119

Baked Red Snapper with Creole Sauce

4 to 6 pound red snapper, cleaned
1 tablespoon shortening

1 teaspoon salt
½ teaspoon black pepper

Combine the shortening with the salt and pepper. Rub the snapper inside and out with shortening and place in a baking pan. Bake at 450° for 30 minutes. Pour creole sauce over snapper. Reduce oven to 350° and continue baking for 30 minutes or until fish flakes easily.

CREOLE SAUCE

½ cup bell pepper, chopped
1 large onion, chopped
2 stalks celery, chopped
1 clove garlic, minced
2 tablespoons butter
1 (16 ounce) can tomatoes, chopped

½ teaspoon sugar
Bay leaf
Dash of thyme
½ teaspoon chili powder (optional)
Salt and pepper to taste

Saute bell pepper, onion, celery and garlic in butter. Add tomatoes and seasonings. Simmer for 30 to 40 minutes. Stir frequently.

To serve, fish may be garnished with fresh chopped parsley and surrounded with mounds of mashed potatoes. Return platter to oven for a few minutes to brown peaks of potatoes. Serves 4.

Mrs. Oney Raines III

Ralph's Flamed Snapper

2 snapper fillets (¼ pound each),
   seasoned
1 slice of bacon
1 tablespoon parsley
3 tablespoons green onion, chopped

4 tablespoons butter
5 thin slices of lemon
Salt to taste
Pepper to taste

SAUCE

1 ounce brandy
1 ounce lemon juice

1 ounce Worcestershire sauce
Tabasco to taste

Saute fillets in butter, together with bacon and lemon slices for 10 minutes. Add green onions and parsley and saute for another 5 minutes. Add sauce to pan, ignite with a long match and stir as long as the flame burns. Serve fillets with residue sauce. Serves 1.

Ralph Clinde
Ralph and Kacoo's Restaurant
New Orleans, Louisiana

Baked Fillets of Fish

6 to 8 fish fillets
½ cup sour cream

1 cup grated Parmesan cheese
Paprika

Salt fillets and place in baking dish. Make a paste of sour cream and Parmesan cheese. Color with paprika. Spread on fish fillets. Bake covered at 350° for 35 minutes.

Mrs. J. C. Ellis, Jr.

Salmon Croquettes

The French word "croquette" stems from "croquer", which means "to crunch". Any croquette without a lot of crunch doesn't deserve the name. Basically, a croquette is finely chopped meat, fish or vegetables bound with a thick sauce or eggs, shaped, then crumbed and deep fried.

1 (1 pound) can salmon (tuna may be substituted)	2 eggs
¼ cup margarine	½ teaspoon salt
¼ cup plus additional flour	1/8 teaspoon pepper
1 cup milk	½ cup plus additional fine dry bread crumbs
1 tablespoon chopped parsley	1 tablespoon water
¼ cup chopped onion	Solid vegetable shortening

Drain salmon, remove center bone and skin. Melt butter. Blend in ¼ cup flour. Stir in milk. Bring to a boil, stirring constantly; boil 2 minutes. Add salmon, parsley, onion 1 egg, salt, pepper and ½ cup bread crumbs. Mix well. Chill 1 hour. Shape into 12 croquettes 3 inches long. Beat remaining egg with water. Roll each croquette in flour, dip in egg mixture, and coat with bread crumbs. Chill 1-2 hours. Fry croquettes in hot shortening until golden brown on all sides, about 3 minutes. Drain and serve hot with cucumber sauce or sauce of choosing.

CUCUMBER SAUCE

Combine 1 cup sour cream, ½ cup diced, peeled cucumber, ½ teaspoon salt, dash pepper, ½ teaspoon Worcestershire, 1 teaspoon lemon juice, ¼ teaspoon sugar and ½ teaspoon dill weed. Mix and chill.

Charlotte Lamey

Cocktail Sauce

1 cup chili sauce (1 bottle)	1 teaspoon Worcestershire sauce
3 or 4 tablespoons catsup	4 to 5 drops Tabasco
1 teaspoon grated onion	1 celery stalk, finely chopped (optional)
2 tablespoons horseradish	

Mix all ingredients together. Add more or less horseradish to taste. Perfect for oysters on the half shell.

Mrs. William E. Smallwood

Tartar Sauce

2 tablespoons minced dill pickle	1 teaspoon onion juice or scraped onion
1 tablespoon minced green olives (stuffed or pitted)	½ cup Kraft mayonnaise (or more to taste)
¼ teaspoon dried tarragon	Salt and pepper to taste
½ teaspoon salad mustard	

Add seasonings to mayonnaise. Stir well. Refrigerate.

Jessie Graves

Poultry

Poultry

Boneless Chicken Breasts

½ cup Parmesan cheese
¼ cup chopped parsley
1 garlic button, crushed
2 teaspoons salt

Red pepper to taste
Melted butter
1 cup bread crumbs or corn flakes
4 chicken breasts, boned
Celery and onions

Mix cheese, parsley, garlic, salt, and red pepper. Dip boned chicken in melted butter and cover completely with cheese mixture. Then coat with bread crumbs or corn flakes. Roll each chicken breast and bake for 1 hour at 350⁰. Boil chicken bones, salt, pepper, celery, and onions in small amount of water to make chicken broth. Use this to baste chicken breasts several times during the hour.

Mrs. William Wise

Party Chicken Breasts

8 chicken breasts, boned and skinned
2 (14 ounce) cans hearts of palm
Melted butter

Salt to taste
White pepper to taste
Chopped chives
Chopped parsley

Wrap chicken breasts around stalks of palm heart. Attach with a toothpick. Place in buttered large, shallow baking dish. Cover breasts generously with melted butter. Season with salt and white pepper. Bake at 400⁰ for 25-30 minutes or until done. Remove from pan and sprinkle with chopped chives and chopped parsley. Serves 8. Especially good served with green rice.

Nancy Mize Sneed

Handsboro Presbyterian Church
Organized in 1877, this church was built in Handsboro, a community founded before the Civil War by Miles and Sheldon Hand. This thriving settlement was noted for timber, charcoal, and brick. The Hand brothers built twin mansions on Bayou Bernard near their foundry. Some of the wrought iron balconies commonly found in New Orleans were cast in their Handsboro foundry.
Photograph by Bill Emore,
Gulf Publishing Co., Inc.

Lura's Chicken Elegante

6 slices dried beef
6 chicken breast halves, deboned
1 clove garlic, pressed
⅓ cup margarine, melted
1½ cups bread crumbs (or corn flake crumbs)

1 cup grated sharp cheddar cheese
⅓ cup Parmesan cheese
½ teaspoon salt

Roll slice of dried beef on each half breast and secure with toothpick. Add garlic to melted butter. Mix bread crumbs, cheddar cheese, Parmesan cheese and salt. Dip rolled chicken into melted margarine and coat with bread crumb mixture. Remove toothpicks. Bake uncovered at 350° for 1 hour.

Susan Gray

Chicken Wrap-Ups

Chicken breasts, boneless and
*   skinned (allow one per person)*
2 slices bacon per chicken breast

Salt, pepper, parsley
Soy Sauce
Lemon Juice

Wrap each chicken breast with two pieces of bacon. Criss-cross slices of bacon and secure with toothpicks. Place in rectangular baking pan. Season with salt, pepper, lots of soy sauce and lemon juice, and a little parsley. Bake at 350° for 45 minutes.

Nancy Mize Sneed

Janet Miller uses small boneless chicken fillets and one piece of bacon. Add Worcester-shire sauce and Morton Nature's Seasons to ingredients and marinate chicken for several hours. Wrap and cook on grill. This makes great appetizers.

Chicken Breasts in Wine

4 chicken breasts, boneless and skinned
½ stick butter (no substitution)
2 tablespoons oil
Salt and pepper
1 tablespoon flour

½ cup dry white wine
2 tablespoons dry red wine
20 large fresh mushrooms, sliced
*   (no substitution)*
3 tablespoons butter
4 slices Munster cheese

Flatten chicken breasts between sheets of waxed paper. Dredge them in flour seasoned with salt and pepper. In a large skillet, saute the chicken in butter and oil until browned and cooked through. Transfer to a shallow flameproof dish. Add flour to pan drippings and brown. Stir in the wines and bring liquid to a boil stirring the brown bits clinging to pan. Add mushrooms that have been sauteed in 3 tablespoons butter. Spoon mushrooms and pan juices over chicken breasts. (May be made ahead to this point and kept at room temperature.) Top each breast with medium-thick slice of Munster cheese. Broil until cheese is melted to cap each breast. If made ahead, heat chicken in 350° oven until juice bubbles and then top with cheese and broil. For 8 chicken breasts, increase butter for browning by 2 tablespoons and use 1 pound mushrooms and same amounts of wine.

Mrs. William E. Smallwood

Chicken Stuffed Eggplant

1 medium eggplant
3 chicken breasts, cooked and boned
1/2 cup diced onion
1/4 cup bell pepper, chopped
1 stalk celery, diced
1 1/2 cups water

1 tablespoon margarine
4 thinly sliced tomatoes
1/2 cup shredded sharp cheese
4 slices cooked bacon
1 teaspoon salt
Soy sauce and Tabasco, if desired

Half eggplant lengthwise. Remove pulp carefully and save shell. Boil chicken breasts in salted water until done. Remove chicken and dice. Boil eggplant in chicken broth for about 5 minutes. Drain. Saute onion, celery, and bell pepper in margarine. Mix chicken, eggplant, sauteed vegetables, Tabasco and soy sauce (if desired) and place in eggplant shells. Top with tomato slices, shredded cheese and bacon. Bake at 375° for 15 minutes. Serves 2 or 3.   *Polly Ladner*

Chicken Gumbo

8 quarts water
1 chicken
1 pound chicken gizzards (optional)
1 tablespoon salt
1 teaspoon black pepper
1 teaspoon garlic powder
10 cubes chicken bouillon
3/4 cup oil

1 1/4 cups flour
1 cup chopped onions
1/2 cup chopped celery
1/2 cup chopped green pepper
1 (14 ounce) can tomatoes, undrained
1/2 pound block bologna from deli,
   cut into bite size chunks

In large stock pot add water, chicken, chicken gizzards, salt, pepper and garlic powder. Bring to boil and cook until chicken is done. Remove chicken and cool. Continue cooking gizzards on medium heat. Add bouillon. Skin and debone chicken. Start roux in large iron pot. Add oil and heat. Add flour, stirring constantly on low heat until dark golden brown. Add onion, celery, and green pepper, stirring until mixed. Add tomatoes and mix. Spoon roux into stock pot. Bring to boil and cook on medium heat, 1 hour. Add chicken and bologna and cook 30 minutes. Serve over rice.   *Mavis Cospelich*

Chicken Spaghetti

1 cup chopped green pepper
1 cup chopped onions
1 cup diced celery
1/2 stick butter or oleo
4 cups diced, cooked chicken
1 large can #3 tomatoes cut up
   with juice (28 ounces)

1 can mushroom soup
1 jar chopped mushrooms, drained
1 (12 ounce) package Vermicelli
3 cups chicken broth
1 cup sliced Spanish olives
2 cups grated cheddar cheese

Saute green pepper, onion, celery in butter. Add chicken, tomatoes, soup and mushrooms. Simmer. Cook one package of Vermicelli in chicken broth. Drain. In large casserole put half of the spaghetti, half of the chicken mix, 1/2 cup of the olives and 1 cup of the cheddar cheese. Repeat layer. Bake 350° for 45 minutes.

Mrs. George D. Slay
Hazlehurst, Mississippi

Curried Chicken

2 tablespoons butter or oleo
2 teaspoons curry powder
1 apple, chopped
1 onion, chopped
6 chicken breasts, boned and skinned

1 can cream of mushroom soup, undiluted
1 cup cream
Salt to taste
Paprika

Melt butter or oleo in a small sauce pan. Saute in it the curry powder, apple and onion until the onion is transparent. Add mushroom soup and cream. Heat without boiling. Sprinkle salt and paprika on chicken breasts and arrange them in a single layer in a shallow, buttered casserole. Pour sauce over chicken. Bake uncovered for 1½ hours at 350°. Check after cooking 1 hour and cover loosely with foil the last 20-30 minutes if necessary. The sauce makes a delicious gravy to serve with rice.

Mrs. Leonard Blackwell

Chicken Garlic

1 tablespoon + 2½ teaspoons salt
1 tablespoon + 1 teaspoon red pepper
1 tablespoon black pepper
4 pounds fryer, skinned and cut up
1 cup (or more) vegetable oil
1 cup (or more) flour
1½ cups chopped onion, divided

2 cups bell pepper, divided
7 cups chicken stock
6 tablespoons finely chopped garlic
2 cups chopped green onions, tops and bottoms
1 cup chopped parsley
4 cups cooked rice

Mix salt and peppers. Sprinkle chicken pieces with 1¼ tablespoons of seasoning mixture. Work in with hands. Cover and refrigerate overnight or for a few hours minimum. Heat oil in heavy 6 quart saucepan. Mix flour and 1 tablespoon of seasoning mixture in shallow pan. As you are ready to fry it, dredge chicken pieces in seasoned flour. Shake off excess. (Save the flour.) Fry chicken on both sides in a single layer in the oil until lightly browned, about 5 minutes per side. Do not overcrowd the pan. Remove browned pieces to a holding bowl while remaining pieces are fried. Pour oil into heat-proof measuring cup, add fresh oil to 1 cup line. Leave browned droppings in the pan. Return oil to pan. Add flour to seasoned flour to equal ½ cup. Add to hot oil. Stir constantly until medium brown. Do not burn! Add ¾ cup of onions, cook and stir for 2 minutes; add 1 tablespoon seasoning mix and 1 cup bell peppers. Cook for 2 minutes. Gradually add 6 cups of stock, blend well, then bring to a boil. Add garlic, fried chicken, remaining vegetables. Return to boil. Cover pan and reduce heat. Simmer 20 minutes. Scrape bottom occasionally. Add green onions and parsley. Simmer uncovered for 15 minutes, stirring and scraping. Add extra stock if mixture is too thick.

Serve over cooked rice for dinner. For appetizers use 3 pounds chicken breast meat skinned, boned and cut into finger sized pieces.

Dr. Gordon Stanfield

King Ranch Chicken

3 to 4 pound hen
1 onion
1 to 2 ribs celery
Salt and pepper
1 large onion, chopped
1 large bell pepper, chopped
1 can cream of mushroom soup

1 can cream of chicken soup
½ pound cheddar cheese, grated
Chili powder
Garlic salt
1 package frozen tortillas
1 can Rotel tomatoes and chilies,
   undrained

Boil hen until tender in water seasoned with onion, celery, salt and pepper. Cool. Cut chicken into small pieces and reserve all stock. Chop onion and bell pepper. Combine soups and grated cheese. Just before putting in casserole, soak the frozen tortillas in boiling chicken stock until wilted. In a 2 quart casserole or 9 x 12 inch baking dish layer ingredients as follows: tortillas (dripping with stock), chicken, onion, bell pepper, chili powder and garlic salt to taste, and soup mixture. Repeat the layers making sure the tortillas are oozing with stock. Top casserole with Rotel tomatoes and all the juice. Juices in the casserole should be about half the depth of the dish, if not, add a little more stock. May be frozen several days ahead, but always make at least one day ahead and refrigerate so that the flavors will blend. Bake casserole uncovered at 375⁰ for 30 minutes. Serves 8-10.

Mrs. J. Robbins Clower, Jr.

Crab-Stuffed Chicken Breast

6 chicken breasts, skinned and boned
¾ cup chopped onion
½ cup chopped celery
¼ cup chopped green pepper
3 tablespoons butter or margarine
3 tablespoons sherry or lemon juice
1 (7½ ounce) can crabmeat,
   drained and flaked
½ cup herb-seasoned stuffing mix

2 tablespoons flour
½ teaspoon paprika
½ teaspoon salt - dash of pepper
2 tablespoons melted butter
1 envelope hollandaise sauce mix
¾ cup milk
2 tablespoons sherry
½ cup (2 ounce) shredded Swiss
   cheese

Pound chicken to flatten. Sprinkle with salt and pepper. Melt butter in pan and saute onions, celery and green pepper. Remove from heat; add 3 tablespoons sherry or lemon juice, the crabmeat, and stuffing mix; toss. Divide mixture among breasts. Roll up and secure with toothpicks. Combine flour and paprika, coat chicken. Place in 11x7-inch baking dish; drizzle with 2 tablespoons melted butter. Bake, uncovered, in 375⁰ oven for 1 hour. Transfer to platter. Blend sauce mix and milk; cook and stir until thick. Add remaining sherry and cheese. Stir until cheese melts. Pour some on chicken; pass remaining. Makes 6 servings.

Charlotte Lamey

Creole Chicken with Mushrooms

1 (3 to 4 pound) chicken, cut up
1/2 teaspoon salt
1/2 teaspoon pepper
1/2 stick margarine (1/4 cup)
1 pound fresh mushrooms, thinly sliced
1 cup water

1/2 cup cooking Sauterne
1 chicken flavored bouillon cube
2 tablespoons tomato paste
1 tablespoon flour
1 tablespoon softened margarine
1/2 cup pimento strips

Sprinkle chicken with salt and pepper. Heat 1/4 cup margarine in large skillet. Add chicken and brown well. Remove from skillet and set aside. Add mushrooms to skillet, cook 3 minutes, stirring frequently. Stir in water, Sauterne, bouillon cube and tomato paste. Add chicken, cover and bring to a boil. Simmer about 40 minutes or until chicken is done. Remove chicken to heated serving dish. Blend together flour and remaining 1 tablespoon margarine. Add to liquid in skillet. Cook until thickened and boiling, stirring constantly. Gently stir in pimentos. Cook one minute. Pour over chicken. Makes 4 servings.

Kathy Russell

Chinese Chicken with Walnuts

1 teaspoon cornstarch, mixed to a thin
    paste with water
1 egg white
4 1/2 ounces diced, skinless chicken
    fillets
4 ounces oil
2 1/2 ounces walnuts

3 1/2 tablespoons chicken stock
1 tablespoon soy sauce
1 teaspoon salt
1 teaspoon sherry
1/4 teaspoon chopped onion
Dash of pepper
Cooked white rice

Mix cornstarch paste with egg white. Toss chicken in mixture until coated. Heat oil and fry walnuts until brown. Remove walnuts and set aside. Brown the coated chicken in heated oil and set aside cooked chicken. Drain all but one ounce of oil and then add chicken stock, soy sauce, salt, sherry, onion and pepper and mix. Return walnuts and cooked chicken to skillet and stir fry until well blended. Serve over cooked white rice. Serves 2. Doubles easily.

This is a 1937 original Chinese recipe from the Sun Ya Restaurant in Shanghai handed down by Mrs. Salloum's mother, Mildred Tootle.

Mrs. Richard P. Salloum

Chicken in Red Sauce

1 chicken, cut up (or favorite
    pieces)
1 cup finely chopped onions
1/3 cup salad oil
1 1/2 cups catsup
1/2 cup water

1/4 cup sugar
1 tablespoon Worcestershire sauce
2 1/2 teaspoons salt
1/4 teaspoon black pepper
1/2 cup lemon juice
Tabasco sauce to taste (optional)

Saute onions in oil. Mix remaining ingredients in bowl and add to onions. Simmer 15 minutes. Place chicken parts in baking dish and pour sauce over them until almost covered. Cover dish with aluminum foil and bake at 350⁰ for 50 minutes. Remove foil and bake an additional 15 minutes. The sauce may be kept in refrigerator or freezer and used in a variety of ways. It is very good on rice or cooked with vegetables as okra or brussel sprouts. The cooked chicken may be removed from the sauce with tongs, placed on a cookie sheet, returned to the oven to dry out a bit and served separately from sauce.

Mrs. Albert E. Fant, Jr.

Raisin and Almond Chicken

3 tablespoons dark raisins
3 tablespoons light or dark rum or
   3 tablespoons boiling water and
   1 teaspoon rum flavoring
½ stick butter or margarine
¼ cup slivered almonds
4 whole chicken breasts about 12 ounces
   each, halved, skinned and boned

1 teaspoon salt
¼ teaspoon pepper
¾ cup chicken broth
1 tablespoon cornstarch
½ cup light cream
Watercress

Soak raisins in rum in small cup while preparing recipe. Heat butter or margarine in a large skillet, add almonds. Cook stirring constantly until almonds are toasted. Remove with slotted spoon to plate. Add chicken breasts to skillet, sprinkle with salt and pepper. Cook over medium heat turning often for 10 minutes or until firm. Remove to plate and keep warm. Add broth to skillet, bring to a boil. Mix cornstarch and cream in a cup, pour into boiling liquid stirring constantly and simmer 3 minutes. Stir in rum and raisins. Taste and add more salt and pepper, if desired. Pour over chicken to serve.

Ann B. Shavers

Chicken Sauterne

2 frying chickens, cut up
1 large onion
¼ cup salad oil
½ cup sauterne
1 clove garlic, mashed

1 teaspoon salt
½ teaspoon celery salt
½ teaspoon pepper
1 teaspoon fresh or ¼ teaspoon dried
   each of thyme, marjoram and
   rosemary

WINE SAUCE: Grate onion in blender. Add salad oil, wine, garlic, and seasonings and blend well. Chill at least 3 hours.

Salt chicken pieces lightly and arrange on broiler pan. Broil several inches from heat, basting with wine sauce and turning several times until fork tender. Serve with wine sauce drippings. If chicken is getting too brown before it is done, turn off broiler and finish cooking in a 375⁰ oven.

Mrs. Gerald Wessler

Chicken and Buttermilk Dumplings

1 fryer
1 1/2 cups flour
Black pepper to taste
1/4 teaspoon baking powder
1/2 teaspoon sugar

4 tablespoons shortening or margarine
1/2 cup buttermilk
1 egg
2 cups chicken stock
3/4 cup or more of milk

Bake chicken in a covered dish in the microwave or oven until just cooked. Reserve juices to be used in place of some of the stock. Mix flour, pepper, baking powder and sugar to blend and then cut in shortening. Add buttermilk and egg (may be done in a food processor). Roll into ball and chill in the freezer (don't forget it's in there). Cut the chicken into bite-size pieces. Roll out the dumpling dough on a floured board as you would for pie crust. Use lots of flour. Cut into 1 inch squares. Place the stock in a 4 quart pan or Dutch oven and bring to a boil. Drop in the dumplings one at a time to keep the stock boiling. Don't let them stick. Place cut-up chicken over the dumplings, pour milk over this. Bring the stock back to a boil. Cover and cook at a fast simmer for 20 minutes. Don't lift the lid! Add pepper and a little more milk if it's too dry. Reheats well covered in the oven at about 350°. If you like onions, add them to the stock while it's boiling.

Marcia Swetman

Mama's Chicken Pie

1 cup plain flour
1/2 teaspoon salt
1 1/2 teaspoons baking powder
2 tablespoons cooking oil
1 1/2 cups milk separated

Self-rising flour
4 cups chicken broth
1 chicken, cooked and deboned
Butter or margarine

Stir plain flour, salt, and baking powder together. Cut in cooking oil, add 1/2 cup milk to make a soft dough. Roll dough out on board floured with self-rising flour, and cut into strips. Hold extra flour on strips for thickening. Pour some of the broth in bottom of casserole dish. Layer strips of dough, chicken and broth until all of chicken and broth are used. Hold enough dough to cover top in strips. Place pats of butter on top and bake in 400° oven until golden brown. Take casserole out of oven and carefully pour 1 cup of milk over top. Set out 10 to 15 minutes before serving. English peas and/or carrots are optional in the broth.

Ellen Thomas

Chicken Tetrazzini I

1 chicken
8 ounces spaghetti
1 can cream of mushroom soup
1/2 cup milk
2 teaspoons chopped pimento

1 small can mushroom pieces
1/2 cup shredded cheddar cheese
Salt and pepper to taste
Grated Parmesan cheese

Place chicken in large kettle, add about 2 quarts cold water. Bring to boil. Reduce heat. Simmer until chicken is tender. Remove chicken from broth and reserve broth. Bone chicken and cut into small pieces. Cook spaghetti in broth until tender, drain well. Blend soup and milk in saucepan. Add chicken, pimento, and mushrooms. Heat throughly. Layer spaghetti, chicken mixture, and cheddar cheese in casserole. Sprinkle each layer with salt and pepper. Top with cheese. Cover and bake at 350⁰ for 30-35 minutes. Serves 8.

Mrs. Terry Loveless

Chicken Tetrazzini II

1 (4 to 5 pound) stewing chicken,
   cooked with seasonings, boned,
   and chopped
12 ounces spaghetti, cooked
3 tablespoons flour
2 onions, chopped
1 green pepper
6 tablespoons butter
1 cup mushroom caps
Grated Parmesan cheese
1 cup pimento, chopped

4 cloves garlic, minced
Salt
Pepper
¼ teaspoon thyme
1 tablespoon Worcestershire sauce
3 cups stock from cooking chicken
¾ cup fine buttered crumbs
3 tablespoons sherry

Saute onion and green pepper in butter. Stir in flour. Add stock, stirring to make a smooth sauce. Add mushrooms, pimento, garlic, thyme and chicken. Season to taste with salt and pepper. Make layers in buttered casserole of spaghetti, chicken in sauce, part of bread crumbs, and Parmesan. Repeat layers. Pour sherry over all and bake 30-45 minutes at 350⁰.

Amye C. Gray

Chicken and Wild Rice Casserole

3 cups cooked chicken
1 package Uncle Ben's Wild Rice
1 cup cream of celery soup
1 medium jar chopped pimento
1 medium onion, chopped

1 cup mayonnaise
2 (16 ounce) cans French style
   green beans
1 can water chestnuts, sliced
Salt and pepper to taste

Boil chicken in seasoned water, bone and chop. Cook wild rice in chicken broth with a little less liquid than directions on package say. Mix with other ingredients; sprinkle with paprika and chopped parsley. Place in large casserole. Bake at 350⁰ for 30 minutes. Serves 16. Very good and colorful for a holiday buffet.

Mrs. Jim Nicholson

Creamy Chicken and Wild Rice

1 cup wild rice ·
1/2 cup chopped onion
1/2 cup butter
1/4 cup flour
1/2 pound fresh mushrooms
1 1/2 cups chicken broth

1 1/2 cups light cream
3 cups cooked chicken breasts, diced
2 tablespoons chopped parsley
1 1/2 teaspoons salt
1/4 teaspoon pepper
1/2 cup slivered almonds

Cook wild rice according to package instructions. Cook onion and mushrooms in butter until tender. Remove from heat and stir in flour. Gradually add chicken broth to mixture. Add cream. Cook and stir until thick. Do not let boil. Add wild rice, chicken, parsley, salt and pepper. Place in 2 quart casserole. Sprinkle with almonds. Bake at 350° for 30 minutes. Use salt and pepper to taste if broth is unseasoned. Serves 6.

Mrs. William E. Smallwood

Aunt Mamie's Old Fashioned Chicken Pot Pie

1 medium onion, finely chopped
1/2 cup celery, finely chopped
1/2 cup margarine
1/3 cup all purpose flour
1 1/2 teaspoons salt

1/4 teaspoon black pepper
3 1/2 to 4 cups chicken broth
4 cups chopped, cooked chicken
1 cup drained English peas (canned)
1 cup drained carrots (canned)

Cook onions and celery in margarine until tender but not brown, blend in flour, salt and pepper. Gradually stir in broth. Cook and stir until thick. Add chicken, peas and carrots. Pour into 3 quart shallow baking dish. Cover with pie crust and bake at 350° to 375° until golden brown.

PIE CRUST

2/3 cup shortening
2 cups sifted all purpose flour

5-7 tablespoons ice water
1 teaspoon salt

Work shortening into flour until it looks like cornmeal. Add ice water. Roll out on floured surface and place on top of pie. You can use Pillsbury All-Ready pie crust.

Mamie Ware
Long Beach, Mississippi

Game

Game

Plantation Dove

20 whole doves or dove breasts
Olive oil
Celery salt
Garlic salt
Onion salt

3 tablespoons dry mustard
3 tablespoons curry powder
2 cups water
Juice of one orange
Juice of one lemon
1 teaspoon Worcestershire sauce

Dip doves in olive oil, saturating doves so that they are well-oiled. Place doves in roasting pan or Dutch oven. Sprinkle with celery salt, garlic salt, and onion salt, dry mustard, and curry powder. Add water. Cover and cook at 275° for approximately 2 hours or until tender. The last 30 minutes of cooking remove top from pan. Pour fruit juices and Worcestershire sauce over doves and continue to cook uncovered. Serve hot or refrigerate and serve cold as hors d' oeuvres. Serves 8.

Mrs. Robert W. King
Jackson, Mississippi

Dove or Quail on Toast

6 to 8 doves or quail
Salt and pepper
1 stick butter

¼ cup water
Toasted bread slices

Generously salt and pepper birds. Melt butter in black iron skillet or Dutch oven. Brown birds in butter. Add water. Cover with a lid smaller than skillet and weight the lid so that birds will be pressed during cooking. Cook over low heat for 1 hour or until birds are tender. Check often during cooking and add additional quarter-cupsful of water as needed. To serve, remove birds from skillet and place on toast. Add water to drippings left in pan to make gravy. Ladle gravy over birds and toast. Serve with grits and hot fruit for a traditionally Southern "special occasions" breakfast. Serves 4.

Holcomb Hector

Walter Anderson, sculptor and painter, lived reclusively in Ocean Springs and on Horn Island. When he died in 1965, his family discovered a stunning room in his cottage with breathtakingly colorful nature scenes covering the walls and ceiling. This mural and other of his paintings, block prints, and pottery may be seen during a visit to Shearwater Pottery and several public buildings in Ocean Springs.

Photograph by Sonny Pippin,
Gulf Publishing Co.

Grilled Doves

16 doves
Bacon to wrap
1½ sticks butter
Salt and pepper

1½ lemons, squeezed
Tabasco
Worcestershire sauce

Wash and dry doves inside and out. Sprinkle cavity with salt and pepper. Wrap one-half piece bacon across each breast and secure with toothpick. Melt butter. Add remaining ingredients. Place doves in ovenproof glass baking dish. Pour sauce over and cover tightly with foil. Bake at 300° for 45 minutes, or until tender, basting three times during baking. To finish; either brown bacon on outdoor grill, basting with sauce, or turn broiler on and brown in oven.

Mrs. Sam Morse

Roasted Quail with Mushrooms

4 quail
4 slices bacon
1 tablespoon butter
¼ cup lemon juice

½ cup hot water
⅓ cup chopped mushrooms
Toast or rice

Prepare quail. Wrap bacon around each quail, securing with skewers or toothpicks. Put birds in shallow buttered pan; cover and bake at 350°, basting with mixture of lemon juice and water.

I usually dot birds with a little more butter to bring out more flavor, if served on bed of rice.

Mrs. Cragin Gilbert

Mississippi Duck Stew

4 ducks
4 tablespoons flour
¾ cup peanut oil
1 teaspoon salt
1 teaspoon pepper
1 cup onion, chopped

1 cup bell pepper, chopped
½ cup flour
4 bouillon cubes (chicken)
4 cups hot water
Celery salt, dash
Garlic salt, dash

Cut ducks into serving pieces. Dredge with flour, salt, pepper, garlic salt and celery salt. Brown in peanut oil in a heavy skillet. Remove ducks. Saute onions and bell pepper and remove. Put ½ cup flour into skillet and brown. Dissolve bouillon cubes in hot water. Add to browned flour mixture, along with ducks and vegetables. Cook at 300° for 1½ hours. Serve with brown, white or wild rice.

Billy Joe Cross
Author of "Cooking Wild Game and Fish - Mississippi Style"

Duck Breasts on Toast Points

Cover duck breasts with French dressing and marinate approximately 12 hours. Drain, but do not wipe dry. Charcoal broil on hibachi or grill in fireplace for 3 to 6 minutes on each side. Slice very thinly at an angle. Serve on toast points.

Delicious as hors d'oeuvres on a cold winter night when having cocktails around the fireplace. Needless to say, guests will be impressed.

Richard C. Nehring
Massapequa, Long Island, New York

Pot Roasted Wild Duck

2 wild ducks	*Vegetable shortening*
1 onion, whole	*Flour*
5 celery tops	*Sliced mushrooms*
½ green pepper	*1 can chicken consomme*
Thyme	*¼ cup Burgundy wine*
3 bay leaves	

Wash, salt, and pepper ducks. Brown well in Dutch oven, using as little fat as possible. Add 2 tablespoons water, cover tightly, and let simmer about an hour, adding water during cooking if needed. Add 1 large onion, celery tops, green pepper, thyme, and bay leaves. In separate skillet, make a roux with equal parts of vegetable shortening and flour; add sliced mushrooms with a little water and cook ten minutes. Add roux and consomme. About fifteen minutes before ducks are finished cooking, add Burgundy. Serve with wild rice.

Mrs. Donnie Riley

Mississippi Mallard

Soak ducks overnight in water to cover to which 3 tablespoons baking soda has been added. Drain and dry inside. Salt inside and stuff with quartered apples, onions, carrots, and celery. Place a piece of bacon on breast. Cover with foil. Roast 1 hour or until done at 400⁰. Remove foil during last 20 minutes of roasting and baste so that skin will brown. Remove stuffing before serving. Serve one-half bird per person. May be served with Duck Sauce.

DUCK SAUCE

1 part Burgundy wine
1 part tomato catsup
1 part currant jelly

Mix ingredients and heat in double boiler. Serve over roast duck.

Richard Nehring
Massapequa, Long Island, New York

Cajun Canard l'Orange

4 wild ducks
½ gallon red port wine
2 tablespoons seasoned salt
2 teaspoons black pepper
1 green pepper, chopped
3 onions, (2 chopped, 1 quartered)
3 stalks celery, chopped
3 carrots, chopped

6 bay leaves
3 pods garlic, slivered
6 oranges (2 quartered, 2 thinly sliced,
*   2 squeezed for juice)*
¼ cup olive oil
1 large can sliced mushrooms
1 pint orange marmalade

Place slivers of garlic in breast and leg portion of each duck. Marinate overnight in refrigerator in red port wine to which seasoned salt, pepper, chopped onions, green pepper, celery, carrots, and bay leaves have been added. Dry ducks, season and brown slowly in olive oil. Place browned ducks in Dutch oven or black iron pot with tight-fitting lid. Fill cavity of duck with quartered oranges and quartered onions. Saute all vegetables from the marinade mixture and sprinkle on top of ducks. Add mushrooms and thinly sliced oranges on each duck. Pour orange juice over the entire mixture. Pour 1 inch of wine marinade mixture in bottom of pot. Ducks should be placed on a rack so that wine does not touch birds while cooking. Cook on top of the stove or in a 325° oven until tender or meat begins to separate from breast bone, approximately 3 hours. After duck is cooked, remove meat from breast bone with carving knife. Remove neck and backbone together which will leave an attractive half of duck. Prepare orange glaze by adding equal parts of gravy to orange marmalade. Bring to a boil. Glaze duck halves with marmalade mixture. Garnish with parsley and thin slices of orange. Remaining gravy may be used to moisten ducks, add to dressing, etc.

Mr. and Mrs. Bubba Oustalet

Ducks 'N Brown Gravy

4-6 large ducks or doves or
*   8-10 small ducks or doves*
2 cups milk for marinade
1 pound lean bacon
¼ cup flour and extra flour
¼-½ cup peanut or olive oil
1-1½ cups milk for gravy

15-20 green onions, chopped
3 medium yellow onions, chopped
1-2 cloves elephant garlic or
*   3-4 regular garlic*
Lowrey's season salt
Cavendar's Greek seasoning

Day before: Breast ducks and cube meat 1 to ½ inch. Marinate in milk overnight. Next day: Cut 1 pound lean bacon into small pieces and brown to medium done. Drain and set aside. After draining from milk, dust duck with extra flour and brown in olive oil or peanut oil. Add ¼ cup flour and additional oil if needed, make roux, stir until golden brown. Add milk to make gravy. Dilute with water to desired consistency (for browning you may add a drop or two of Kitchen bouquet). Add duck, bacon, onions and garlic back to gravy. Season with Lowrey's season salt and Cavendar's to taste. Simmer on top of stove 3-4 hours covered, stirring every 30 minutes. This can be frozen.

Richard and Faye Williams

Venison Chili

1½ pounds ground beef
1½ pounds ground venison
1 teaspoon salt
½ teaspoon pepper
½ teaspoon garlic powder
2 cloves chopped garlic
4 medium chopped onions

Approximately 2 tablespoons olive oil
6 ounces tomato paste
2 cans kidney beans
4 cans tomatoes
2 tablespoons chili powder
½ teaspoon cloves
3 bay leaves

Brown beef and venison with salt, pepper and garlic powder. Drain thoroughly. Saute garlic and onions in olive oil. Add all remaining ingredients, including the meat, and cook at least two hours over low heat, stirring frequently. Adjust seasoning to taste and add cloves and bay leaves. This freezes beautifully.

Mrs. Sherman Muths, Jr.

Leg of Venison

1 leg or large roast of venison
1 pound bacon cut into 2" pieces
1 (4½ ounce) jar stuffed olives

Garlic powder
Salt
Lemon pepper marinade

Trim all fat from meat. Pierce holes in meat and stuff an olive into each hole. Sprinkle each piece of bacon generously with garlic powder, salt, and lemon pepper marinade. Roll up and stuff into cavity with remaining olives. Do this on both sides of the meat. Sprinkle entire leg or roast with salt, garlic powder, and lemon pepper to taste. Put on spit and grill over hot coals for approximately 2½ hours. If venison has been frozen, cover with water and one-half can evaporated milk to thaw.

Mrs. Gordon Allen

Roast Venison

Rump of loin venison roast
Flour
Salt
Pepper
Bacon, sliced

1 small onion, chopped
1 clove garlic, chopped
1 stalk celery, chopped
1 cup beef bouillon
½ cup dry wine

Soak roast in mild salt water solution overnight. Before roasting, salt, pepper, and flour roast. Put on rack in roasting pan and completely cover roast with bacon slices. Place in 450° oven for 15 to 20 minutes, or until bacon begins to brown. Lower oven to 325° and continue roasting for 20 minutes to each pound for medium rare. During last 45 minutes of baking, add chopped onion, garlic, and celery. Let brown about 10 minutes; add beef bouillon and wine. Correct gravy for seasonings.

Mrs. Hoshall Barrett

Meats

Meats

Baked Sirloin Steak

1 large sirloin steak, 3" thick
1 teaspoon salt
¼ teaspoon black pepper
1 cup catsup
3 tablespoons Worcestershire sauce
½ cup melted butter or oleo

1 tablespoon lemon juice
1 clove garlic, minced
1 large onion, sliced
24 ounces sliced canned mushrooms,
    drained, or 1 pound fresh

Brown meat in oil and place in shallow, rectangular pan. Combine salt, pepper, catsup, Worcestershire, butter or oleo, lemon juice, and garlic and pour over the steak. Arrange slices of onion on top of this. Sprinkle with mushrooms. Bake covered at 350⁰ for 1½ hours for medium rare steak. Baste occasionally. Can be made day ahead and baked at serving time.

Mrs. Tom Simmons

Steak Au Poivre for Two

2 rib eye or strip sirloin steaks
Medium cracked pepper
Steak fat
¼ cup brandy

1 cup brown stock or beef broth
½ cup heavy cream
¼ cup butter, sliced
Green peppercorns, pounded (optional)

Press cracked pepper into both sides of the steaks. Rub a heavy skillet with piece of steak fat over moderately high heat, heat the fat until it is very hot, and sear the steaks for 1½ minutes on each side. Reduce the heat to moderate, cook the steaks for 1 to 2 minutes more on each side for rare meat, and transfer them to a heated platter. Pour the fat from the pan, add brandy to pan and ignite it. Shake the pan until the flames go out. Add brown stock or beef broth and heavy cream. Reduce the liquid by half over high heat. Add salt to taste and pounded green peppercorns. Swirl in sliced butter and pour sauce over the steaks.

Mrs. William E. Smallwood

FORT MASSACHUSETTS

Located on Ship Island, twelve miles from the mainland, is historic Fort Massachusetts, captured by Union Forces during the Civil War and used to house Confederate prisoners. Because of shallow inland waters, Ship Island was used as a harbor by the French as early as 1699; from this point coastal exploration and settlement emanated until 1720. This strategic island was also used as a military base by the British in the War of 1812. Tour boats provide visitors excursions to the island.

Photograph by Vernon Matthews, Gulf Publishing Co., Inc.

Beef Fillet Wellington

2 packages Pepperidge Farm patty
   shells, thawed
1 egg yolk
Whole fillet of beef
1½ pounds veal, ground twice
2 slices bread
Milk to soak bread

4 tablespoons butter
3 tablespoons chopped parsley
1 bunch green onions, chopped
3 tablespoons cream and 2 eggs, beaten
   together
Salt and pepper to taste

Remove outside fat from fillet and sinews and fold small end up to make fillet uniform in size. Roast uncovered at 350⁰ until meat thermometer registers desired doneness. Cool.

VEAL PATE: After bread has soaked in milk, squeeze dry. Saute onions in butter over low heat for 5 minutes. Add parsley, bread, eggs and cream to onions and cook 2 minutes. Remove from heat and add veal, salt, and pepper. Blend mixture well.

CRUST: Form ball of thawed patty shells and roll into a rectangle large enough to enclose fillet. Spread veal pate on pastry evenly. Put fillet in center and wrap veal-covered pastry around it, pinching off excess pastry. The ends are enclosed, but avoid too thick pastry overlapping. Place seam side down on greased pan. Decorate with shapes cut from left-over pastry. Brush over all with egg yolk mixed with about 1 table-spoon water. Refrigerate until 45 minutes before serving.

Bake at 350⁰ for 30 minutes and then at 400⁰ for 10 minutes or until crust is nicely browned. Fillet, protected by the pate and crust, will not cook anymore. When sliced, the meat should be completely surrounded by pate and crust. Serves 8 amply.

Mrs. Ernest G. Martin, Jr.

Beef Parmigiana

1½ pounds round steak (3/8" thick)
1 egg, beaten
⅓ cup grated Parmesan cheese
⅓ cup fine dry bread crumbs
⅓ cup cooking oil
1 medium onion, minced
1 teaspoon salt

¼ teaspoon pepper
½ teaspoon sugar
½ teaspoon marjoram or oregano
Dash of Italian seasoning
1 (6 ounce) can tomato paste
2 cups hot water
½ pound mozzarella cheese, sliced

Place meat between pieces of wax paper; lay on board and pound until thin, about ¼ inch. Trim and cut into 6 or 8 pieces. Dip meat in egg and roll in mixture of Parmesan cheese and crumbs. Heat cooking oil in large skillet; brown steak on both sides over medium heat until golden brown. Lay in wide, shallow baking dish. In same skillet, cook onion over low heat until soft; stir in seasonings and tomato paste. Gradually add hot water stirring constantly. Boil 5 minutes scraping browned bits from pan. Pour most of sauce over meat. Top with cheese slices and remaining sauce. Bake at 350⁰ for about 1 hour or until tender. Garnish with parsley. Serves 4 to 6.

Deborah Mills Rosetti

Beef Stroganoff

1½ pounds round steak
Flour
Salt and pepper
1/8 pound butter or oleo or more as
    needed
1 onion, chopped

¼ pound mushrooms
½ cup consomme
1 tablespoon vinegar
½ pint sour cream
Paprika

Slice steak in thin strips, then flour, salt and pepper. Brown lightly in butter, adding more as needed. Add onions, mushrooms, and consomme. Simmer 30 minutes or until tender. Just before serving, add the vinegar and sour cream. Sprinkle with paprika. Serve over rice or noodles. Serves 6.

Mrs. J. Robbins Clower, Jr.

Beef Tips La Duke

1 large sirloin, cubed, or 2 pounds
    boneless chuck, cubed
1 tablespoon cooking oil
1 large onion, finely chopped
1 tablespoon minced onion flakes
2 cloves garlic, chopped
1 tablespoon parsley, chopped

10 to 12 fresh mushrooms, cleaned
    and sliced
1 package beef gravy mix
½ cup red wine
2 cans beef broth
1½ tablespoons Worcestershire
Salt and pepper to taste

In Dutch oven brown meat in oil. Add onion, garlic, and parsley. Cook until transparent. Add onion flakes and sliced mushrooms. Fry a short time, until mushrooms are tender. Cover meat with beef broth and wine. A small amount of water may be used, if needed. Bring to boil, cover, and place heat on low. Cook 2 hours or until meat is very tender. When tender, add package of gravy mix and dash of Worcestershire. Cook until gravy is very thick, about 3-4 minutes. Salt and pepper to taste. May be served with white rice or curry rice. Serves 4. Check meat often during cooking since a better cut of meat may require less cooking time.

Duke Drown

Beef and Green Bean Stew

1 pound fresh snap beans
1 pound cubed beef
1 tablespoon oil
1 medium onion, chopped

1 pound canned tomatoes
¼ teaspoon pepper
1 teaspoon salt
¼ teaspoon cinnamon

Wash and prepare beans, drain and set aside. Saute meat until lightly browned. Add onion to meat and saute. Place washed, prepared beans over meat. Add salt, pepper, and cinnamon. Cover and simmer for 30 or 40 minutes on low heat. Add tomatoes and a small amount of water (enough to cover beans and meat). Cook, covered, on low heat for 1 hour or more. Serve over cooked rice. Serves 4 to 6.

Mrs. Joe Salloum

Hungarian Gulasch (Goulash)

3 to 4 pounds veal or beef shank (if
   not available chuck roast or
   similar kind may be substituted)
4 to 5 onions
2 to 3 tablespoons Hungarian
   Rose Paprika

2 large garlic cloves, crushed
1 to 2 tablespoons caraway seeds,
   crushed
Salt to taste
Marjoram to taste

Peel and slice onions and saute in fat in large pot until tender but not brown. Add meat cut into 1½ to 2 inch cubes to onions. Then add paprika, crushed garlic cloves, and crushed caraway seeds, salt and marjoram (not too much). Cover the pot with a tight fitting lid and simmer slowly for 2 to 3 hours, checking for doneness after 2 hours. There is no need to add water since the meat will make its own gravy. After the meat is done, test for salt or other needed seasoning. Add paprika, if desired. Serve with wide noodles or dumplings.

Evelyn P. Floyd

Chili

1 pound ground beef
1 tablespoon shortening
1 large onion, chopped
1 pound can tomatoes
2 (1 pound) cans kidney beans

¼ cup catsup
2 teaspoons salt
1 tablespoon sugar
1 to 2 teaspoons chili powder
¼ teaspoon pepper

Brown meat slowly in Dutch oven in hot shortening. Add onions and saute 1 minute. Mix in remaining ingredients. Simmer covered 2 hours or longer. More chili powder may be added according to taste. Serves 6.

Mrs. J. Robbins Clower, Jr.

Rouladen (German Meat Rolls)

4 thin slices beef sirloin tip or
   sandwich steak
Salt and pepper to taste
Prepared mustard (optional)
4 slices bacon
2 small carrots, sliced in thin strips

2 medium onions, 1 chopped and 1
   thinly sliced
Parsley
1 tablespoon butter
1 tablespoon flour
1 cup water

Have butcher slice steak about ¼ inch thick and about size of dessert plate. Sprinkle meat with salt and pepper, spread with mustard. Place bacon strips about 1 inch apart on meat slice and then place carrot strip between bacon strips. Cover with chopped onion and parsley. Roll up like jelly roll and fasten with toothpicks. Heat butter in skillet and brown meat rolls on all sides. Add sliced onion and lightly brown. Remove meat and onions, stir flour into skillet. Replace meat and onions; add water. Cover tightly and cook about 15 minutes. Serves 2.

Mrs. William Wise

Green Pepper and Tomato Steak

1 medium sirloin steak (1½ to
   2 pounds)
½ teaspoon salt
½ teaspoon Accent
½ to ¾ cup diced onion
1 can beef bouillon, broth,
   or consomme

1 clove garlic, finely minced
1 or 2 green peppers, cut in 1 inch
   pieces
2 tablespoons cornstarch
¼ cup cold water
3 tablespoons soy sauce
2 tomatoes, cut in pieces

Cut meat in ½ inch strips. Sprinkle with Accent. Trim off any excess fat and use it to grease skillet. Or, use 1 tablespoon cooking oil. Brown meat on one side. Turn and sprinkle with half the salt. Brown other side and sprinkle with remaining salt. Push meat to side of skillet, add onion, and cook until tender. Add bouillon or consomme, soy sauce, and garlic. Cover and simmer approximately 10 minutes or until meat is tender. Add green pepper, cover and simmer 5 minutes. Blend cornstarch with water and gradually stir into meat mixture. Cook over low heat stirring constantly until mixture thickens and boils. Add tomatoes, heat thoroughly, and serve over hot rice.

Mrs. Ruth Stringfellow

Enchilada Casserole

1 package chopped frozen spinach
2 pounds ground chuck
1 large onion, chopped
1 (16 ounce) can whole tomatoes
   or 1 can Rotel tomatoes
Salt to taste
Freshly ground pepper to taste
1 can cream of mushroom soup

1 can golden mushroom soup
1 carton sour cream
½ cup milk
¼ teaspoon garlic powder
12 to 16 tortillas
½ cup butter, melted
1 or 2 cans chopped green chilies
½ pound grated cheddar cheese

Cook spinach according to package directions and squeeze dry. Cook meat, drain, and stir in onions, tomatoes, spinach, salt and pepper. Combine soups, sour cream, milk and garlic in a bowl. Dip half of tortillas in melted butter. Arrange on bottom and sides of large shallow casserole. Spoon in meat mixture. Scatter chopped chilies on top. Cover with all but ½ cup of cheese. Add remaining tortillas also dipped in butter. Spread sauce over top. Cover and refrigerate overnight. Sprinkle remaining ½ cup cheese on top and bake in 350° oven for 35-45 minutes or until bubbly. Serves 12. Freezes well.

Mrs. Robert H. Walker

Tamale Pie

1 pound ground chuck
¾ cup chopped onion
½ cup chopped green pepper
1 teaspoon cumin
Salt and pepper to taste
1 (10 ounce) can Rotel diced tomatoes
   and green chilies

1 (8 ounce) can tomato sauce
1 (10 ounce) can whole kernel corn
   or Mexicorn
1½ tablespoons sugar
4 teaspoons chili powder
10 ounces shredded cheddar cheese
1 small package corn bread mix

In a 10 inch iron skillet brown chuck, onions and green pepper. Add cumin, salt and pepper while browning. Drain. Add diced tomatoes and sauce, corn, sugar and chili powder. Simmer 15 minutes. Remove from heat and stir in cheese. Prepare corn bread mix according to package directions. Spread over top of meat mixture. Bake in iron skillet at 375° for 30 minutes until corn bread is done.

Anna Mellen

Bolichi
(Stuffed Eye of Round)

3 to 4 pounds eye of round
1 Chorizo sausage, chopped
  (or mild linked sausage)
1 medium slice of cured ham, chopped
1 clove minced garlic
1 medium spanish onion, chopped

½ green pepper, chopped
Salt and pepper
Paprika
3 tablespoons bacon drippings
¾ cup hot water
4 whole cloves

Ask butcher to cut lengthwise pocket in center of beef (or do it yourself with a sharp knife), leaving opposite end closed. Mix sausage, ham, garlic, onion and green pepper. Stuff roast, packing well but not too tightly. Secure open end with skewers or wire. Salt and pepper all over and sprinkle generously with paprika. Brown well in bacon drippings over medium heat. Turn often to get an even browning, because the better the browning, the more delicious the sauce. When browned, add hot water, scraping the pan well. Add bay leaf and cloves to liquid. Cover and place in 325° oven. Baste occasionally and cook about 3 hours or until the meat is fork tender. During the last 30 minutes, potatoes may be added. Serve cut in round slices and pass gravy separately. Serves 8 to 10.

Missy Kennedy Allen

Veal Parmigiana

6 tablespoons olive oil, divided
3 cloves garlic, minced
1 chopped onion
1 #2 can tomatoes
1¼ teaspoons salt
¼ teaspoon pepper
1 (8 ounce) tomato sauce

¼ teaspoon dried thyme
1 pound veal cutlet, thinly sliced
1 egg
¼ cup dried bread crumbs
¼ cup grated Parmesan cheese
½ pound Mozzarella cheese, shredded
Parmesan cheese

Heat 3 tablespoons of the oil in saucepan. Add garlic and onion and saute until golden. Add tomatoes, salt and pepper. Use spoon to break up tomatoes. Simmer, uncovered for 10 minutes. Add tomato sauce and thyme and simmer an additional 20 minutes. Begin heating oven to 350°. While sauce cooks, prepare veal: Beat egg with fork in pie plate. Combine bread crumbs and Parmesan cheese and place on sheet of waxed paper. Dip each piece of veal first into egg, then into crumb mixture. Heat 1 tablespoon oil in skillet and saute 2 or 3 pieces of veal at a time, adding remaining oil as necessary. Saute until golden brown, turning one time with bread spatula. Place browned veal in 12 x 8 x 2 inch baking dish in a single layer. Pour ⅔ sauce over veal, (strain sauce if desired). Arrange Mozzarella on top. Spoon on rest of sauce. Sprinkle with additional Parmesan. Bake in 350° oven for 30 minutes. 4 generous servings.

Mrs. James LaRose

Hamburger Casserole

1 pound good ground beef
1 tablespoon margarine
1 chopped onion
1 clove garlic, minced
2 (8 ounce) cans tomato sauce
1 teaspoon salt

½ teaspoon pepper
1 (6 or 8 ounce) package small egg
  noodles
1 carton sour cream
1 carton cottage cheese
1 cup (or more) Mozzarella cheese,
  shredded

Brown beef, drain. Add margarine for flavor, onion, garlic, tomato sauce, salt and pepper. Simmer 15 minutes on low heat. Cook and drain noodles as package directs. Arrange noodles in bottom of casserole, pour in meat sauce, sour cream, cottage cheese, and mix. Top with Mozzarella cheese and bake uncovered at 350⁰ for 20-30 minutes or until bubbly. Serves 6-8. May be made ahead and freezes well.

Mrs. Larry Watkins,
Macon Mississippi

Jalapeno Cornbread and Ground Beef Casserole

MEAT MIXTURE

1 pound ground beef
1 large onion, chopped

1 (16 ounce) can tomatoes
3 chopped jalapenoes, or more to taste

BATTER

1 cup cornmeal
1 tablespoon salt
1 cup milk plus 1 teaspoon soda

1 small can cream style corn
1 egg, beaten
½ cup bacon grease

Brown and drain ground beef. Add remaining meat mixture ingredients. Mix batter ingredients together in another bowl. Pour scant half of batter into greased large casserole or oblong pan. Spoon all of beef mixture over batter and top with remaining batter. Bake at 375⁰ for 1-1¼ hours or until brown.

Bonnie Davis

Moussaka

1 pound ground beef
1 clove garlic, minced
1 (16 ounce) can stewed tomatoes
2 (8 ounce) cans tomato sauce
1 envelope onion soup mix
½ teaspoon oregano

1 medium eggplant
2 eggs beaten with 1 tablespoon water
1 cup bread crumbs
Olive oil for frying
½ cup Parmesan cheese
½ pound Mozzerella cheese, cubed

Brown meat. Stir in garlic, stewed tomatoes, tomato sauce, onion soup mix, and oregano. Cover and simmer 15 minutes. Pare eggplant. Cut crosswise in ¼ inch slices. Dip eggplant into egg-water mixture and then into bread crumbs. Brown in hot olive oil. Alternate layers of eggplant, cheeses, and sauce in a 9 x 13 inch pan or casserole dish. Bake at 350⁰ for 30 minutes. Serves 8.

Mrs. Kaleel Salloum

Red Beans and Rice

1 package red beans, cooked
  according to package directions
2 large onions, chopped
1/2 green pepper, chopped
Butter

2 pounds ground meat
1 teaspoon garlic salt
2 tablespoons chili sauce
1 teaspoon Worcestershire
Tabasco to taste

Saute onions and pepper in butter. Add ground beef and lightly brown. Do not overcook. Add remaining ingredients and simmer 1 hour. Serve on bed of rice.

Donnie Riley

Lasagna

1 pound ground beef
3 cloves garlic, minced
1 large chopped onion
1 teaspoon oregano
1 tablespoon Worcestershire
1 teaspoon thyme
1 (16 ounce) can tomatoes, chopped
  and drained
2 (6 ounce) cans tomato paste

10 ounces lasagna noodles, cooked
2 eggs
1/2 cup grated Parmesan cheese
1 teaspoon pepper
3 cups fresh ricotta cheese
2 tablespoons parsley
1 pound Mozzarella cheese,
  thinly sliced

Brown meat slowly; drain excess fat, add garlic, onion, oregano, Worcestershire and thyme. Cook until onions are translucent. Add tomatoes and tomato paste. Simmer uncovered for about 30 minutes. Beat eggs; add remaining ingredients except Mozzarella and noodles. Spread a large tablespoonful of tomato sauce on the bottom of a 13 x 9 x 2 inch baking dish. Layer half the noodles, spread with half the ricotta filling, add half the Mozzarella cheese, top with half the tomato sauce. Repeat. Bake at 375° for about 30 minutes or assemble early, refrigerate and bake for 45 minutes. Let stand 10 minutes before serving.

Marcia Swetman

Spaghetti Ala Carbonnara

1 chopped onion
1 can mushroom slices
1/2 stick melted butter
1 small can evaporated milk
2 raw eggs

12 ounces spaghetti, cooked and drained
1 pound bacon, cooked and broken
  into pieces
Salt, pepper, garlic powder to taste
3/4 cup Parmesan cheese

Saute onion and mushrooms in butter until tender. Heat milk until warm. Add eggs to spaghetti after it is drained. Mix all other ingredients and serve.

Peggy Harrington

Spaghetti Pizza

4 ounces thin spaghetti, cooked
  and drained
2 tablespoons melted butter
1 (15 ounce) can tomato sauce
1 medium onion, chopped and
  sauteed in 3 tablespoons butter

1/2 pound grated Swiss cheese
1/2 pound sliced or grated Mozzarella
  cheese
1 (3.5 ounce) package sliced pepperoni
1 large can sliced mushrooms, drained
Pinch of basil and oregano

Boil pepperoni for 5 minutes, drain. In a 2 quart oblong baking dish combine cooked spaghetti and 2 tablespoons melted butter. In order, top with half of tomato sauce, Swiss cheese, pepperoni, and Mozzarella cheese and all of mushrooms, sauteed onions, basil and oregano. Repeat using remaining ingredients. Bake at 350° about 30 minutes or until bubbly. Serves 6. May be made day ahead and refrigerated.

Mrs. George W. Taylor

Creole Liver

1 pound calves liver, sliced
4 slices onion
½ green pepper, chopped
1 pint tomatoes, chopped

1/8 teaspoon red pepper
1½ teaspoons salt
1/8 teaspoon chili powder
3 slices bacon

Cut bacon small and fry until crisp. Dip sliced liver in flour and brown in bacon fat. Add remaining ingredients. Cover and simmer for 25 minutes. Serve with fluffy white rice. Liver may be diced, if preferred. Serves 4.

Barbara Harvey

Grillades

7 pounds veal (I use baby beef round
    steak run through tenderizer)
½ cup bacon grease
½ cup flour
3 medium onions, chopped
3 cloves garlic, minced

2-3 bell peppers, chopped
½ cup parsley
3 teaspoons salt
1½ teaspoons pepper
2 quarts water
Tabasco to taste

Brown meat in grease. Lift out and brown flour in same grease. Saute onions and green pepper in above. Add other ingredients and simmer about two hours. Serves 14. Freezes well. Serve grillades with cheese grits, scrambled eggs, French bread, and green salad for a traditional New Orleans brunch.

Mrs. Donnie Riley

Veal Scaloppine a la Francais

1½ pounds veal, pounded thin
    and cut into small pieces
2 eggs, beaten
Flour
¼ cup butter

Salt and pepper
Garlic powder
Fresh parsley, chopped
½ cup white wine
Mushrooms (optional)

Dip veal in beaten egg, then flour, and egg again. Brown in melted butter in large skillet. Turn once. Add salt and pepper, garlic powder, and a lot of chopped parsley. Continue browning and add wine and sliced mushrooms. Cover and simmer 15 minutes. Serves 4.

Mrs. William J. Juliana

Herbed Leg of Lamb

6 to 8 pound leg of lamb
½ cup Dijon mustard
1½ teaspoons soy sauce
1 clove garlic, mashed

1 teaspoon ground rosemary
Pinch ginger
2 tablespoons olive oil

Preheat oven to 325°. Place leg of lamb on rack in roasting pan. Prepare mustard coating by combining mustard, soy sauce, garlic, rosemary, and ginger in mixing bowl. Add olive oil a few drops at a time, and beat well after each addition. With basting brush, paint outside of lamb evenly. Roast uncovered in oven for 35-40 minutes per pound. Baste several times while roasting. Mustard coating also good on a baked ham.

Mrs. Donnie Riley

Shish Kebobs

2 pounds boneless lamb or veal
1/4 cup fresh lemon juice
1 teaspoon salt
1/2 teaspoon oregano
1/2 cup olive oil
1 large onion, sliced
3 cloves garlic, pressed

1 bunch parsley, finely chopped
10 bay leaves
Lemon wedges
Small boiled onions
Green pepper, cut in chunks
Cherry tomatoes
Mushroom caps

Trim all fat from meat and cut in 2 inch cubes. In bowl large enough to hold meat, beat lemon juice, salt, and oregano. Whisk in oil. Stir in onion, garlic, parsley, bay leaves, and meat. Toss thoroughly with hands, cover. Marinate overnight in refrigerator. Drain meat, and string it on skewers, alternating with lemons, onions, mushroom caps, and pepper chunks. Put tomatoes on ends. Cook over grill or broil in oven to desired doneness. Turn once during cooking.

Mrs. Kosta Vlahos

Lou's Stuffed Pork Tenderloin

1 1/2 pounds ground pork tenderloin
1 teaspoon each salt, pepper
1 egg white
3 pods garlic, ground
3 tablespoons Grey Poupon mustard
12 ounces fresh mushrooms, chopped
1 large white onion, chopped

2 1/4 tablespoons olive oil
2 (10 ounce) frozen chopped spinach cooked and drained well
2/3 to 1 cup Italian breadcrumbs
1 (10 1/4 ounce) Smuckers low sugar apricot spread

Have on hand 1 jelly roll pan and Saran wrap
Mix ground pork, salt, pepper, egg white, garlic and mustard. Place in freezer until lightly frozen. (About 30 minutes) Saute mushrooms and onions in olive oil. Stir in spinach and breadcrumbs. Place in freezer to cool–not freeze. Place Saran wrap inside jelly roll pan. Take pork mixture from freezer and spread in jelly roll pan, patting well, leaving a one inch border around all sides. Next fill with spinach mixture. Gently roll mixture up, removing Saran wrap, and seal ends together. Bake at 400° for 20 minutes. Reduce oven to 350° and glaze with the apricot spread. Cook an additional 25 to 30 minutes.

Susan Oustalet

Barbeque Ham

½ cup oil	2 teaspoons soy sauce
½ cup wine vinegar	3 bay leaves
½ cup garlic vinegar	2 cloves garlic
⅔ cup brown sugar	1½″ thick center cut ham steak

Mix all ingredients in a saucepan. Boil for 3 minutes. Pour over 1½″ thick center cut ham steak in an ovenproof glass dish. Marinate overnight, turning at least once. Place on grill and baste with marinade. Do not overcook.

Mrs. Mike Achee

Ham Loaf

2 pounds center cut ham, ground	2 beaten eggs
1½ pounds lean pork, ground	1 cup milk
Salt and pepper	1 cup cracker meal

Mix all ingredients and shape into loaf. Bake at 350° for 1½ hours. After 30 minutes of baking, add the following sauce:

1½ cups dark brown sugar	½ cup apple cider vinegar
1 tablespoon dry mustard	½ cup water

Mix sauce ingredients and cook 5 minutes. Pour over loaf and continue cooking for remaining hour.

Mrs. Kenneth Layton

Irish Baked Ham

3-5 pound uncooked ham	20 whole cloves
Water (to cover ham)	½ cup brown sugar
Apple cider (enough to cover ham in a Dutch oven) (room temperature)	1 teaspoon mustard

Cover ham with cold water and bring slowly to a boil. Discard water and replace with cider. Bring this just to a boil and lower the heat, keeping it barely simmering for 20 minutes to the pound. Remove from heat and allow to stand in the cider for 30 minutes. Take out the ham, skin it and score the fat with a sharp knife in a diamond pattern. Stud the ham with the whole cloves. Mix the sugar and mustard and rub well into the surface of the ham. Bake in a preheated oven for 10 minutes per pound, at 400°.

Dixie Boyd

Red Beans and Sausage

6 tablespoons butter
3 medium yellow onions, peeled and
   thinly sliced
1 large green pepper, finely chopped
1 clove garlic, minced
3 (15¼ ounce) cans kidney beans,
   drained
2 pounds "little" pork sausages

2 cups red wine
1 bay leaf
2 cloves
3 tablespoons tomato paste
Salt
Freshly ground pepper

Thoroughly butter a 3 quart casserole, set aside. Melt remaining butter in large skillet. Add onions and green pepper and cook over moderate heat for 5 minutes. Stir in garlic and then combine with beans. Meanwhile, cook the sausages according to package directions. Bring the wine to boiling point with bay leaf and cloves. Stir in tomato paste, discard bay leaf and cloves. Set aside 6 cooked sausages. Put ⅓ of the bean mixture into buttered casserole. Sprinkle with salt and pepper. Add half of the remaining sausages, then another layer of ⅓ of beans, second half of sausages, and remaining ⅓ of beans. Place 6 sausages on top of beans in spoke design. Strain the hot wine mixture over the top. Place in oven and bake at 350° for 1 hour. Serves 6. Long cooking improves the taste. Reheats well.

Mrs. Martin Miazza

Sunday Omelet

½ pound good quality pork sausage
2 cups frozen French fries, diced
Chopped green onions
Grated sharp cheddar cheese

3 well-beaten eggs
Salt and pepper to taste
2 tablespoons oil

In small black iron skillet, fry sausage till done. In large black iron skillet cook potatoes in oil until slightly brown. Lower heat and add cooked sausage and green onions and stir. Sprinkle cheese on top and then pour eggs over entire mixture in skillet. Tilt skillet till eggs settle evenly, and use spatula to lift omelet and let uncooked egg run to bottom. Be certain fire is low. When egg seems set, fold omelet over. You may want to turn it once to insure doneness. This is great after church on Sunday!

Ann Barker Matthews

Scotch Eggs

4 hard-boiled eggs
1 egg, beaten

1 pound sausage
Cracker meal or bread crumbs

Peel eggs, then dip in beaten egg. Wrap each egg in a thick coat of sausage meat. Dip again in egg. Roll in cracker meal. Fry in hot deep fat (375°) for 5-6 minutes. Drain well on paper towel. Excellent for a brunch. May be made the night before and fried just before time to serve.

Gay Graves

Sweet & Tangy Sauce

18 ounces orange marmalade
5 tablespoons horseradish

5 tablespoons Creole mustard

Combine ingredients and mix well. Use to spice up ham, turkey, sliced beef or sandwiches or dip for fried shrimp.   *Dr. Gordon Stanfield*

High Plains Barbeque Spice

1½ to 1¾ ounces ground cumin
¼ cup each salt and pepper
3½ tablespoons celery salt

½ cup butter or margarine, melted for
    basting (optional)

Mix all dry ingredients. Store in sealed container. Sprinkle heavily on chicken, ribs, or pork in preparation for grilling on the barbecue. Baste with melted butter while on grill.   *Bill Boyd*

Orange Barbeque Marinade

3 ounce can frozen orange juice
    concentrate
3 tablespoons brown sugar
1 tablespoon soy sauce

⅓ cup catsup
2 tablespoons lemon juice
½ teaspoon onion powder

Combine ingredients in a large zip-top plastic bag. Seal and mix. Use to marinate shrimp or chicken over night in refrigerator. Baste with marinade when grilling.
                    Mrs. John Edgar Johnson III

Barbeque Marinade

⅓ cup vinegar
¼ cup catsup
2 tablespoons cooking oil
2 tablespoons soy sauce
1 tablespoon Worcestershire sauce

1 teaspoon prepared mustard
1 teaspoon salt
¼ teaspoon pepper
¼ teaspoon garlic powder

Sprinkle a 4 pound roast with monosodium glutamate (and tenderizer for less expensive cuts of meat). Mix all ingredients well. Pour over meat, turning once or twice. Use to baste while grilling. This can be used in the oven as well as the grill.
                    Mrs. William M. Rainey

Strawberry Glaze For Baked Ham

1 cup strawberry jelly
1 teaspoon dry mustard

½ teaspoon ground allspice
2 tablespoons vinegar

Combine all ingredients. Beat with fork until foamy. Baste ham with glaze during the last 30 minutes of baking.   *Mrs. Gerald Phillips*

Jezebel Sauce

1 small jar prepared mustard
1 jar horseradish

1 (18 ounce) glass apple jelly
1 (18 ounce) glass pineapple preserves

Combine all ingredients. Refrigerate. Delicious with ham, pork, and roast beef. It is also excellent to give for Christmas.   *Margaret Murdock*

Desserts

Desserts

Fool-Proof Apple Dumplings

6 to 8 small apples
2 cups all-purpose flour
1 teaspoon salt
2 teaspoons baking powder

¾ cup Crisco
½ cup milk
Sugar, cinnamon and nutmeg
Butter

Wash, pare, and core apples. Sift flour, salt, and baking powder. Cut in shortening. Add milk all at once and stir until flour is just moistened. Roll the dough to ¼ inch thick. Cut in 5 to 6 inch squares and place one apple in each square. Sprinkle generously with sugar, cinnamon, and nutmeg. Place ½ teaspoon butter on apple. Fold corners and seal edges together. Place 1 inch apart in greased baking dish. Pour on sauce. Bake at 375⁰ for 35 minutes. Serve with hot cream.

SAUCE

2 cups sugar
2 cups water
¼ teaspoon cinnamon

¼ teaspoon nutmeg
¼ cup butter

Combine sugar, water, cinnamon, and nutmeg. Simmer 5 minutes. Add butter and stir until melted. Pour over dumplings.

Mrs. Robert A. Mitchell

Pommes a la Poele

6 to 8 apples
½ cup sugar

4 to 6 tablespoons butter
4 to 6 tablespoons rum

Peel and core apples. Slice into eighths. Mix apples in large bowl with sugar. Melt butter in heavy skillet and add apples. Do not stir. Bake at 350⁰ until apples are tender and sugar has caramelized somewhat. Remove from oven and sprinkle with rum to taste. If apples are tart, sugar may be added accordingly.

Evelyn P. Floyd

The monarch butterfly arrives by the thousands each fall on the Mississippi Coast. This spectacle enhances the beauty of the entire coast as the butterflies pause for a few weeks during their long trek from Canada to Mexico, where they will spend the winter months. This monarch rests briefly on a marigold found in the garden at Beauvoir

Photograph by Vernon Matthews

My Grandmother's Banana Pudding

5 to 6 bananas, sliced
1 package vanilla wafers
1½ cups sugar
¼ cup flour
4 eggs, separated
2 cups milk

1 can evaporated milk
Dash salt
1 teaspoon vanilla extract
¼ cup sugar
1 teaspoon cream of tartar

Layer bananas and vanilla wafers in large baking dish. Mix sugar, flour, and egg yolks. Add milk, evaporated milk, salt, and vanilla extract. Beat with mixer. Cook over low heat, stirring constantly until thickened. Pour over bananas. Add salt, sugar and cream of tartar to egg whites and whip to make meringue. Top pudding with meringue and broil until brown. Refrigerate.

Mrs. Edward Gaines

Banana Split Dessert

2 cups vanilla wafers, crushed
1 box confectioner's sugar
2 sticks oleo
2 eggs
5 to 6 bananas, split lengthwise

1 large can crushed pineapple, drained
1 large carton Cool Whip
1 cup chopped pecans
1 small bottle cherries, chopped

Mix vanilla wafers and 1 stick of melted oleo. Press into a 9 x 15 inch pan. Make and add layers in the following order. Combine confectioner's sugar, eggs, and 1 stick oleo and beat with mixer on high speed for 15 minutes. Smooth on crust. Layer bananas, pineapple, and Cool Whip. Sprinkle with pecans and cherries. Refrigerate until chilled. Serves about 20.

Hazel Herrington
Mrs. Anthony Ruggier

Satsuma Ice

8 large tree-ripened satsumas or
    more smaller ones
2 tablespoons lemon juice

Red food coloring
2 cups water
1 cup sugar

Cut a slice off tops of satsumas, and juice carefully on a reamer, preserving shells. Work the membranes loose from the skins and put the shells in the freezer. Dissolve sugar in water and boil 5 minutes. Stir in the fruit juice and cool. Tint with a drop or two of red food coloring. Pour into refrigerator trays and freeze until mushy. Transfer to a bowl and beat with mixer; then return to trays and freeze solid. Heap the frozen mixture into the satsuma shells. May be wrapped and kept in freezer for several weeks. Tangerines or oranges may be used the same way. Adjust sweetness to taste. To be used as a sorbet (to be served with main course or between courses).

Ricky Graves

French Pears

8 fresh, ripe, large pears
8 ounces cream cheese

½ to 1 cup chopped pecans
2 tablespoons to ¼ cup powdered sugar

Carefully peel pears. Slice in half lengthwise and remove core. Do not break pear in the process. Set aside. Mix remaining ingredients according to taste. The mixture should have enough nuts to look pretty and provide enough crunch and enough powdered sugar to be slightly sweetened. Carefully stuff mixture into each pear half. Put stuffed pear halves together to form each whole pear again and wrap individually with plastic wrap. Store in covered container in refrigerator until serving time, preferably serve within 12 hours. To serve, place one pear in stemmed sherbet glass, pour warmed chocolate sauce over top, and sprinkle with crushed pecans, if desired.

CHOCOLATE SAUCE

1 stick good margarine
4 squares semi-sweet baking
   chocolate

3 cups sugar
1 large can evaporated milk
1 teaspoon vanilla

In double boiler melt margarine and chocolate. Gradually add sugar. Stir constantly and blend well. Add canned milk. Bend well. Cook 10 minutes or until chocolate forms soft ball (has some body) when small amount is dropped in cup of cool water. Remove from heat. Stir in 1 teaspoon vanilla. Cool. Serve warm over pears. Store in refrigerator.

Mrs. Jack Kornmeyer,
Washington, D.C.

Biscuit Tortoni

¼ cup sugar
½ cup milk
2 egg yolks, slightly beaten
1/8 teaspoon salt

½ cup crushed almond macaroons
2 teaspoons sherry
¼ teaspoon vanilla
1 cup heavy cream, whipped

Combine sugar, milk, egg yolks, and salt in heavy saucepan and heat stirring until slightly thickened. Cool. Add macaroons, sherry and vanilla. Fold into whipped cream. Pour into paper souffle cups and freeze. Should not be frozen too hard when served. May be topped with maraschino cherries cut in flower shape.

ALMOND MACAROONS

6 ounces blanched almonds, finely
   ground
⅔ cup sugar

2 egg whites
1/8 teaspoon salt

Work almonds and sugar together, then add egg whites one at a time. Add salt and work thoroughly together. Form into small balls, bake on unglazed paper in 300° oven for 30 minutes or until very lightly browned. Turn paper over immediately and dampen thoroughly. Pull macaroons off paper. Let cool and dry before crumbling for Biscuit Tortoni.

Louise Graves

Brandy Velvet

1/2 cup brandy
1/4 cup strong cold coffee
1/4 cup chocolate syrup

1 quart coffee ice cream
Additional chocolate syrup for topping

Combine brandy, coffee, and 1/4 cup chocolate syrup. Put in blender with ice cream and whirl until just blended. Pour in tall glasses. Keep in freezer until ready to serve. Top with additional chocolate syrup. If desired, turn mixture into pan and freeze.

Mrs. Donald Sutter

Sherry Trifle

3 or 4 stale lady fingers
1 tablespoon strawberry jam mixed
   with 1/4 or 1/2 cup hot water
1 small package strawberry gelatin
1 to 2 tablespoons sherry

Sweetened fresh or frozen strawberries
  or a mixture of fruits as peaches,
  cherries, fruit cocktail (reserve liquid)
Custard
Sweetened whipped cream

Crumble lady fingers in a large bowl. Pour strawberry jam and hot water mixture over lady fingers. Dissolve gelatin in 1 1/2 cups liquid (reserved fruit juices and water). Mix approximately 1/3 of the gelatin mixture with sherry and pour over the lady fingers. Congeal. Add fruit on top and pour on the remainder of the gelatin. Congeal again. Make the custard and when cool but still runny, pour over gelatin. Chill. Just before serving decorate with whipped cream, nuts, and strawberries.

CUSTARD

1/2 cup sugar
2 tablespoons flour
1/4 teaspoon salt

2 cups milk
3 egg yolks
1 teaspoon vanilla

Combine sugar, flour and salt in top of double boiler. Stir in milk. Cook over boiling water stirring constantly until thickened. Cook uncovered an additional 15 minutes stirring occasionally. Beat egg yolks. Add small amount of hot milk mixture to egg yolks, then gradually add egg yolk mixture to milk mixture stirring constantly. Cook 5 minutes continuing to stir. Remove from heat. Add vanilla.

Christine King,
Birmingham, England

Syllabub

1 cup whipping cream
1 cup milk
1 cup white wine or white
  grape juice

1/4 teaspoon grated orange rind
2 to 3 tablespoons frozen orange
  juice concentrate
Nutmeg

Chill glasses. Whip all ingredients except nutmeg until foamy. Pour into glasses. Top with sprinkle of nutmeg. Refrigerate until served.

Mrs. Adron Swango

Cold Zabaglione

...lks
... sugar
... Marsala wine

½ teaspoon vanilla
Grated rind of ½ lemon
1 cup heavy cream, whipped

In top of double boiler over hot water, beat the yolks and sugar until thick and pale in color. Gradually add the wine and as soon as it forms soft mounds, remove from fire and beat until cool. When at room temperature, add rind and vanilla. Place pan in larger bowl filled with cracked ice. Beat until thoroughly chilled. Fold in whipped cream. Pour into individual serving dishes and chill until served. May be served plain or topped with frozen fruit.

Mrs. Victor T. Bazzone

Bread Pudding with Rum Sauce

6 slices day old bread
2 tablespoons plus ½ cup sugar
1 teaspoon cinnamon
4 eggs

2 cups milk
2 tablespoons melted butter
½ cup seedless raisins
1 teaspoon vanilla extract

Break bread in small pieces in baking dish (about 1½ quart size). Sprinkle cinnamon over bread and add raisins and melted butter. Lightly toast bread mixture in 350⁰ oven. Add mixture of eggs, sugar, milk and vanilla. Bake about 30 minutes at 350⁰ or until set. Serve with rum sauce. Serves 8.

RUM SAUCE

2 cups milk
½ stick butter
½ cup sugar
1 tablespoon nutmeg

1 tablespoon vanilla
Rum to taste
1 tablespoon oil
2 tablespoons flour

Place milk, butter and sugar in saucepan; let come to a boil. Thicken with roux made of the oil and flour. Remove from fire; add nutmeg, vanilla and rum to taste. Serve over pudding.

Mary Mahoney

Built in 1737, Mary Mahoney's Old French House Restaurant and Slave Quarters Lounge in Biloxi is one of the Coast's most popular places for dining in Old World tradition. Diners will also enjoy the courtyard and gardens with a magnificent live oak estimated to be over three hundred years of age.

Honey Custard

3 eggs
½ cup honey
Dash salt

1 teaspoon vanilla extract
2½ cups milk
Ground cinnamon

In medium bowl beat together eggs, honey, salt and vanilla. Heat milk until a tiny rim of bubbles forms around edge of pan. Slowly stir hot milk into egg-honey mixture, beating constantly with wire whisk while pouring. Pour egg-milk mixture into 6 custard cups. Sprinkle with cinnamon. Place cups in baking pan. Pour very hot water into pan until 1 inch deep. Bake at 350° for 40-45 minutes or until a knife inserted halfway between center and edge of custard comes out clean. Remove cups from water. Serve warm or cold.

Mrs. Donnie Riley

Flan

¾ cup granulated sugar	*1 teaspoon vanilla*
1 can condensed milk	*1/8 teaspoon salt*
3 cans whole milk	*Nutmeg*
5 eggs, beaten until well blended	

Caramelize sugar by heating slowly in heavy pot until melted. Pour quickly into a 2 quart baking dish and set aside. Mix condensed milk, whole milk, eggs, vanilla, and salt. Pour over caramelized sugar in baking dish. Sprinkle top with nutmeg. Place in larger baking pan filled with warm water and bake at 325° for 1 hour or until knife comes out clean. Serves 10-12.

Mrs. Arthur V. Hays

Garnette's Bread Pudding

Extra margarine	*3 tablespoons vanilla extract*
4 (½ pints) whipping cream	*3 tablespoons margarine cut in*
1 pint half and half	*¼ sections*
2 eggs	*16 slices white bread torn in*
3 cups sugar	*¼ sections*
4 dashes each cinnamon, nutmeg and allspice	

Preheat oven 350°. Prepare 9 x 13 pan with extra margarine. Mix thoroughly whipping cream, half and half, eggs and sugar. Add spices, vanilla and margarine. DO NOT OVER STIR. Add bread last. Add ½ cup milk if it appears too dry. Bake at 350° for 1 hour.

Garnette Wetzel

Sherry Cups

4 egg yolks	*1 cup chopped nuts*
1 cup sugar	*1 pint whipping cream*
½ cup sherry	*Coconut macaroons, crumbled*

Cook eggs, sugar, and sherry in top of double boiler until thickened. Cool. Whip whipping cream. Fold whipped cream and nuts into egg mixture. Place in paper muffin cups. Top with crumbled macaroons and freeze.

Millie Ross

Chocolate-Butterscotch Ice Cream Squares

1 cup sifted all-purpose flour
1/4 cup quick-cooking rolled oats
1/4 cup brown sugar
1/2 cup butter or margarine

1/2 cup chopped nuts
1 (12 ounce) jar butterscotch or caramel
   ice cream topping
1 quart chocolate ice cream

Combine flour, oats, and brown sugar; cut in butter or margarine until mixture resembles coarse crumbs. Stir in nuts. Pat mixture in 13 x 9 x 2 inch baking pan. Bake at 400° for 15 minutes. Stir while still warm to crumble; cool. Spread half the crumbs in 9 x 9 x 2 inch baking pan; drizzle about half the topping over crumbs in pan. Stir ice cream to soften; spoon over crumbs and topping. Drizzle with remaining topping and top with crumbs. Freeze. Garnish with whipped cream and cherry if desired. Serves 8.

Mrs. Alben N. Hopkins

Cream Cheese Ice Cream

1 cup evaporated milk
2 pints Creole cream cheese
1 cup sugar

1/2 teaspoon vanilla extract
1 egg white, stiffly beaten

Blend milk and cream cheese. Add sugar, vanilla. Fold in egg white. Pour into chilled tray and freeze.

Mrs. Edmund Crane

Lemon Ice Cream I

2 cups sugar
4 eggs
1 (13 ounce) can evaporated milk
1 teaspoon flour

1 teaspoon pure lemon flavoring
1 teaspoon pure vanilla flavoring
Dash salt
Milk

Whip 1 cup sugar with eggs in blender or mixer. Add evaporated milk and whip well. Add flour, salt, and flavoring and whip. Add the other cup of sugar and whip. Pour into freezer can and finish filling to fill line with milk. If more color is desired, add a drop or two of yellow food coloring. If imitation flavoring is used, use 1 tablespoon instead of 1 teaspoon. Freeze according to freezer directions.

Mrs. Ruth Stringfellow

Lemon Ice Cream II

Rind of one lemon, finely grated
1 cup sugar
1/8 teaspoon salt

3 tablespoons lemon juice
2 cups half and half cream

Combine rind, juice, and sugar, and stir to mix. Gradually stir in cream and salt, mixing well. Pour into an ice cube tray and freeze for an hour or so, until solid on the edges and mushy in the middle. Stir well with a wooden spoon. Cover and continue to freeze until firm. This recipe is so flavorful that a little bit goes a long way.

Rob Barber

Low Calorie Frozen Lemon Custard

1 egg, separated
1/3 cup sugar
1/4 teaspoon grated lemon rind

3 tablespoons lemon juice
1/3 cup water
1/2 cup nonfat dry milk

Mix egg yolk, sugar, lemon rind, and 2 tablespoons lemon juice. In electric mixer beat remaining lemon juice, water, egg white and milk at high speed until stiff. Gradually beat egg yolk mixture into egg white mixture. Spoon into refrigerator tray and freeze without stirring. There are approximately 508 calories in entire recipe.

Gay Graves

Mamma Pott's Peppermint Ice Cream

1 pound King Leo Peppermint Sticks
   or good quality peppermint
1 1/2 quarts whole milk

1 cup sugar
1 cup whipping cream
2 cups half and half

Crush peppermint sticks with hammer in clean dish towel. Melt peppermint in 1 cup milk in double boiler, (or in microwave on low power) stirring often until dissolved. Stir sugar in mixture to melt. Add remaining milk and creams. Freeze in ice cream freezer turning until hard. Serve with Chocolate Sauce.

Anna Stanfield

Buttermilk Sherbet

2 cups buttermilk
1 cup sugar
1 (8 ounce) can crushed pineapple,
   undrained

1 tablespoon vanilla extract
2 egg whites

Combine buttermilk, sugar, pineapple and vanilla mixing well. Place in an airtight container and freeze mixture until slushy. Place egg whites in medium size mixing bowl and beat until stiff but not dry. Add buttermilk mixture and beat well. Pour into airtight freezer container and return to freezer. Freeze until firm. Yield about 1 quart.

Mrs. Dan M. Russell, Jr.

Regal Chocolate Sauce

1/2 cup lite corn syrup
1 cup sugar
1 cup water

3 (1 ounce) squares unsweetened
   chocolate
1 teaspoon good real vanilla
1 cup evaporated milk

Combine corn syrup, sugar, and water and cook to a soft ball stage (235° on candy thermometer). Remove from heat. Add chocolate stirring, until melted. Add vanilla. Slowly add milk, mixing thoroughly. Cool and store covered in refrigerator. Yield 2 cups. Doubles easily.

Missy Kennedy Allen

Ruby Fire Over Diamond Ice

¼ cup sugar
1 tablespoon cornstarch
⅓ cup tangerine or orange juice
3 cups fresh strawberry halves

3 tablespoons Cointreau or any
* orange flavored liqueur*
1 quart French vanilla ice cream
Whipped cream (optional)

In a chafing dish, skillet, or flambe pan, mix cornstarch and sugar. Gradually add tangerine or orange juice stirring constantly so it doesn't become lumpy. Place pan on direct heat, stirring constantly. When the mixture begins to thicken, add strawberries. Mix the strawberries in the orange mixture until well immersed. Heat the liqueur in a side pan; when warm, ignite and pour flaming liqueur over strawberries. As the strawberries flame, spoon mixture over ice cream balls in serving dishes. To make ice cream balls, place balls on cookie sheet and return to freezer. When ready to serve, place ball in serving dish. Whipped cream may be added to the top of each serving if desired.

Vern Lanegrasse

Strawberries Chantilly

1 quart fresh strawberries
½ cup plus 4 tablespoons powdered
* sugar*

2 tablespoons rum
2 egg whites
Whipped cream

Wash and stem berries. Cut berries in half and cover with powdered sugar (½ cup) and rum. Chill 30 minutes. Whisk egg whites until stiff, adding 4 tablespoons powdered sugar. Fold in chilled berries. Serve in sherbert glasses. Top with whipped cream.

Mrs. Adron Swango

Strawberries-Cherries Jubilee

1 quart strawberries
3 tablespoons granulated sugar
1½ quarts vanilla ice cream

1 (1 pound 13 ounce) can pitted
* Bing cherries*
¾ cup currant jelly
½ cup brandy

Wash and hull strawberries and sprinkle with sugar. Refrigerate. Make and freeze 8 ice cream balls. Drain strawberries and cherries. In chafing dish over direct heat, melt jelly stirring constantly. Add drained fruits and heat slowly, constantly stirring till simmering. Pour warmed brandy into center of fruits. Do not stir. Heat undisturbed for 1-2 minutes. Light carefully; immediately spoon flaming fruits over ice cream balls in individual dishes.

Gay Graves

Wine Jelly

2 packages peach or apricot gelatin
1¼ cups juice from canned blue plums
¼ cup juice from canned peaches
½ cup dry sherry, Madeira or Marsala

10 to 12 blue plums, pitted and split
2 cups cold ginger ale
½ pint whipping cream (optional)

Strain through cheesecloth the juice from peaches and plums. Put in saucepan and add sherry. Heat to boiling and dissolve gelatin in boiling juices. When dissolved, stir in cold ginger ale and set aside. When cool, refrigerate until slightly thickened. Take plums and place in design on ring mold. Carefully pour in gelatin mixture so as not to disturb design. Chill for several hours. Unmold and garnish with whipped cream if desired. A perfect ending to a heavy meal.

Mrs. Victor T. Bazzone

Date Meringues

1 cup dates, chopped
1 cup chopped nuts
Flour

3 egg whites, room temperature
1 cup sugar

Flour nuts and dates so that they won't stick together. Beat egg whites until stiff. Add sugar gradually. Fold in nuts and dates. Line rectangular shallow pan with brown paper or foil and grease. Put meringue in pan and bake at 275⁰ for 1 hour. While warm cut into squares. Serve warm or at room temperature with whipped cream or topping.

Mrs. H. H. Albritton

Peach Supreme

16 canned peach halves, drained
2 egg yolks, beaten
Whipping cream

24 coconut macaroons, crushed
½ cup oleo, softened
4 tablespoons sugar

Mix together the egg yolks, macaroons, oleo, and sugar. Put peach halves in shallow baking pan. Put a large tablespoon of macaroon filling in each peach. Bake at 325⁰ for 30 minutes. Serve warm with whipped cream. Serves 8.

Mrs. Bert Allen

Pineapple-Peach Melba

1 quart vanilla ice cream, softened
1 (8½ ounce) can crushed pineapple,
  well drained

3 fresh peaches
¼ cup brandy
1 (10 ounce) package frozen raspberries,
  thawed

In chilled large bowl of mixer beat ice cream at low speed until mushy. Quickly stir in pineapple until well mixed. Turn mixture into 8 x 8 x 2 inch pan, cover with foil and freeze until firm. Wash and peel peaches. Cut in half and remove pits. Place in medium bowl and sprinkle with brandy. Press raspberries and juice through sieve to make a puree. Pour over peaches. Refrigerate covered for several hours or overnight. To serve use a slotted utensil to remove peach halves to individual serving dish. Place a scoop of pineapple ice cream in center of each and spoon raspberry sauce over top.

Gay Graves

Meringue Dessert

3 egg whites
1 teaspoon cream of tartar
1 cup sugar
1 teaspoon vanilla

1 cup pecans, chopped
18 saltine crackers, broken into bits
1 small jar pineapple preserves
1/2 pint whipping cream, whipped

Beat egg whites until very dry. Add cream of tartar, sugar, and vanilla. Combine. Fold in pecans and crackers. Bake in a 9 x 9 ungreased pan for 20 minutes in 375° oven. Cool. Then top first with layer of pineapple preserves and then with layer of whipped cream. Sprinkle with coconut. Refrigerate. Serves 9-12. May be frozen for a few weeks.

Mrs. Lorne A. Davis

Microwave Pralines

1 box brown sugar
1 small container whipping cream

2 tablespoons butter or margarine
1 cup pecans

Mix brown sugar and whipping cream together in a large microwave safe mixing bowl. Cook in microwave for 8 minutes. Take out and stir. Place back in microwave for 5 minutes. Take out, stir in butter and pecans until mixture begins to lose gloss. Spoon quickly onto wax paper. Let stand until candy sets and remove from wax paper. Makes about 30 pieces when dropped by tablespoon.

Debbie Daughtrey

Divinity

3 cups granulated sugar
1/2 cup white corn syrup
2/3 cup water
1/4 teaspoon salt

2 egg whites
1 teaspoon vanilla
1 cup chopped pecans
Butter

Boil sugar, syrup, water and salt together until syrup forms hard ball when dropped in cold water, (about 13 minutes) or if using candy thermometer cook to 270°. Just before removing syrup from stove, place unbeaten egg whites in large bowl and beat until eggs are stiff but not dry. Slowly pour the hot syrup over the egg white, beating while adding syrup, being careful not to pour too much at a time, or egg whites will curdle. After the syrup is all added, continue to beat until mixture becomes stiff. Add vanilla and pecans and continue to beat until mixture holds shape. Drop by teaspoonfuls on a buttered surface, or pour mixture into a buttered dish and cut into squares when cool.

"Aunt Jack" Shaw

Pistachio Cake

1 package white cake mix
1 (3 ounce) package Royal Pistachio
   instant pudding
4 eggs

1 cup orange juice
1/2 cup oil
1 small can Hershey Chocolate syrup
Powdered sugar

Add all ingredients except syrup at one time and beat 4 minutes. Pour 2/3 of batter in a well greased spring form pan (not a tube pan). Mix remaining batter with 1 small can Hershey Chocolate syrup and pour over top of other mixture. Bake 1 hour at 350° or until done. Sprinkle with powdered sugar while hot. Cool 2 hours before removing from pan. Do not invert cake.

Sue Dalto

Spiced Pecans

1 cup sugar
½ cup water
¾ teaspoon salt

½ teaspoon cinnamon
1 teaspoon vanilla
1 quart pecans

Cook mixture (first five ingredients) four minutes or until thick. Remove from stove and immediately stir in 1 quart pecans. Cool on wax paper.

Rachel J. Price

Raw Apple Cake

2 cups sugar
1½ cups Wesson oil
3 eggs, beaten
3 cups plain flour
1 teaspoon salt

1½ teaspoons baking soda
1½ teaspoons vanilla
3 cups raw, unpeeled, diced apples
1 cup walnuts, chopped
¾ cup coconut

Mix sugar and oil. Add eggs and mix again. Combine flour, salt, soda, and add to above mixture. Add vanilla, coconut, apples, and nuts. Bake at 350° in greased tube pan for about one hour until done.

New River Inn,
Blowing Rock, North Carolina

Almond Crunch Cake

2 cups Swansdown cake flour
2 cups sugar
1 cup Crisco

6 eggs
½ teaspoon salt
2 tablespoons almond extract

Add all ingredients and blend with electric mixer at low speed. Turn to high speed and beat 12 minutes. Put in greased and lightly floured tube pan. Bake at 350° for 1 hour.

Mrs. Edward R. Gaines

Stacy's Cupcakes

1 package chocolate cake mix
8 ounces cream cheese
½ cup sugar

Dash of salt
1 egg
1 package chocolate chips

Mix cake mix according to directions. Cream sugar and cream cheese; add salt, egg, and chocolate chips. Fill cup cake pans ⅔ full with cake mixture. Drop 1 tablespoon cream cheese mixture in middle of batter in cupcake pans and bake at 350° for 25 minutes. It's such a nice surprise to have the frosting in the middle!

June Hearn

Company Cheesecake
(Crowd Pleaser Size)
CRUST

2 cups graham cracker crumbs   ½ cup melted butter
½ cup granulated sugar

Mix crumbs and sugar. Mix in melted butter. Line sides and bottom of spring form pan with mixture. Refrigerate.

CAKE

40 ounces cream cheese   1½ teaspoons vanilla
1¾ cups granulated sugar   5 eggs
3 tablespoons plain flour   2 egg yolks (or use total of 6 eggs)
¼ teaspoon salt   ¼ cup whipping cream
3 tablespoons lemon juice

Beat cheese until fluffy. Mix sugar, flour, and salt and gradually blend into cheese, keeping mixture smooth. Add lemon juice and vanilla. Add eggs (and egg yolks) one at a time, beating well after each. Stir in ¼ cup cream. Pour into crust. Bake at 475° for 15 minutes, reduce heat to 225° and bake for additional hour. Turn off heat and let stand for 15 minutes with oven door cracked. Remove from oven and cool. Remove sides of pan and refrigerate. Serves 14-16.

Mrs. William G. Wise

Regina's Cheese Cake

This procedure is done in 3 separate bowls.

BOWL 1: *2 eggs (whites only, beat until stiff)*
Add 6 tablespoons sugar and ½ teaspoon vanilla

BOWL 2: *8 ounces cream cheese, softened and creamed*

BOWL 3: *2 egg yolks, 1 teaspoon lemon juice. Beat until fluffy.*

Combine all three mixtures. Mix gently until well combined. Pour into graham cracker pie shell. Bake 20-25 minutes at 350°. Cool completely.

TOPPING

½ pint sour cream   1 teaspoon vanilla extract
¼ cup sugar

Blend ingredients by hand. Pour on cool pie. Bake at 350° for 5 minutes only. Chill. Serves 8-10. This recipe is delightful for freezing. Thaw in warm oven for unexpected guests.

Mrs. Duane Hanks

Irresistible Cheesecake

CRUST
1¾ cups graham cracker crumbs
¼ cup walnuts, chopped
½ teaspoon cinnamon
½ cup softened butter
(Save 3 tablespoons crumb mixture
   for topping)

FILLING
3 eggs
16 ounces cream cheese
1 cup sugar
1 teaspoon vanilla extract
3 cups sour cream

TOPPING
Frozen Strawberries

Press crust into spring form pan on bottom and sides. Combine eggs, softened cream cheese, sugar, and vanilla; beat until smooth. Blend in sour cream. Pour into crust. Top with reserved crumbs. Bake 1 hour at 375°. Chill 4 to 5 hours. Serve with strawberries for topping.

Mrs. William E. Smallwood

Hershey Bar Pound Cake

2 sticks butter
2 cups sugar
7 Hershey Bars (1.65 ounces each)
4 eggs
½ teaspoon salt

¼ teaspoon soda
2½ cups flour
1 cup buttermilk
2 teaspoons vanilla

Cream butter and sugar until light. Add melted Hershey Bars and eggs. Beat well. Stir in dry ingredients. Add buttermilk and vanilla, beating well. Pour into greased and sugared Bundt Pan or two loaf pans. Bake at 300° for 1 hour and 10 minutes or until the center springs back when touched. When baked in loaf pans the cooking time should be reduced.

Marcia Swetman

Chocolate Fudge Cake

4 eggs, beaten
2 cups sugar
2 cups sifted plain flour
2 level teaspoons baking powder

1 stick melted oleo
¼ square chocolate (3 blocks) or
   6 tablespoons cocoa
1 cup chopped nuts
1 teaspoon vanilla

Stir only. Do not beat. Bake in greased and floured 9 x 3 pan at 350° for 25 minutes. A winner in the Clarion-Ledger cooking contest in 1950.

Mrs. C. D. Hutchison
Yazoo City, Mississippi

"Best Ever" Chocolate Cake

3 squares unsweetened chocolate
2¼ cups sifted cake flour
2 teaspoons baking soda
½ teaspoon salt
2¼ cups firmly packed light
   brown sugar

3 eggs
1½ teaspoons vanilla
1 cup dairy sour cream
½ cup (1 stick) butter
1 cup boiling water
Chocolate Fudge Frosting

Preheat oven to 350⁰. Melt chocolate in a small bowl over hot, not boiling water; cool. Grease and flour two 9 x 1½ inch pans. Beat butter until soft in large bowl. Add brown sugar and eggs; beat with mixer at high speed until light and fluffy, 5 minutes. Beat in vanilla and cooled melted chocolate. Sift flour, baking soda, and salt onto wax paper. Stir dry ingredients into butter mixture alternately with sour cream, beating well with wooden spoon after each addition. Stir in boiling water. Batter will be thin. Pour at once into prepared pans and bake for 35 minutes. Frost with chocolate fudge.

CHOCOLATE FUDGE FROSTING

4 squares unsweetened chocolate
½ cup butter
1 package 10x sugar

½ cup milk
2 teaspoons vanilla

Combine chocolate and butter in small heavy saucepan. Place over low heat, just until melted. Remove from heat. Combine 10x sugar, milk and vanilla in medium size bowl; stir until smooth; add chocolate mixture. Set bowl in pan of ice water; beat with wooden spoon until frosting is thick enough to spread and hold its shape.

Gay Graves

Perfect Chocolate Cake

1 cup unsifted unsweetened cocoa
2 cups boiling water
2¾ cups sifted all-purpose flour
2 teaspoons baking soda
½ teaspoon salt

½ teaspoon baking powder
1 cup butter
2½ cups sugar
4 eggs
1½ teaspoons vanilla extract

CAKE: In medium bowl, combine cocoa with boiling water, mixing with wire whisk until smooth. Cool completely. Sift flour with soda, salt, and baking powder. Preheat oven to 350⁰. Grease and flour three 9 x 1½ inch layer cake pans. Beat butter, sugar, eggs, and vanilla at high speed until light (about 5 minutes). At low speed, beat in flour in fourths, alternately with cocoa mixture in thirds, beginning and ending with flour. Do not overbeat. Divide evenly into pans; smooth top. Bake 20-25 minutes. Cool in pans for 10 minutes, loosen sides with spatula; remove from pans, cool on racks.

FILLING

1 cup heavy cream, chilled
¼ cup unsifted powdered sugar

1 teaspoon vanilla extract

FILLING: Whip cream with sugar and vanilla; refrigerate.

FROSTING

1 (6 ounce) package semisweet
   chocolate pieces
½ cup light cream

1 cup butter
2½ cups unsifted powdered sugar

FROSTING: In medium saucepan, combine chocolate pieces, cream, butter; stir over medium heat until smooth. Remove from heat. With whisk, blend in powdered sugar. In bowl set over ice, beat until it holds shape.

TO ASSEMBLE CAKE: On plate, place a layer, top side down; spread with half of cream filling. Place second layer, top side down; spread with rest of cream filling. Place third layer top side up. TO FROST: With spatula, frost sides first, covering whipped cream; use rest of frosting on top. Refrigerate at least 1 hour before serving. Store in refrigerator. Serves 10 to 12.

Mrs. William E. Smallwood

Mississippi Mud Cake

2 sticks butter or oleo
½ cup cocoa
4 eggs, lightly beaten
2 cups sugar
1½ cups flour

1½ cups chopped nuts
Pinch of salt
1 teaspoon vanilla
Miniature marshmallows

Melt butter with cocoa, cool and add sugar and eggs and vanilla. Mix thoroughly. Add flour and salt slowly to mixture. Mix well and pour into 9 x 13 inch pan. Bake at 350° for 35-45 minutes. While hot, push marshmallows into cake.

ICING

1 box confectioners' sugar
½ cup whole milk

¼ cup cocoa
½ stick butter or oleo

Beat butter and sugar, then add cocoa and milk. Mix until smooth and spread on hot cake. Cut in squares after cooling.

Bess Lindsey
Mrs. Tom Rand

Coconut Sour Cream Pound Cake

½ pound butter
3 cups sugar
3 cups flour
¼ teaspoon soda
6 eggs at room temperature

½ pint sour cream
1 teaspoon vanilla
2 cups chopped pecans
1 cup Angel Flake coconut

Cream butter and sugar. Sift dry ingredients and add to creamed mixture. Add remaining ingredients and mix until well blended. Bake in prepared tube pan for 1 hour at 350° or until done.

Ame Deen

Coconut-Pineapple Cake

2 cups crushed pineapple and juice
1½ cups grated coconut
1 cup chopped pecans (optional)

1 box yellow cake mix
2 sticks margarine sliced in ¼ inch
   squares

Pour crushed pineapple and juice into a greased 10 x 14 inch pan (or two 8" pans). Cover with coconut and pecans. Spread dry cake mix over mixture. Place squares of margarine over entire top of cake. Bake at 350⁰ about 25 minutes or until brown. Serve with ice cream or whipped topping.

Mrs. Cragin Gilbert

Italian Cream Cake

2 cups flour
1 stick margarine
½ cup Crisco
5 egg yolks
1 teaspoon soda
2 cups sugar

1 cup buttermilk
1 teaspoon vanilla
1 small can Angel Flake Coconut
1 cup chopped pecans
5 egg whites, stiffly beaten

Beat egg whites and set aside. Cream margarine and shortening. Add sugar and beat until mixture is smooth. Add egg yolks and beat well. Combine flour and soda and add to creamed mixture alternately with buttermilk. Stir in vanilla. Add coconut and nuts. Fold in beaten egg whites. Pour batter into 2 greased and floured 8" cake pans. Bake at 350⁰ for 25-30 minutes. Frost with cream cheese frosting.

CREAM CHEESE FROSTING

8 ounces cream cheese, softened
1 stick margarine, softened

1 box powdered sugar
1 teaspoon vanilla

Combine ingredients. Sprinkle chopped pecans between layers and on top.

Mrs. Judy Pate

Date Nut Cake

1 pound dates, chopped and pitted
4 cups pecans, chopped
½ pound cherries, chopped
   (Maraschino or candied)
1 cup sugar

1 cup flour
4 eggs
2 teaspoons baking powder
½ teaspoon salt

Mix all ingredients in large bowl by hand. Place in prepared tube pan. Bake in 325⁰ oven for 1 hour or until done. Cook slowly as it is easily burned.

Mrs. E. C. Tutor
Grenada, Mississippi

Festive Cake

3 cups sifted flour
1 teaspoon baking soda
1 teaspoon cinnamon
2 cups sugar
1 teaspoon salt
1 cup chopped almonds

3 eggs
1 teaspoon almond extract
1 (8 ounce) can crushed undrained
   pineapple
2 cups chopped firm bananas
1½ cups vegetable oil

Mix first 6 ingredients together and set aside. Beat eggs and combine with rest of ingredients. Add wet ingredients to dry and mix thoroughly but do not beat. Spoon into well oiled 10 inch tube pan. Bake at 325° for 1 hour and 20-25 minutes. Invert cake on wire rack and cool. Frost with cream cheese frosting.

FROSTING

8 ounces cream cheese
½ cup margarine

1 pound powdered sugar
1 tablespoon instant cocoa

Combine all ingredients and beat until smooth. Frost and refrigerate until ready to serve.

Mrs. A. Ruggier
McKeesport, Pennsylvania

Fig Cake

2 cups plain flour
1 teaspoon salt
1 teaspoon soda
1½ cups sugar
1 cup oil
3 eggs
1 cup buttermilk

2 cups chopped nuts
1 pint fig preserves, drained and
   chopped
1 teaspoon vanilla
1 teaspoon cloves
1 teaspoon cinnamon
1 teaspoon nutmeg

Sift dry ingredients, add oil and beat well. Add sugar, eggs, buttermilk and other ingredients. Bake in well-greased and floured tube pan at 325° for 1 hour or until cake tests done.

GLAZE

½ cup sugar
1 stick oleo
1 teaspoon Karo

1 teaspoon vanilla
¼ cup buttermilk
¼ teaspoon soda

Mix well and boil 3 minutes. Pour over cake while warm. Let cake cool in pan 15 minutes. Remove and take ice pick and stick holes over top and sides of cake so glaze goes down into cake.

Millie Ross

For PLUM CAKE use this recipe and substitute 1 jar Junior Baby Food Plums in place of fig preserves.

Mrs. Bert Allen

Aunt Bertha's Old Fashioned Molasses Cake

2½ cups flour
1½ teaspoons soda
1 teaspoon salt
1 teaspoon cinnamon
1 teaspoon allspice
1 teaspoon cloves

½ teaspoon ginger
1 cup melted butter
1 cup sugar
1 cup molasses
2 eggs, well beaten
1 cup boiling water

Sift flour, then measure. Add dry ingredients and resift. Combine butter, sugar, molasses, eggs; blend well. Add flour mixture; beat smooth. Add boiling water; stir smooth. Bake in prepared tube pan at 350⁰ for 50 minutes or until done. Let cool 10 minutes in pan.

Mrs. W. R. Clement

Prune Cake

½ pound butter
4 eggs
2 cups sugar
1½ cups prunes, chopped
2⅔ cups flour
1 teaspoon soda

1 teaspoon baking powder
1 teaspoon cinnamon
1 teaspoon nutmeg
1 teaspoon cloves
1½ cups buttermilk

Cream butter and sugar and add eggs, one at a time. Add dry ingredients, alternately with milk. Add prunes. Bake at 350⁰ for 45-50 minutes.

ICING

Juice and rind of 1 orange and 1 lemon   ⅓ stick butter
1 box confectioner's sugar

Add only amount of juice necessary for icing consistency. This cake is also very good uniced.

Margaret Gillespie
Jackson, Mississippi

Bourbon Pecan Cake

1 (17 ounce) package pound cake mix
½ teaspoon ground nutmeg
⅔ cup bourbon

4 eggs, separated
2 cups chopped pecans

Combine cake mix and nutmeg in a large bowl. Add bourbon and beat 1½ minutes on low speed. Add egg yolks and beat 2 minutes. Add nuts. Beat egg whites stiff, but not dry, and fold gently into batter. Bake in well greased Bundt pan at 325⁰ for 45-50 minutes. Cool in pan 10 minutes. Then invert. Ice if desired.

Mrs. A. E. Lombardo
McKeesport, Pennsylvania

Christmas Nut Cake

1 (15 ounce) package raisins
½ cup grape juice or wine
2 sticks butter or margarine
2½ cups sugar
6 eggs
4 cups sifted flour

1 quart pecans
1 teaspoon cinnamon
1 teaspoon cloves
1 teaspoon nutmeg
1 teaspoon soda
1½ teaspoons vanilla
1 cup molasses or dark Karo

Soak raisins overnight in grape juice. Cream butter and sugar; add beaten eggs a small amount at the time and beat well after each addition. Mix all dry ingredients except soda. Mix soda and vanilla with molasses. Alternately add dry ingredients and molasses mixture to creamed mixture. Drain raisins and dredge in flour, add nuts, fold into batter. Bake in two stem pans in very slow oven (250°) for 2 hours. Wrap cooled cake in wine or whiskey-soaked cloth and store in tin box. This makes two cakes. Keep one and give one as a gift.

Mrs. Letha Reed
Itta Bena, Mississippi

English Shortbread

⅓ cup sugar
1½ sticks butter

1¾ to 2 cups all-purpose flour

Rub sugar, butter and flour together with hands until it resembles bread crumbs. Gently knead into a soft dough. Press into two 8 x 8 inch pans and prick all over top with fork. Bake at 325° for 25-30 minutes or 320° for 40 minutes. Be sure to use dairy butter, not margarine. Cooking slowly is important. This recipe is straight from England.

Mrs. William Sheen
McComb, Mississippi

White Fruit Cake

1 pound candied cherries
1 pound candied pineapple
1 pound white raisins
1 quart pecans
Dredge in 1 cup flour

8 eggs, separated
3 cups unsifted flour
1 teaspoon baking powder
1½ cups sugar

2 sticks butter
1 teaspoon lemon flavoring
1 teaspoon vanilla flavoring
1 teaspoon almond flavoring

Cream butter and sugar, add yolks of eggs and beat until fluffy. Beat egg whites separately. Mix flour with baking powder. Then mix egg whites and flour alternately with butter and sugar mixture. Add flavoring and fruits. Cook at 250° for four hours. Test with a toothpick for doneness after 3½ hours.

Shirley H. Bergfield

June's Butter Pound Cake

2 cups sugar
2 sticks oleo
4 to 5 eggs

2 cups plain flour
2 teaspoons vanilla

Cream margarine and sugar until creamy. Add eggs, one at a time. Blend well. Add flour and vanilla. Pour in prepared tube pan. Put in cold oven at 325° and bake for 50 minutes or until a straw comes out clean. Turn out to cool.

Mrs. John Cotten

Buttermilk Pound Cake

2 cups sugar
1 cup butter
4 eggs
3 cups flour

½ teaspoon baking powder
½ teaspoon soda
1 cup buttermilk
1 teaspoon vanilla

Cream butter and sugar. Add eggs, one at a time. Mix together flour, baking powder, and soda. Add to batter alternately with milk. Add vanilla. Bake 1 hour at 325° in a greased and floured tube pan.

Mrs. Virgil Gillespie

Sour Cream Sweet
(Coffee Cake)

1 cup butter
1¼ cups sugar
2 eggs, lightly beaten
1 cup sour cream
1 teaspoon vanilla

2 cups sifted flour
1 teaspoon baking powder
½ teaspoon baking soda
Cinnamon sugar

Cream butter with sugar. Add eggs, sour cream, and vanilla; beat thoroughly. Sift together sifted flour, baking powder, and baking soda. Gradually stir the dry ingredients into sour cream mixture. Butter a 9" round cake pan. Pour in half the batter and sprinkle it with cinnamon sugar. Add the remaining batter and top with a little more cinnamon sugar. Bake the cake in moderate oven (350°) for about 40 minutes or until a toothpick inserted in the center comes out clean. Freezes well.

Mrs. H. C. Thompson

Brown Sugar Pie

3 eggs
1 stick butter

2 cups brown sugar
1 teaspoon vanilla

Beat sugar and eggs well. Add melted butter and vanilla, beating slightly. Bake in one unbaked 9 inch pie shell for 30 minutes or until firm in a 350° oven. Serves 6.

Mrs. William H. Murdock
Greenwood, Mississippi

Never Fail Pie Crust

1 scant cup shortening
2 cups flour
1 teaspoon salt

⅓ cup milk
1 tablespoon vinegar

Preheat oven to 475⁰ if recipe calls for baking before filling. Bake 8-10 minutes. This recipe is enough for two 8 inch or 9 inch pie pans. Sift flour and salt together. Cut shortening into flour mixture. Mix milk and vinegar together and add to flour and shortening. Form a ball and roll out using half of the mixture at a time to form two pie crusts.

Mrs. William J. Juliana

Apple Custard Pie

1 cup applesauce
3 tablespoons lemon juice
1 cup sugar
4 eggs, slightly beaten
2 tablespoons butter, melted

½ teaspoon salt
½ teaspoon nutmeg
½ teaspoon cinnamon
1 unbaked pie shell

Combine ingredients thoroughly. Pour in pie shell. Bake in moderate oven until set.

Mrs. H. Jerry Pettit
Branson, Missouri

Impossible Pie

1¾ cup sugar
2 cups milk
½ cup self-rising flour
4 eggs, well beaten

1 teaspoon vanilla
½ stick oleo, melted
7 ounces coconut

Mix sugar, flour, and well beaten eggs blending with a mixer. Add the remaining ingredients. Pour into two greased pie plates and bake in a 350⁰ oven for 35 minutes or until golden brown. This recipe makes two 9 inch pies. It is very delicious, quick, and requires no crust.

Dayonne McGuire

Egg Custard Pie

3 eggs
½ teaspoon vanilla
3 teaspoons butter
½ teaspoon salt

¾ cup sugar
1½ cups milk
1 nine inch pie crust
Nutmeg to taste

Heat milk and butter to boiling point in a saucepan. Beat whole eggs lightly in a bowl. Add sugar and vanilla to egg mixture. Stir in milk. Bake at 475⁰ for 10 minutes. Reduce heat to 350⁰ and cook until pie is firm. If the pie browns too fast, cover the entire pie with foil until the pie is done.

Mrs. Mike Achee

Buttermilk Pie

¼ cup butter
1¼ cups sugar
1 tablespoon flour
2 whole eggs
½ teaspoon vanilla

1 teaspoon lemon extract
1 cup buttermilk
Pinch of salt
Nutmeg, if desired

Cream butter and sugar. Blend in remaining ingredients, except for the nutmeg, and pour into an unbaked 9 inch pie shell. Bake at 450⁰ for 10 minutes. Reduce the heat to 350⁰ and bake for 30 minutes more. If desired, the pie can be dusted with grated nutmeg before baking. This is easy to make, very rich, and delicious.

Sandra Cain

Fruit-In-Crust Cheesecake Pie

1 cup all-purpose flour
1 cup quick-cooking oats
½ teaspoon baking powder
⅔ cup brown sugar, firmly packed

½ cup butter or oleo, softened
10-12 ounce jar apricot (or any kind
    of fruit) preserves

Mix flour, oats, sugar, baking powder, and butter until crumbly. Reserve 1 cup of crumbs. Pat remainder on the bottom and sides of an ungreased 9 inch pie pan. Spread the preserves over the unbaked crust. Top with the reserved cup of crumbs. Bake until golden brown at 350⁰ for 20-25 minutes. Serves 8.

TOPPING

½ cup powdered sugar
2 tablespoons milk
1½ teaspoons vanilla

3 ounces cream cheese, softened
2 cups whipping cream, whipped

Blend in a small mixer bowl all topping ingredients, except whipped cream, until smooth. Fold 2 cups whipped cream into this mixture. Spoon into baked pie crust. Keep in refrigerator.

Mrs. James O. Dukes

Chocolate Chess Pie

2½ tablespoons cocoa
1 cup sugar
2 tablespoons flour
1 teaspoon vanilla

3 eggs, separated
2 cups milk
2 tablespoons melted butter

Mix cocoa, sugar, and flour. Beat egg yolks and add milk. Add to sugar mixture. Cook until thick. Add melted butter and vanilla. Pour mixture into baked pie crust. Top with meringue and brown in a 400⁰ oven. Serves 6.

Mrs. Guy Lewis

Mrs. Martin Miazza adds 1 heaping teaspoon instant coffee to above recipe to make a Mocha Chess Pie.

Jeff Davis Pie

3 eggs
1½ cups sugar
1 can regular size Pet milk or
   1 cup rich cream

1 rounded teaspoon flour
1 teaspoon melted butter
¼ teaspoon lemon extract
¼ teaspoon nutmeg

Put sugar and flour in a small bowl of a mixer. Add eggs and beat until creamy. Stir in melted butter. Add the flavorings. Add cream last. Pour into an unbaked pie shell and bake at 325⁰ until set (about 45 minutes). This is a very old family recipe.

Mrs. J. Robbins Clower, Jr.

Chocolate Chip Pie

1 (6 ounce) package chocolate chips
2 tablespoons sugar
3 tablespoons milk

4 eggs, separated
Pie shell
Whipped cream

Melt the chocolate chips, sugar, and milk. Let cool. Add egg yolks. Whip the egg whites until stiff and fold into the chocolate mixture. Fill the pre-baked pie shell with chocolate mixture and top with whipped cream. Chill for several hours.

Mrs. John DeLuca

Chocolate Hershey Pie

6 Hershey almond bars
16 large marshmallows
½ cup milk

½ pint heavy cream, whipped
9 inch graham cracker crumb crust

Melt Hershey bars and marshmallows in milk in the top of a double boiler. Cool. Fold in whipped cream. Pour in shell and chill in refrigerator for 8-10 hours. May be decorated with shaved chocolate. This freezes beautifully.

Rivers Wallace

Chocolate Pie

2 squares Baker's unsweetened
   chocolate
2 cups milk
1 cup sugar
⅓ cup flour
Pinch of salt

Large lump of butter
3 egg yolks
3 egg whites
1 teaspoon vanilla
1 nine inch pie shell

Heat milk and chocolate until chocolate is melted. Add these ingredients to a mixture of sugar, flour, and salt. Cook in the top of a double boiler until thickened. Beat egg yolks. Add some of the hot mixture to the eggs, mix, and return to the pan stirring well. Add butter and cook for about 5 minutes stirring constantly. Cool and add vanilla. Pour into pie shell. Beat egg whites adding a pinch of salt and a small amount of vanilla. Add 6 tablespoons of sugar slowly. Spread meringue over pie and bake for 15 minutes at 350⁰.

Willa Vae Biggs

Quickie Fudge Pie

1 stick oleo
1 square chocolate
1 cup sugar

½ cup flour
2 eggs
Vanilla ice cream

Melt oleo and chocolate. Add sugar and flour. Add eggs. Bake at 325⁰ for 25 minutes. This is so quick and may be put in the oven while finalizing dinner. It must be served while hot with a large helping of vanilla ice cream on top. Serves 6-8. This pie makes its own crust.

Mrs. Ted Hearn

Three Layer Pie

FIRST LAYER

1 stick oleo
1 cup plain flour

1 cup chopped nuts

SECOND LAYER

8 ounces cream cheese
1 cup confectioner's sugar

1½ cups Cool Whip

THIRD LAYER

1 small box instant chocolate
  pudding mix
1 small box instant vanilla
  pudding mix

3 cups cold milk
Hershey bar
Cool Whip
Pecans

Preheat oven to 350⁰. Mix oleo, flour, and nuts. Press into a 9 by 13 inch pan. Bake 30 minutes or until medium brown. Cool. Mix cream cheese, confectioner's sugar, and Cool Whip.Spread on cooled first layer. Mix chocolate pudding mix and vanilla pudding mix with the cold milk until semi-thick. Spread on second layer. Top with more Cool Whip and garnish with grated Hershey bar and/or pecans. If desired, 2 boxes of chocolate pudding may be used instead of 1 chocolate and 1 vanilla.

Mrs. L. Lamar Clark
Mrs. Larry Watkins, Macon, Mississippi
Mrs. Webb Mize
Mrs. Wallace Long

Southern Pecan Pie

½ cup sugar
½ stick oleo
1 cup white Karo syrup
3 beaten eggs

1 teaspoon vanilla
1 cup chopped pecans
Unbaked pie shell

Cream sugar and oleo. Add Karo syrup. Add eggs. Stir. Add vanilla and pecans. Pour into the raw pie shell. Bake 30-40 minutes at 325⁰. This pie is not as sweet as most pecan pies.

Mrs. Duane Hanks

Peach Cobbler

2 cups sliced fresh peaches
2 cups sugar
1 stick oleo or butter
¾ cup flour

2 teaspoons baking powder
¼ teaspoon salt
¾ cup milk

Mix peaches with 1 cup sugar and let stand. Put butter in a two quart casserole and place in the oven to melt. Combine remaining sugar, flour, baking powder, salt, and milk. Pour over melted butter. Do not stir. Spoon peaches on top of batter. Bake for one hour at 325⁰.

Mrs. Henry M. Thomas

Peach Pie

1 stick butter
2 tablespoons flour
1 teaspoon vanilla
1 cup sugar

1 large can homestyle peaches,
  halves or sliced (drained)
2 eggs
1 nine inch pie shell

Combine sugar and flour. Add melted butter. Add beaten eggs and vanilla and mix well. Pour over peaches in pie shell and bake for one hour at 350⁰. Serves 6 to 8.

Willa Vae Biggs

Pecan Cracker Pie

1 cup saltine crackers, crushed
  in a plastic bag
1 cup nuts, chopped medium fine
1 teaspoon baking powder

3 large eggs, whites only, beaten stiff
1 cup granulated sugar
2 teaspoons vanilla

Preheat oven to 350⁰. Mix crackers, nuts, and baking powder. Beat egg whites adding sugar 1 teaspoon at a time until stiff. Add vanilla. Fold cracker mixture into egg white mixture. Butter a Pyrex pie pan and pour mixture into the pan. Bake 20-25 minutes. Serve with a topping of vanilla ice cream or sweetened whipped cream. This pie makes its own crust. It does not need to be refrigerated and will keep for several days covered.

Doris Riemann

Blueberry Pie

Two 9 inch pie shells
12 ounces cream cheese
Pecan pieces
¾ box powdered sugar

½ large container of Cool Whip
½ large container Cool Whip for topping
1 can blueberry pie mix

Sprinkle pecan pieces in pie shells and bake. Spread blended cream cheese and ½ of a large container of Cool Whip in baked pie shells. Top with can of blueberry pie·mix. Cover with remaining ½ of a large container of Cool Whip. This pie will keep in the refrigerator for a week or so or it may be frozen.

Mrs. Webb Mize

Peacheesy Pie
CRUST

2 cups good flour
2/3 cup shortening (not oil)
1 teaspoon salt

6-7 tablespoons peach syrup
2 tablespoons butter or oleo

PEACH FILLING

1 (1 pound 13 ounce) can cling
   peach slices, reserve liquid
½ cup sugar
2 tablespoons cornstarch
2 tablespoons corn syrup
2 teaspoons cinnamon
2 teaspoons vanilla extract

CHEESE TOPPING

2 eggs, slightly beaten
1/3 cup sugar
2 tablespoons lemon juice
2 tablespoons peach syrup
8 ounces cream cheese

FILLING: Drain peaches, but save the syrup. Combine peach slices, ½ cup sugar, corn syrup, corn starch, cinnamon, and vanilla.

CHEESE TOPPING: Combine eggs, 1/3 cup sugar, lemon juice, 2 tablespoons peach syrup in a small saucepan. Cook, stirring constantly, until thick. With electric beater, soften cream cheese and gradually add hot mixture. Beat until smooth.

TO MAKE PIE: Combine flour and salt. Cut in shortening and sprinkle peach juice over mixture while stirring with a fork. Roll half of the dough on floured surface about 1½ inches larger than pan. Fit in pan and flute the edge. Fill with peach filling. Dot with butter. Cover with cheese topping. Roll out remaining dough and cut into circles using a juice glass. Brush with peach syrup and arrange on cheese topping. Brush crust edges with peach juice. Check during the 30-35 minutes baking time that the crust does not get too brown. Should it occur, cover edges of the crust with foil. Bake in pre-heated oven at 425° for the first 10 minutes and at 350° for 30-35 minutes. This recipe is time consuming, but good. The pie is better the second day and freezes well if properly sealed.

Mrs. William M. Rainey

Cherry Cream Cheese Pie

1 package Dream Whip
1½ cups confectioner's sugar
8 ounces cream cheese
½ cup chopped pecans

2 teaspoons lemon juice
1 can Lucky Leaf Cherry Pie filling
1 nine inch pie crust

Prepare Dream Whip according to directions and then add confectioner's sugar. In a large mixing bowl, beat until smooth cream cheese with lemon juice. Combine Dream Whip mixture with cream cheese mixture and pour into a 9 inch cooked pie crust into which chopped and toasted pecans have been sprinkled. Let stand in refrigerator until firm and then add Lucky Leaf Cherry Pie filling for topping.

Doris Hogue

Amaretto Pie

3 cups chocolate chips
1/4 cup plus 2 tablespoons butter
1 (14 ounce) sweetened condensed milk
1/4 teaspoon salt

1/4 cup water
1/4 cup Amaretto
1/2 pint whipping cream
Whipped cream and almonds for garnish

Line a 9 inch pie plate with foil (very smoothly). Melt 1 cup chips with 2 table-spoons butter and pour into pie plate, rolling around evenly. Refrigerate until chilled. Carefully remove the chocolate shell from the foil and place in the bottom of the pie plate. Combine 2 cups of chips, 1/4 cup butter, sweetened condensed milk, and salt, and cook until melted. Add water and cook at low heat for 5 minutes. Add Amaretto and cook 2 minutes. Cool. Whip cream and fold into the chocolate mixture. Fill the pie plate. Chill for 3 to 4 hours. Garnish with whipped cream and almonds. Serves 12.

Sue Dalto

Buttermilk Coconut Pie

1 stick butter or margarine
3 eggs
1 1/2 cups sugar

1/2 cup buttermilk
1 can coconut
1 unbaked pie shell

Melt margarine or butter; pour into mixing bowl. Add eggs, sugar and other ingredients. Beat well for 2 minutes. Pour into unbaked pie crust. Bake at 350° for 45 minutes or until firm.

Hiawatha Evans

Cranberry Pie

1 cup whole cranberry sauce
1/2 cup light brown sugar
1 small box orange gelatin

1 cup whipping cream
1/2 cup walnuts, finely chopped
Vanilla wafers

Mix cranberry sauce and brown sugar in pan. Bring to a boil. Remove from heat. Add package of gelatin and stir until dissolved. Let cool. Whip cream until stiff. Add nuts and cranberry mixture to whipped cream. Line a 9 inch pie plate with vanilla wafers arranging them in the bottom and along the sides of the plate. Pour in cranberry mixture. Chill thoroughly. If desired, additional whipped cream may be used for garnish. This pie is especially good with Thanksgiving or Christmas dinner.

Mrs. Alben N. Hopkins

Key Lime Pie

9" graham cracker crust, prepared and
  baked
1 can sweetened condensed milk

1/2 cup Key Lime Juice
4 eggs, separated

Combine condensed milk, egg yolks, and Key Lime Juice. Pour into crust. Top with stiffly beaten egg whites for meringue. Brown quickly and lightly. Refrigerate. Serves 6-8.

Mrs. Jack Thompson

Fresh Dewberry Pie

cups berries
1 1/2 cups sugar
3 tablespoons cornstarch

Pinch of salt
1/2 stick butter or oleo
Pie shell for two crust pie, unbaked

Wash and drain berries. Place berries in pie shell. Cover with sugar to which you have added the cornstarch and salt. Dot with butter. Cover with top crust. Seal edges well and pierce top crust. Place on middle rack in the oven and bake at 375° until brown, about 30-40 minutes. This pie is delicious when served warm. Cream may be poured on top of each serving as an added treat. Dewberries and blackberries are indigenous to this area. They are usually ready for picking in late April and early May. The effort of picking the berries makes the anticipation of the pie that much greater and the reward ever so delicious.

Mrs. Adron Swango

Deep Dish Pie

1 cup Bisquick
1/2 cup sugar
1 cup milk

1 stick of butter
2 cups fruit (sugar to taste)

Melt butter in a 1 1/2 quart casserole while pre-heating the oven to 350°. Mix Bisquick, sugar, and milk. It will be lumpy. Add the mixture to the butter. Add fruit, but do not stir. Bake for 1/2 hour. Serves 6. It is quick and easy. Blackberries or peaches are good.

Mrs. Jack C. Thompson

Millionaire Pie

1 cup Eagle Brand milk
1 small can crushed pineapple, drained
1 cup chopped pecans
1/2 cup cherries
1/4 cup lemon juice

1 can flake coconut
9" baked pie shell, cooled
1 carton whipping cream
2 tablespoons sugar

Mix all ingredients except whipping cream and sugar. Pour into pie shell. Whip cream with 2 tablespoons sugar and put on pie right before serving.

Margie McFarland

Ice Cream Pie

1/2 stick butter or oleo, melted
25 plain chocolate or vanilla wafers
1 cup sugar
1/2 gallon ice cream, any kind

1/2 cup water
1/4 teaspoon salt
1/4 tablespoon cream of tartar
4 egg whites

Crush cookies. Add melted butter and pat into a standard pie pan, 9 or 10 inch, and set aside. Beat egg whites until stiff and set aside. Cook the sugar, water, and cream of tartar until thick and stringy. Pour this mixture into the egg whites while beating with a beater until it holds high peaks. Spread the ice cream in the shell and cover completely with meringue. The meringue draws up in cooking so be sure to overlap the meringue to crust. Place in a 450° oven and brown meringue quickly. Freeze pie until ready to use.

Lynndee Rainey

Girdle Buster Pie

⅓ cup melted butter
24 crushed Oreo cookies
2 quarts Jamoka or Pralines and
    Cream ice cream

2 tablespoons butter
1 cup sugar
1⅓ cups evaporated milk
4 squares unsweetened chocolate

Use two 9 inch pie pans. Mix butter and cookies. Press into pie pans and freeze. Fill each with 1 quart of ice cream. Melt squares of chocolate with butter and sugar. Stir in evaporated milk. Cook until thickened. Pour over frozen ice cream. Return to freezer. This may be served with whipped cream and toasted almonds on top. It is rich, but good.

Mrs. Ted Hearn

Mrs. David Manifold uses semi-sweet chocolate squares for a slightly sweeter version.

Angel Pie

MERINGUE
4 egg whites
1 cup sugar
Pinch of salt
Pinch of cream of tartar

FILLING
Grated rind and juice of 1 lemon
1 cup sugar
2 egg yolks, beaten
½ pint heavy cream, whipped

Make a stiff meringue with the egg whites, sugar, salt, and cream of tartar. Grease a 9 inch pie pan well and fill with meringue, having it level on top. Bake at 250⁰ for 1 hour. After it has cooled, fill with alternate layers of lemon filling and whipped cream, ending with whipped cream. For the filling, combine sugar, lemon rind and juice, and beaten egg yolks. Cook carefully in a heavy saucepan or double boiler, stirring constantly, until clear. Cool. Serves 8.

Sue Foley

Mrs. Bert Allen has a similar recipe where she layers whipped cream and fresh fruit over the meringue.

"Show Off" Frozen Lemon Pie

1 large can evaporated milk, very cold
1 cup sugar

⅓ to ½ cup lemon juice
1 teaspoon grated lemon peel
Saltines

Crush 2 saltines and sprinkle crumbs in the bottom of a 9 inch pie plate. Whip chilled evaporated milk until stiff and add sugar. Fold in lemon juice. Spoon into pie pan and top with grated lemon peel and one or two more crushed saltines. Freeze. This makes a spectacular "show off" dessert.

Mrs. Charles R. Galloway

Pineapple Ice Box Pie

2 nine inch pie shells, baked

FILLING
1 (13½ ounce) carton of Cool Whip
1 (14 ounce) can Eagle Brand
condensed milk
1 (20 ounce) can crushed pineapple,
well drained
Juice of 1 lemon or the equivalent
of 2 tablespoons

TOPPING
½-1 cup finely chopped pecans
Chopped maraschino cherries as
desired for color

Bake two 9 inch pie shells and cool thoroughly. Prepare filling by mixing the filling ingredients in a large bowl. Mix in order as listed. Use a rubber spatula and mix gently. Pour into pie shells. Freeze. Remove from the freezer 15-20 minutes prior to serving. Sprinkle chopped nuts and cherries on top or wedges of pineapple to add color. This recipe makes 2 pies or approximately 16 slices. It is a very refreshing dessert.

Mrs. W. M. Brewer

Quick Pineapple Cheese Pie

8 ounces softened cream cheese
¼ cup sugar
1 cup heavy cream, whipped

1½ cups drained crushed pineapple
(1 pound 4 ounce can)
1 nine inch Graham cracker pie shell

Whip cream cheese and sugar together. Fold in the whipped cream and then the pineapple that has been drained. Spoon into the pie shell. Chill for about 2 hours or until set.

Gay Graves

Rum Pie

6 tablespoons butter
1 cup flour
2 tablespoons powdered sugar
3 eggs, separated
Scant ½ cup sugar

1 tablespoon gelatin, dissolved in a
little cream
Scant ¼ cup Jamaican rum
1½ cups heavy cream, whipped
Nutmeg

Make a crust by working together the butter, flour, and powdered sugar. Pat into pie pan, prick with a fork, and bake for 20 minutes at 300⁰. For the filling, combine egg yolks and sugar in a double boiler and cook, stirring constantly, until yolks thicken. Add gelatin softened in cream to hot mixture and stir to dissolve. Add rum and fold into beaten egg whites. Cool. Fold in ⅔ of the whipped cream. Pour into the cooled crust. Chill. Top with the remaining whipped cream and sprinkle with nutmeg. Serves 8.

Sue Foley

Black Bottom Pie

½ cup sugar plus 2 teaspoons flour
1 tablespoon cornstarch
2 cups milk, scalded
4 beaten egg yolks
1 teaspoon vanilla
1 (6 ounce) package semi-sweet
   chocolate pieces, melted

1 nine inch pie shell, baked
1 tablespoon unflavored gelatin
¼ cup cold water
Bourbon to taste (½ cup)
4 egg whites
½ cup sugar
1 cup heavy cream, whipped
Chocolate pieces, grated for garnish

Combine sugar, flour and cornstarch. Slowly add scalded milk to beaten egg yolks. Stir in sugar mixture. Cook and stir in top of double boiler until the custard coats a spoon. Add vanilla. To 1 cup of the custard add the melted chocolate. Pour in bottom of cooled pie shell. Chill. Soften gelatin in cold water and add to remaining hot custard. Stir until dissolved. Chill until slightly thickened. Beat egg whites, adding sugar gradually until mixture stands in peaks. Fold in custard-gelatin mixture to which bourbon has been added. Pour over chocolate layer and chill until set. Garnish with whipped cream and chocolate pieces grated on top.

Mrs. Sam D. Stennis
DeKalb, Mississippi

Fresh Strawberry Pie

¾ cup sugar
3 tablespoons cornstarch
2 tablespoons water
Pinch of salt
1 cup boiling water

1 tablespoon lemon juice
½ teaspoon red food coloring
1½ pints sliced strawberries
Whipped cream

Make a paste of sugar, cornstarch, 2 tablespoons water, and salt. Heat 1 cup water to boiling and stir slowly into paste. Cook until clear and thick. Remove from heat. Add lemon juice, red food coloring, and strawberries. Turn into a pre-baked pie shell. Chill. Serve with whipped cream.

Mrs. Edward R. Gaines

Frozen Strawberry Pie

1 (10 ounce) package frozen
   strawberries
1 cup sugar
2 egg whites
1 tablespoon lemon juice

1/8 teaspoon salt
1 cup whipping cream
1 teaspoon vanilla
1 cup nuts
2 Graham cracker crusts

Place the defrosted strawberries, sugar, egg whites, lemon juice, and salt in a large bowl of an electric mixer. Beat at a high speed for 15 minutes. Whip cream. Add vanilla. Fold into strawberry mixture with nuts. Put into 2 pie shells. Freeze for several hours or overnight. Serves 16. Makes 2 pies.

Mrs. Carlisle Carothers

Camellia's Own Lemon Meringue Pie

1 (4¾ ounce) package lemon pie filling
¾ cup sugar (additional sugar to taste)
1½ teaspoons grated lemon peel
2 tablespoons freshly squeezed
   lemon juice

3 large beaten egg yolks at room
   temperature
1⅔ to 1¾ cups water
1 baked 9" pie shell

Put pie filling and ¾ cup sugar in sauce pan. Mix in lemon peel, fresh juice, beaten egg yolks and water. Taste and adjust sugar as needed. Follow package directions for cooking filling. DO NOT STIR FILLING AFTER COOKING (causes weeping meringue!!) Spoon cooled filling into baked pie shell.

MERINGUE

4 egg whites (at room temperature)
¼ teaspoon cream of tartar
Pinch of salt

6 tablespoons sugar
½ teaspoon freshly squeezed
   lemon juice

Beat egg whites until frothy. Add cream of tartar and salt and beat until whites just hold peak. Add ½ the sugar gradually while beating. Beat in lemon juice. Gradually add remaining sugar. Continue to beat until stiff (meringue rubbed between fingers is not grainy). Spread meringue over filling, sealing the edges to pastry to avoid shrinkage. Bake at 350° 10 to 12 minutes or just to a light, golden brown. DO NOT OVER BAKE MERINGUE. (This also causes weeping.)

Camellia Ricks
The French Connection
Biloxi, Mississippi

Refrigerator Lemon Pie

1 large carton Cool Whip
1 can Eagle Brand milk

1 small can of frozen lemonade
   concentrate
1 eight or nine inch pie shell or
   graham cracker crust

Bake a pie shell. Combine 2 cups Cool Whip with Eagle Brand milk and lemonade, thawed, but not diluted. Pour into cooled pie shell and refrigerate for several hours or several days. Garnish with more Cool Whip, if desired. This can also be done with individual tart shells.

Mrs. Sherman Muths, Jr.

Cocoa Brownies

¾ cup sifted flour
1 cup sugar
5 tablespoons cocoa
½ teaspoon salt

½ cup soft shortening
2 eggs, unbeaten
1 teaspoon vanilla
½ cup chopped nuts

Place all ingredients in a large bowl and beat for three minutes. Do not add nuts until at the end of three minutes. Then stir in nuts. Grease the bottom of a 8 x 8 x 2 inch pan and pour mixture in pan. Bake in 350° oven for 30 minutes. Let cool in baking pan before cutting. Do not double recipe. It will not be as good.

Mrs. John Stringer

Best Brownies

½ cup oleo
1 cup sugar
4 eggs, beaten

½ cup nuts (optional)
1 pound can Hershey's syrup
1 cup plain flour

Cream butter and sugar. Add eggs and other ingredients beating well. Pour in 11 x 16 inch greased pan and bake. While brownies are baking assemble the ingredients for the icing. Bake for 25 minutes at 350⁰.

ICING

1½ cups sugar
6 tablespoons milk

6 tablespoons oleo
1 (6 ounce) package semi-sweet chocolate
     morsels

Boil the sugar, milk, and oleo for 1 minute. Then add the chocolate morsels. Spread on brownies while warm.

Mrs. George Thatcher

Butter Cookies

1 cup softened butter
½ cup sugar
1 egg yolk

3 tablespoons vanilla
3 cups all-purpose flour
½ teaspoon baking powder
Almonds (optional)

Cream sugar and butter. Add sifted flour and baking powder and mix until dough "follows" spoon. Chill dough overnight. Roll out and cut into shapes. Place on ungreased baking sheets. Press blanched almonds into top of each cookie. Brush with beaten mixture of 1 egg yolk and 2 tablespoons water. Bake until lightly brown, about 5 to 7 minutes at 425⁰.

Mrs. Henry Thomas

Color Me Cookies

1 stick softened butter or margarine
½ cup sugar
¾ cup flour
¼ teaspoon vanilla

COOKIE PAINT
Confectioner's sugar
Water
Food coloring

Heat oven to 375⁰. Put butter and sugar in mixing bowl. Stir with wooden spoon. When well blended, break egg and mix it in with sugar and butter mixture. Add flour and vanilla and mix until dough is nice and yellow. Drop rounded teaspoons of dough on greased cookie sheet, leaving spaces between the cookies. Bake 15 to 18 minutes, but do not let cookies get brown.

COOKIE PAINT: Place a few spoons of sugar in a cup. Add just a few drops of water to make thin icing. Color with food coloring. Spread on cooled cookies.

Amy Gillespie

Golden Brownies

¾ cup vegetable oil
1 box light brown sugar
3 eggs
2 cups unsifted flour

1 tablespoon baking powder
1 teaspoon salt
2 teaspoons vanilla
1 cup chopped nuts

Mix together oil, sugar, and eggs. Add eggs one at a time. Add vanilla, then dry ingredients and nuts. Pour into greased pan and bake for 25 minutes at 350⁰.

Mrs. C. H. Brandon

Chess Squares

1 stick softened butter
1 Duncan Hines butter cake mix

4 eggs
8 ounces cream cheese
1 box confectioner's sugar

Combine with mixer: butter (room temperature), cake mix and 1 egg. Pat into 11 x 14 inch pan. Combine with mixer: cream cheese, 3 eggs, confectioner's sugar. Pour cream cheese mixture over cake mixture. Bake at 350⁰ for 35 to 45 minutes. When golden brown, check the center with a toothpick. If it comes out clean, it is ready. Cut into squares. Serves 20. If you like lemon squares, you'll love this, and it is easier. Cake may be served warm or cool. Freezes well.

Mrs. John Sneed

Chocolate Chip Cookie Bars

2 cups flour
1 teaspoon baking powder
¼ teaspoon soda
1 teaspoon salt
⅔ cup margarine, melted

2 cups brown sugar
2 eggs, slightly beaten
2 teaspoons vanilla
1 (12 ounce) package chocolate chips

Mix margarine with sugar. Cool slightly. Add eggs and vanilla. Sift flour, baking powder, soda, and salt. Add all at once to sugar mixture. Add ½ package of chocolate chips to batter. Mix well. Spread batter in a 9 x 13 inch Pam-coated pan. Sprinkle remaining chocolate chips over the top. Bake at 350⁰ for 25 to 35 minutes. Bake only until brown on edges. They will look slightly underdone in the center. DON'T OVER BAKE. Delicious cut and served while warm.

Betty Sheffield

Date Cake Squares

1 cup sugar
1 cup flour
1 cup chopped nuts
1 cup dates, chopped

1 teaspoon baking powder
3 eggs
Dash salt
1 tablespoon vanilla

Mix dry ingredients. Beat in eggs and vanilla. Add nuts and dates. Bake in a 9 inch square greased cake pan in a preheated oven at 350⁰ for 20 minutes or longer until done. Cut in squares while warm and roll in powdered sugar. Makes about 3 dozen.

Mrs. Frank Scott

Caramel Layer Squares

1 (14 ounce) bag (50) light caramels
1/3 cup evaporated milk
1 package Pillsbury German
   Chocolate Cake Mix
1 teaspoon water

1/2 cup butter or margarine
1 cup chopped nuts
1 (6 ounce) package chocolate chips

Combine first 2 ingredients in heavy saucepan and cook over low heat stirring constantly until caramels are melted. Keep warm. Combine remaining ingredients except chocolate chips in bowl and stir with fork until dough is crumbly and holds together. Press half of dough into a 9 x 13 inch greased and floured pan. Reserve the remaining dough for topping. Bake for 6 minutes. Sprinkle chocolate chips over partially baked crusts and spread caramel over all. Bake at 350° for 15 to 20 minutes. Cool completely. Do not overbake. Makes 3 dozen bars.

Mrs. Gayler Hajek
McKeesport, Pennsylvania

Ben's Chess Pie Cookies

2 sticks melted oleo
1 pound box brown sugar
1 cup white sugar
4 eggs, separated
2 cups plain flour

2 teaspoons baking powder
1/4 teaspoon salt
1 cup chopped nuts
1 1/2 teaspoons vanilla
Powdered sugar

Mix by hand margarine and sugars. Blend well. Add egg yolks and beat well. Sift dry ingredients and add to sugar and margarine mixture. Fold in nuts and vanilla. In a mixer beat egg whites until they are stiff and fold into batter. Spread batter evenly in a 9 x 13 inch pan which has been greased and floured. Bake at 350° for 30 to 45 minutes. When done sprinkle with powdered sugar. Cut when cool.

Mrs. James O. Dukes

Palmiers (Prussians)

1 package frozen patty shells

Granulated sugar

Defrost frozen patty shells in refrigerator overnight. Place three patty shells on a floured board or pastry cloth. Stack and press together. Roll out into a 7 x 9 inch rectangle. Fold the 7 inch wide edges of the rectangle inward, to meet at center. Sprinkle heavily with sugar. Fold in half again to resemble a closed book measuring 2 1/4 x 9 inches. Sprinkle with sugar and press down firmly. Cut crosswise into 1/2 inch strips, making fourteen strips in all. Place cut side down on an ungreased baking sheet. Bake at 400° for 8 to 10 minutes or until lightly browned. Turn over and bake other side for 2 to 5 minutes. Repeat with remaining three patty shells. Makes 28.

Mrs. H. G. McCall
New Orleans, Louisiana

Gingerbread Men

½ cup butter or margarine, softened
¾ cup sugar
1 egg yolk, beaten
¼ cup molasses
Juice of ½ orange (3 or 4 tablespoons)
3½ to 4 cups all-purpose flour
½ teaspoon salt

1 teaspoon soda
1 teaspoon ground cinnamon
1 teaspoon ground ginger
Raisins
Decorator candies
Decorator icing

Cream butter and sugar; beat in egg yolk. Add molasses and orange juice to creamed mixture. Combine dry ingredients and blend into creamed mixture. Chill dough about 1 hour or until stiff enough to handle. Work with ½ of dough at a time; store remainder in refrigerator. Roll dough ¼ to 1/8 inch thick between two pieces of waxed paper. Cut with a gingerbread man cutter and remove excess dough. Place greased cookie sheet on top of gingerbread men; invert and remove waxed paper. Press raisins into dough for eyes and nose. Decorate with desired candies. Bake at 350⁰ for 10 minutes. Cool for 1 minute. Remove to rack and finish cooling. Trim with decorator icing. Children like to make these, but will need some help.

Amy, Jamie and Ricky Graves

Lace Cookies

1 cup sugar
1 cup oatmeal
1 tablespoon flour

¼ teaspoon salt
¼ teaspoon baking powder
1 stick margarine
1 egg, slightly beaten

Melt margarine and add first five ingredients. Mix well. Add egg. Heat oven to 325⁰. Cover a cookie sheet with foil and grease foil well. Drop by ½ teaspoons, 2 inches apart onto greased foil. Bake for about 10 to 12 minutes. Watch carefully. Allow to cool before removing from foil. MUST BE BAKED ON GREASED FOIL. Store in air-tight container.

Alden and Kent Lovelace

Pecan Thins

1 cup butter
1 cup sugar
1 egg yolk
2 egg whites

2 cups sifted flour
1 teaspoon cinnamon
½ teaspoon vanilla
Sliced pecans

Cream butter and sugar thoroughly. Beat in egg yolk. Stir in flour, cinnamon, and vanilla. Spread dough on bottom of 2 ungreased cookie sheets as thinly as possible. Be sure dough covers all of pan. Put enough egg white over surface of dough to cover. Drain off all excess egg white with finger tips. Sprinkle dough generously with thinly sliced (or chopped) pecans and lightly press down. Bake at 375⁰ until lightly browned. Remove from oven and immediately cut into squares or bars with a sharp knife and remove from pan. Store in air-tight container. Makes 6 to 7 dozen.

Mrs. Cecil Kilpatrick
Mobile, Alabama

Peanut Butter Cookies

1 cup brown sugar
1 cup sugar
3 cups flour
1 1/4 sticks margarine or 3/4 cup butter

1 cup peanut butter
1 1/2 teaspoons soda
1/2 teaspoon salt
1 1/2 teaspoons vanilla
2 eggs

Mix butter (or margarine), sugars, and peanut butter. Heat in double boiler. Add vanilla. Beat in eggs one at a time. Sift together the flour, soda and salt. Add gradually to the egg mixture. Roll into balls and place on ungreased cookie sheet. Flatten with a fork by criss-crossing. Bake 12 to 15 minutes at 350°. Makes about 3 dozen cookies.

Holly Thomas

Pecan Crisp

1 egg white
1 cup light brown sugar

1 teaspoon vanilla
1 cup pecan halves

Beat egg white until frothy, but not stiff. Add sugar and stir. Add flavoring and nuts. Coat pecans with mixture. Grease cookie sheet and put lightly coated pecan halves about 1/2 inch apart on cookie sheet. Bake at 300° for 20 minutes. Let cool before lifting from pan.

Jacqueline Krass

Mama's Christmas Cookies

1 stick softened butter
3/4 cup confectioner's sugar
1 1/4 cups flour
1/8 teaspoon salt
1/4 teaspoon almond extract

1/4 teaspoon vanilla extract
1/4 cup chopped candied cherries,
   red and green
Milk to moisten

Cream butter, add sugar. Add sifted flour and salt. Add extracts to mixture beating well. Then stir in chopped candied cherries. Add milk as needed, to keep mixture moist. Roll mixture into a log and wrap in wax paper. Refrigerate until chilled (2 hours) (may be kept in the refrigerator for 2 to 3 weeks). Slice 1/4" thick and bake on ungreased cookie sheet at 400° for about 10 minutes or until the bottom browns. Freezes well. Yield: 3 dozen.

Kitty McGuire

Toffee Bar Cookies

1/2 box graham crackers
1/2 cup brown sugar
1/2 cup butter

1 teaspoon vanilla
1/2 cup chopped pecans
Pinch of salt

Spread crackers unbroken on cookie sheet. Melt butter and sugar in 1 quart saucepan. Cook exactly 2 minutes. Remove from heat and add vanilla and nuts. Pour over graham crackers. Spread evenly. Bake 10 minutes at 350°. Cool and divide. Try a 275° oven if cookies seem to cook too fast.

Tara and Ashley Bazzone

Pineapple Oatmeal Cookies

½ cup granulated sugar
½ cup brown sugar
½ cup shortening
1 egg
1 cup crushed pineapple, drained
1½ cups oatmeal

½ teaspoon soda
½ teaspoon salt
½ teaspoon cinnamon
1/8 teaspoon nutmeg
½ cup chopped nuts
1 cup sifted flour

Preheat oven to 375⁰. Cream shortening and sugars until fluffy. Beat in egg and pineapple. Add remaining ingredients and drop on ungreased cookie sheet. Bake 15 minutes.

Gay Graves

Sand Tarts

2 sticks butter
4 tablespoons sugar

2½ cups flour
1 teaspoon vanilla
1 cup pecans, chopped

Cream butter and add sugar slowly. Then add flour while still stirring. Add vanilla and pecans. Shape into cresents on a large cookie sheet. Bake in a slow oven until light brown (250⁰ for about 45 minutes). After cookies cool roll in powdered sugar.

Lee Ann Riley

Super Duper Clock Cookies

½ cup shortening
4 ounces unsweetened chocolate
2 cups sugar
2 teaspoons vanilla
4 eggs, unbeaten

2 teaspoons baking powder
2 cups flour
1/8 teaspoon salt
½ cup chopped nuts

Melt shortening and chocolate. Add sugar and vanilla. Mix well. Add eggs one at a time, beating after each addition. Sift flour, baking powder and salt together. Add to the above with the nuts. Mix well. Chill dough for several hours. Form in small balls. Roll in powdered sugar. Bake at 350⁰ for 12 to 15 minutes. Do not overcook.

Anna Margaret Bergfield

Stay Up All Night Cookies

2 egg whites at room temperature
⅔ cup sugar
Pinch of salt

½ teaspoon vanilla
1 (6 ounce) package chocolate bits
¼ cup pecans (optional)

Preheat oven to 375⁰. Beat egg whites to hold stiff points, and gradually add sugar and salt. Add vanilla. Fold in chocolate bits and pecans. Drop by teaspoon onto cookie sheet covered with brown paper. Place in oven and turn off heat. Leave overnight or may be used any time after one hour.

Mrs. William J. Hough

Top of Stove Cookies

1 stick oleo
½ cup milk
¼ cup cocoa
2 cups sugar

1 teaspoon vanilla
½ cup coconut (optional)
½ cup peanut butter
3 cups quick-cooking oatmeal

Melt oleo in small pan. Add milk, cocoa, and sugar; bring to a boil and cook one minute. Add vanilla, coconut, peanut butter, and oatmeal. Stir and drop from teaspoon onto waxed paper. No baking; a quick and easy treat. Pecans or walnuts may be added for variety.

Michael Tate
Kathy Brandon Hays, Jackson, Mississippi

Butterscotch Candy

1 large package butterscotch morsels
1 can salted peanuts

1 can chow mein noodles

Melt morsels over low heat. Stir in peanuts and noodles carefully. Drop by teaspoonsful onto waxed paper. Let harden.

Jill Smallwood

Chocolate Candy

4½ cups sugar
1 tall can Carnation milk
1 stick margarine or butter

1 pint jar marshmallow cream
3 giant Hershey bars (9¾ ounces)
2 quarts pecan halves

Put sugar, milk and margarine on low fire until sugar dissolves well. Turn up heat and let bubbly boil for 3 to 5 minutes. Take off fire and stir in broken-up Hersheys and marshmallow cream. Mixture will get real creamy. Cool some and add pecans. Drop from spoon on waxed paper. Makes about 200 small pieces.

Kim Edwards

Banana Bits

2 bananas
3 tablespoons honey

1 tablespoon wheat germ
3 tablespoons chopped nuts

Peel the bananas and place them on a cutting board. Use a knife to slice the bananas into 1 inch chunks. Cover a cookie sheet with a piece of aluminum foil. Put honey in a shallow dish. Mix the wheat germ with the chopped nuts and sprinkle it on the waxed paper. One at a time, dip the banana chunks in the honey. Then roll them in the chopped nuts and wheat germ and place them on the cookie sheet. Set the cookie sheet in the freezer for about 1 hour, or until the banana chunks are hard. Then put them in a plastic bag and keep the bag in the freezer. Eat the banana bits frozen.

Katina Krass

INDEX

the Gulf Gourmet
WESTMINSTER ACADEMY
5003 Lawson Avenue
Gulfport, Mississippi 39507

Send me _____ copies of **the Gulf Gourmet** at **$14.95** per copy plus $3.00 per copy for postage and handling. (Mississippi residents add $1.05 sales tax per book.)

Enclosed is my check for $ _____ .

NAME _____

PLEASE PRINT

ADDRESS _____

CITY _____ STATE _____ ZIP _____

Make checks payable to The Gulf Gourmet.

the Gulf Gourmet
WESTMINSTER ACADEMY
5003 Lawson Avenue
Gulfport, Mississippi 39507

Send me _____ copies of **the Gulf Gourmet** at **$14.95** per copy plus $3.00 per copy for postage and handling. (Mississippi residents add $1.05 sales tax per book.)

Enclosed is my check for $ _____ .

NAME _____

PLEASE PRINT

ADDRESS _____

CITY _____ STATE _____ ZIP _____

Make checks payable to The Gulf Gourmet.

the Gulf Gourmet
WESTMINSTER ACADEMY
5003 Lawson Avenue
Gulfport, Mississippi 39507

Send me _____ copies of **the Gulf Gourmet** at **$14.95** per copy plus $3.00 per copy for postage and handling. (Mississippi residents add $1.05 sales tax per book.)

Enclosed is my check for $ _____ .

NAME _____

PLEASE PRINT

ADDRESS _____

CITY _____ STATE _____ ZIP _____

Make checks payable to The Gulf Gourmet.

If you would like to see *the Gulf Gourmet* in your area, please send the names and addresses of your local gift and book stores.

- -

If you would like to see *the Gulf Gourmet* in your area, please send the names and addresses of your local gift and book stores.

- -

If you would like to see *the Gulf Gourmet* in your area, please send the names and addresses of your local gift and book stores.

the Gulf Gourmet

WESTMINSTER ACADEMY
5003 Lawson Avenue
Gulfport, Mississippi 39507

Send me _____ copies of *the Gulf Gourmet* at **$14.95** per copy plus $3.00 per copy for postage and handling. (Mississippi residents add $1.05 sales tax per book.)

Enclosed is my check for $ _____ .

NAME _____
PLEASE PRINT

ADDRESS _____

CITY _____ STATE _____ ZIP _____

Make checks payable to The Gulf Gourmet.

the Gulf Gourmet

WESTMINSTER ACADEMY
5003 Lawson Avenue
Gulfport, Mississippi 39507

Send me _____ copies of *the Gulf Gourmet* at **$14.95** per copy plus $3.00 per copy for postage and handling. (Mississippi residents add $1.05 sales tax per book.)

Enclosed is my check for $ _____ .

NAME _____
PLEASE PRINT

ADDRESS _____

CITY _____ STATE _____ ZIP _____

Make checks payable to The Gulf Gourmet.

the Gulf Gourmet

WESTMINSTER ACADEMY
5003 Lawson Avenue
Gulfport, Mississippi 39507

Send me _____ copies of *the Gulf Gourmet* at **$14.95** per copy plus $3.00 per copy for postage and handling. (Mississippi residents add $1.05 sales tax per book.)

Enclosed is my check for $ _____ .

NAME _____
PLEASE PRINT

ADDRESS _____

CITY _____ STATE _____ ZIP _____

Make checks payable to The Gulf Gourmet.

If you would like to see *the Gulf Gourmet* in your area, please send the names and addresses of your local gift and book stores.

- -

If you would like to see *the Gulf Gourmet* in your area, please send the names and addresses of your local gift and book stores.

- -

If you would like to see *the Gulf Gourmet* in your area, please send the names and addresses of your local gift and book stores.

the Gulf Gourmet

WESTMINSTER ACADEMY
5003 Lawson Avenue
Gulfport, Mississippi 39507

Send me _____ copies of *the Gulf Gourmet* at **$14.95** per copy plus $3.00 per copy for postage and handling. (Mississippi residents add $1.05 sales tax per book.)

Enclosed is my check for $ _____ .

NAME _____

PLEASE PRINT

ADDRESS _____

CITY _____ STATE _____ ZIP _____

Make checks payable to The Gulf Gourmet.

the Gulf Gourmet

WESTMINSTER ACADEMY
5003 Lawson Avenue
Gulfport, Mississippi 39507

Send me _____ copies of *the Gulf Gourmet* at **$14.95** per copy plus $3.00 per copy for postage and handling. (Mississippi residents add $1.05 sales tax per book.)

Enclosed is my check for $ _____ .

NAME _____

PLEASE PRINT

ADDRESS _____

CITY _____ STATE _____ ZIP _____

Make checks payable to The Gulf Gourmet.

the Gulf Gourmet

WESTMINSTER ACADEMY
5003 Lawson Avenue
Gulfport, Mississippi 39507

Send me _____ copies of *the Gulf Gourmet* at **$14.95** per copy plus $3.00 per copy for postage and handling. (Mississippi residents add $1.05 sales tax per book.)

Enclosed is my check for $ _____ .

NAME _____

PLEASE PRINT

ADDRESS _____

CITY _____ STATE _____ ZIP _____

Make checks payable to The Gulf Gourmet.

If you would like to see *the Gulf Gourmet* in your area, please send the names and addresses of your local gift and book stores.

- -

If you would like to see *the Gulf Gourmet* in your area, please send the names and addresses of your local gift and book stores.

- -

If you would like to see *the Gulf Gourmet* in your area, please send the names and addresses of your local gift and book stores.